THE NEW AMERICAN

Dream
Dictionary

THE NEW AMERICAN

Dream
Dictionary

The Complete Language of Dreams
in Easy-to-Understand Form

JOAN SEAMAN
and TOM PHILBIN

 NEW AMERICAN LIBRARY

New American Library
Published by New American Library, a division of
Penguin Group (USA) Inc., 375 Hudson Street, New York,
New York 10014, USA
Penguin Group (Canada), 90 Eglinton Avenue East, Suite 700, Toronto,
Ontario M4P 2Y3, Canada (a division of Pearson Penguin Canada Inc.)
Penguin Books Ltd., 80 Strand, London WC2R 0RL, England
Penguin Ireland, 25 St. Stephen's Green, Dublin 2,
Ireland (a division of Penguin Books Ltd.)
Penguin Group (Australia), 250 Camberwell Road, Camberwell, Victoria 3124,
Australia (a division of Pearson Australia Group Pty. Ltd.)
Penguin Books India Pvt. Ltd., 11 Community Centre, Panchsheel Park,
New Delhi - 110 017, India
Penguin Group (NZ), cnr Airborne and Rosedale Roads, Albany,
Auckland 1310, New Zealand (a division of Pearson New Zealand Ltd.)
Penguin Books (South Africa) (Pty.) Ltd., 24 Sturdee Avenue,
Rosebank, Johannesburg 2196, South Africa

Penguin Books Ltd., Registered Offices:
80 Strand, London WC2R 0RL, England

First published by New American Library,
a division of Penguin Group (USA) Inc.

First Printing, January 2006
10   9   8   7   6   5   4   3   2

NEW AMERICAN LIBRARY and logo are trademarks of Penguin Group (USA) Inc.

LIBRARY OF CONGRESS CATALOGING-IN-PUBLICATION DATA

Seaman, Joan.
  The New American dream dictionary: the complete language of dreams
in easy-to-understand form/by Joan Seaman and Tom Philbin.
     p.   cm.
  ISBN 0-451-21747-0
  1. Dream interpretation—Dictionaries.   I. Philbin, Tom, 1934–   II. Title.
  BF1091.S34 2006
  154.6'3'03—dc22   2005014375

Set in Granjon
Designed by Victoria Hartman

Printed in the United States of America

PUBLISHER'S NOTE
While the author has made every effort to provide accurate telephone numbers and Internet
addresses at the time of publication, neither the publisher nor the author assumes any
responsibility for errors, or for changes that occur after publication. Further, publisher does
not have any control over and does not assume any responsibility for author or third-party
Web sites or their content.

We sincerely hope that you,
our fellow dreamers, find this book useful.

—Joan Seaman and Tom Philbin

Using the Book

This book is set up as a dictionary, and hopefully will give readers—dreamers—the means—and meanings—to interpret their dreams more easily.

The terms provided—over three thousand—list the ideas, feelings and things that commonly show up in our dreams and what they commonly mean. In some cases, the term can have a single meaning, but in most, there will be multiple meanings. The terms and meanings have been culled from a wide variety of sources, including great psychiatric thinkers like Jung and Freud, as well as cultural traditions.

To determine what your dream means, we suggest you start by looking up the ideas, feelings or things that occur in your dream, and read the meanings provided. This may be enough for you to make an interpretation. If this isn't enough for you to discern what is going on, then use the technique of free association: let your mind play over the terms and the meanings and pay attention to the associations you make until you are able to assemble, like pieces in a puzzle, a relevant interpretation. It's that simple.

For example, let's say you experienced the first term, "abandoned." Read the meanings—in this case, three—and see how any of this material applies to your own life. Is someone abandoning or neglecting you? Are you doing that to someone? If there is no direct correlation—none of the meanings apply to your life—then use the free-association technique, focusing on the term and meanings until new meanings emerge that do make sense to you.

—*Joan Seaman and Tom Philbin*

THE NEW AMERICAN

Dream
Dictionary

A

abandoned 1. feeling neglected. 2. if actually abandoned, a sense that bad news is on the way. 3. abandoning someone else may mean an affirmation of one's independence.

abbey (church) 1. one's inner state is peaceful, anxiety free. 2. if the abbey is damaged, something is intruding on one's ability to achieve peacefulness. 3. if the structure is seen in clear weather, a hint good things are on their way, which will result in a diminution of anxiety. 4. if the abbey is seen in fog or bad weather, then bad news is on the way which may result in sadness, but this will fade.

abdomen 1. if hurting, it may mean one senses success in business. 2. if abdomen is exposed, treachery is close by. 3. a distaste or dissatisfaction with something.

abduction 1. under the control of someone else, or circumstances. 2. generally feeling powerless in the face of obstacles. 3. watching someone get abducted may also indicate the dreamer, and the meanings above would apply.

abhorrence 1. dislike of a person. 2. dislike of something else.

abnormal if the dream does not reflect waking reality, but includes images such as trees that are purple or a dog that purrs, then one is struggling to come up with a solution to difficult-to-understand problems.

aborigine 1. longing to travel to a foreign country, get away from it all. 2. raw sexual power, hidden while awake. 3. overindulgence in food or drink.

abortion 1. if male, failure at whatever one is trying. 2. if female, a health issue is in question. 3. a hard fight over something is about to occur.

above if looking up, a sign to set one's goals higher.

abroad 1. may be slang, disguised expression of desire for a particular female. 2. traveling abroad means one longs to be free from a current situation. 3. if actually traveling overseas, the desire to be financially well-off. 4. experiencing something that is difficult to handle which may indicate a need for a move to another area. 5. if traveling by ship to some place, indicates one may have found an important new friend.

abscess 1. need to express something painful. 2. need to get rid of a particular problem.

abstinence 1. practicing abstinence from sex, drink, drugs or other things that are not necessarily desirable may be a warning that one is overconfident and such habits may quickly return. 2. sign that one's life in general needs toning down.

abundance 1. conserve physical or mental energies for a trying event to come. 2. a general satisfaction with life.

abuse 1. if a character in the dream has been mistreated by the dreamer, fear of repercussions for the dreamer. 2. fear of being abused or taken advantage of. 3. if dreamers witness someone being abused and liking it, it may be themselves if they were abused early in life (abuse equals love—attention—however represented). 4. if being attacked by an animal or other creature, the creature may represent someone who abused the dreamer when a child.

abyss 1. a feeling of being lost, or with no way out of one's life. 2. a project the dreamer is devoting time to isn't worth it. 3. danger coming from someone the dreamer is dealing with, such as a business contact. 4. male fear of getting romantically involved.

academy 1. potential for new friendships. 2. warning to take care when getting new friends. 3. take an advanced degree in education.

Academy Awards 1. to receive an Academy Award is to fulfill one's dreams, whatever they may be. 2. if one is up for the award but does not win, then this may confirm one's feelings of inadequacy.

accelerator 1. a warning to slow down. 2. if in control of an accelerator (whether it be on a car, boat or aircraft), then one is in control of his/her destiny. 3. if accelerator is jammed, part of one's life is out of control (e.g., drinking).

acceptance 1. if yearning for acceptance, one does not feel worthy. 2. if accepted for something, one's sense of worth is confirmed.

accessory one feels incomplete without something being added.

accident 1. warning to avoid whatever was dangerous in the dream. 2. if another person has an accident, a wish to be free of that person.

accomplice 1. guilt over having done the wrong thing. 2. feeling strong but negative influence by someone else.

accordion 1. hearing the music is an attempt to feel better about some downbeat situation in waking life. 2. playing the accordion (or any other instrument) suggests one finds it easier to express deepest feelings musically rather than orally.

accountant 1. situation is being viewed objectively. 2. the need to put order in one's life. 3. one is responsible for one's actions. 4. take care not to project too much emotion into the solving of a problem.

accounts 1. if money is owed by the dreamer, indicates he/she is worried about how well or badly the business will be going. 2. an attempt by collectors to extract payments from the dreamer indicates one has very deep concern about business's viability.

accuse 1. if the dreamer is accused of something, he/she is feeling guilty. 2. if the dreamer accuses, he/she sees the accused as guilty of something.

ace 1. one needs luck to survive something. 2. one needs top-notch help.

ache a deep longing for someone or something.

acid 1. warning to beware of touching (getting involved) in something. 2. anger at someone. 3. if drinking acid, one is probably swallowing (i.e., hiding) his/her feelings.

acne 1. low self-esteem. 2. inability to cope—self-conscious—in a particular situation. 3. feeling of alienation from a group.

acorn 1. potential. 2. a sign not to be dissuaded in one's quest for greatness by small beginnings.

acquittal 1. one feels that he/she is guiltless in a particular situation. 2. one is willing to try very hard.

acrobat 1. if the dreamer is performing, he/she feels as if a test of his/her abilities is being conducted. 2. if one gets the feeling of always being an acrobat, then one is feeling that his/her life is an act. 3. it is alright to take a risk on a project. 4. one must bring balance into one's life or risk falling. 5. one is insecure about taking a certain step.

actor 1. if one is acting, it can refer to feeling that one's true self will not be accepted by others. 2. being generally dishonest.

acupuncture 1. worry about something that the dreamer is not familiar with. 2. someone is ministering to someone.

Adam and Eve 1. feeling some sort of guilt. 2. longing for a simpler way of life.

addict 1. a situation has gone out of control. 2. inability to control one's impulses. 3. low self-esteem.

addition 1. life is getting better as one adds to one's house. 2. solving a math problem in addition indicates one is involved in an adversarial situation.

adhesive 1. afraid to get involved. 2. afraid a relationship will break and have to be repaired.

adieu 1. bidding someone goodbye with deep feeling, happy or sad. 2. desire to be better educated.

admire 1. if one feels like the object of admiration, he/she feels that he/she will achieve his/her goals. 2. if someone is admired by the dreamer, he/she may be the budding object of romantic interest.

admission 1. if one can't get into a place because of lack of money, this may mean some sort of obstruction, emotional or actual, is in place. 2. one owes a loved one some emotional debt. 3. if one can't gain entry, this means a poor self-image. 4. need to unburden guilt.

adolescent longing for carefree days.

adoption 1. if adopting a child, dreamer is accepting some proposal made in waking life, such as a new idea. 2. if child is rejected, a new idea is rejected. 3. if dreamer feels adopted, he/she is feeling out of place. 4. not being dealt with honestly by someone. 5. feeling that one wants to be adopted by and protected by someone.

adulation to seek adulation signifies one will arrogantly step up to an undeserved position of honor.

adultery 1. if watching a lover engage in sex with someone else, this reflects the dreamer's feelings of unworthiness and/or sexual inadequacy. 2. if engaging in sex with someone other than his/her mate, it reflects a desire to change one's love object. 3. the dreamer's defiance that cannot be expressed when awake. 4. reaffirms one's sexual self-confidence. 5. expression of the adulterer's feeling of being neglected by partner. 6. his/her spouse or boyfriend/girlfriend is being unfaithful. 7. one feels that he/she has been found out re unfaithfulness.

advertisement if looking at an ad, a message is contained in it that one must interpret.

advice 1. giving advice may indicate an arbitrary personality. 2. taking advice indicates an open, flexible mind.

aerobics watching someone do this is a hint that one needs to exercise more.

affair if having one, one is not completely happy in one's current romantic relationship.

agency a sense that a government organization will soon be involved in one's life.

aggression 1. one dislikes someone. 2. way of letting go of hidden anger present in reality.

agitated the source of one's pain is unknown.

air 1. if outside breathing freely, the indication is that one should express beliefs that are being privately held. 2. being released from a confining situation. 3. desire to be free.

airborne desire to be proud of oneself.

airplane 1. one wants to fly away, be free. 2. if one wants to fly the plane, he/she wants to control his/her own destiny.

airplane crash feeling helpless in the face of major tragedy.

airport 1. the need to be free, to "fly" away, as it were. 2. if the airport is not busy, the dreamer is questioning his/her own actions.

aisle (walking down) 1. various pathways in one's life. 2. commitment, dedication. 3. if walking among a crowd, one feels admired.

alarm something in one's life needs attention.

albatross 1. fear of death. 2. fear of luck going bad. 3. freedom.

alchemy 1. something in one's life needs changing from poor to good, base metal to gold. 2. one has hope for change, even though it seems impossible.

alcohol 1. one must cut down on his/her drinking. 2. one is engaging in some sort of unhealthful activity. 3. hint that one should speak the truth on some issue. 4. if drinking, a deep-seated urge to escape the pummeling of life. 5. if drinking, guilt and alienation. 6. watching someone drink to the point of inebriation signifies a negative feeling on the part of the dreamer toward the person. 7. not drinking in a crowd of people who are drinking indicates one is feeling alienated. 8. not drinking in a drinking crowd may indicate a feeling of superiority.

alcoholic unable to cope.

alfalfa one needs protection against poverty.

alien(s) 1. if one fears being abducted, it signifies a deep fear of losing one's home and family. 2. if the dreamer pictures self as an alien, it means that ideas about the supernatural are getting outlandish. 3. if aliens appear, they symbolize specific fears which can be determined by the context of the dream. 4. deceased persons. 5. fear of alienation.

alimony 1. not getting one's due in a relationship. 2. fear that a relationship with someone might not work out well.

Allah 1. looking for answers for a very difficult problem or problems. 2. if one is not Muslim, one is considering changing religions.

allergy 1. sensitivity to a particular situation. 2. unable to do something.

alley taking shortcut may lead to danger.

alligator 1. if surrounded by alligators, the dreamer has to make a choice among equally distasteful choices. 2. if attacked by an alligator, there is a problem that will not go away and must be dealt with. 3. to be able to manage an alligator means that one is in control of one's problems. 4. an attack is imminent, and it will come in a cunning way, perhaps by best friends.

allowance 1. if receiving, one feels like a child. 2. hint to make allowance for someone's behavior.

aloe vera 1. female beauty. 2. related to intuition. 3. related to the moon.

alone 1. standing alone means feeling deserted. 2. feeling a lack of support from friends and relatives.

alphabet, letters of individual letters usually stand for something, such as a person: for example, the letter "g" or the sound of a "g" may stand for "George," or some other significant person or object in a person's life.

altar 1. religious feelings. 2. ready to "sacrifice" someone to achieve an end. 3. symbol of god. 4. desire to be Christian.

altar boy desire to return to a state of innocence, a religious way of life.

ambassador 1. if one feels that one is this, he/she feels that he/she is doing a good job (being diplomatic) in a delicate situation. 2. deep-seated desire to take a trip to a foreign country, perhaps to escape from one's present life.

amber (color) 1. fear that one's child might be abducted. 2. one is receiving a warning to slow down.

ambulance 1. worry about having a disease (the ambulance can carry one to a place to get treatment for it). 2. worry about having created a situation where very bad results can follow.

Amish 1. a need in one's own life to focus on and live the fundamentals, the important things in life. 2. a desire to simplify one's life.

ammonia 1. need to "clean up" one's life in some area. 2. caution to wake up and be aware of something.

ammunition 1. get ready for some sort of conflict. 2. someone is gathering emotional and/or factual ammunition against one.

amplifier one realizes that to be heard one will have to find a special way.

amputation 1. need to eliminate part of one's personality, like aggression. 2. need to work on eliminating part of someone else's personality.

amusement park 1. yearning for childhood and all the good things that it represents. 2. yearning to have more fun in one's life. 3. yearning to regain lost innocence. 4. fear of scary rides (roller coaster, etc.) could signify inability to take chances in life.

anatomy one's overall view of oneself.

anchor 1. one needs to be grounded. 2. something is holding one back from progressing.

anesthetic 1. if receiving an anesthetic, it may mean that one is trying to escape from reality. 2. need for a vacation.

angel 1. a sense that someone should watch over one. 2. seeking a power to help one that is higher than human. 3. longing to be a better person for someone else.

angelica (plant) one should go to where it's hot and sunny to get away from it all.

anger 1. if the dreamer is angry at something or someone, chances are the dreamer is also afraid of the person or thing, but can't vent in waking life. 2. if someone is angry at the dreamer, it may indicate that the dreamer is afraid of that person, but doesn't allow him/herself to experience this in waking life.

angling 1. trying to achieve something, but not with a solid plan (as unpredictable as fishing). 2. creating a crafty plan to succeed.

animal(s) 1. if killing, the desire to eliminate a certain aspect of one's personality as symbolized by the particular animal (e.g., one might kill a lion to eliminate aggressiveness). 2. aspects of one's own or another's personality as reflected in the characteristics of a certain animal. 3. religious or spiritual representations.

annex 1. a choice is available. 2. desire to take control of something ("annex" it).

announcer 1. desire to express deep-seated views long held close to the vest. 2. someone has a high degree of ego.

annuity 1. need to make some sort of fiscal plan. 2. need to make long-range plans of some sort.

anorexia 1. fear that one is too compulsive about something. 2. fear that one has adopted too healthy a lifestyle.

ant(s) 1. hardworking, industrious. 2. one knows his/her place in a community. 3. unselfish. 4. willingness to work for the common good.

anteater 1. phallic symbol. 2. one who works against group efforts.

anteroom 1. if standing in, one feels like a second-class citizen. 2. what one sees is not the whole, open, honest picture.

anthill regrets that people can't work as well.

antiaircraft guns one feels under attack, but is ready to fight back.

antidote 1. need for some sort of psychotherapy to eliminate poisonous feelings. 2. need for a quick fix of some sort.

antifreeze 1. one needs to protect oneself against possible enemies. 2. one needs to be a little warmer toward others. 3. being prepared will help one avoid problems.

antique 1. one feels very old. 2. one feels old—but valuable.

antlers 1. it is time to make sure others understand one's identity. 2. if necessary, one knows one will fight—and has the means to.

anvil 1. if necessary, willingness to take punishment for others. 2. need to hammer out solutions to certain things.

apart need to be separated from someone.

apartment reflects one's fiscal condition (if the apartment is lavish, one is well-off; if poorly furnished, one is not).

ape 1. someone is tricky, mischievous, perhaps trying to fool the dreamer in some way. 2. the dreamer is trying to trick someone else. 3. the desire to imitate someone else. 4. strength.

Aphrodite 1. beautiful. 2. having qualities that are magical.

apology 1. one wants to apologize for something. 2. another action is necessary to correct something.

apparition someone or something one is afraid of.

appendix something that is not useful but can cause problems.

applause 1. a good job. 2. desire to be acknowledged for what one has accomplished. 3. the need for love ("like waves of love coming across the footlights"—*All About Eve*).

apple 1. feeling healthy, good. 2. willingness to offer something to someone to influence the behavior toward one. 3. if apple has a worm, it is a warning to be alert to being deceived. 4. guilt over something (Adam and Eve). 6. love. 7. peace and harmony.

apply need for a new job.

apricot sexually attracted by the behind of someone (description of a woman having a behind like a "perfect apricot"—*Portnoy's Complaint*).

April 1. one has hope that one's life will become better. 2. sad memories will emerge (idea from "The Love Song of J. Alfred Prufrock," by T. S. Eliot).

apron before attempting something, wear appropriate protection.

aquarium peace, harmony and beauty in one's life.

Aquarius one feels one is at the beginning of a new age ("Age of Aquarius").

arbor a place to retreat to.

arch or archway 1. rite of passage. 2. doorway to something significant.

archaeologist look to the past to find answers to the present.

Archangel someone is available for helping one that one is not aware of.

architecture (parts of a building) 1. body parts. 2. strengths and weaknesses of an individual.

Arctic or Antarctica 1. one's emotional life is empty and cold. 2. one is isolated from others.

argument 1. reflection of an argument one is having with someone in waking life. 2. problem that must be decided. 3. parts of one's personality are in conflict.

Aries a mirror of oneself (people under this zodiac sign are ruthless and need to win).

arm 1. if damaged, a feeling that one cannot "reach out" to get help as well as one used to. 2. if in good condition, one should reach out.

armadillo one may feel odd, but also well-protected by personal assets.

Armageddon (end of world) deep worry about one's own world, including job, family, romantic relationships—everything.

armaments 1. weapons. 2. protection. 3. love. 4. perception of hostility.

armchair take time to relax every now and then.

armor make sure one is well-protected in some upcoming encounter.

army officer 1. one wants to get respect from one's colleagues. 2. not a run-of-the-mill person.

arrested 1. fear of being caught for something one has done secretly. 2. fears of medical problems (cardiac arrest).

arrow 1. one wants to be regarded as straightforward ("straight arrow"). 2. some sort of hostility may be in the offing.

artist 1. hints at untapped potential as an artist, cameraman, etc. 2. artistic achievement. 3. picturing oneself living in a garret could mean that one is being too vain, considering self above others.

ash hard, tough (like a baseball bat).

ashes 1. one's waking dreams of achievement or promise have failed. 2. the loss of one's ideals. 3. one has stopped being ambitious. 4. a sign that one is working too hard.

ass 1. one feels like a beast of burden in certain situations. 2. one sometimes feels like a fool. 3. sexual attraction (slang).

assassin if coming after the dreamer, he/she feels guilty over something.

assassination desire to eliminate something that is painful in one's life.

assault one feels hostility toward someone.

astrologer one feels that the answer to his/her problems may be extraterrestrial.

astronaut 1. one would love to be admired like an astronaut. 2. one knows that a certain situation will require courage.

atlas 1. looking for a way to get from one place to another. 2. questioning one's overall direction in life. 3. looking to be stronger.

attacked 1. if attacked by a person, one's unconscious mind is sensing danger and sending a warning. 2. if attacked by an animal, see "animal(s)." 3. if successful in repelling any attack, one sees he/she is capable of handling a crisis in life.

attic 1. if a person lives in an attic, he/she may feel isolated. 2. one has reached the top of something. 3. one is getting the "big picture" in life.

attorney one senses a difficult problem is going to occur.

auction 1. desire to possess something, no matter how great the odds against it. 2. desire to get rid of something, such as a problem or relationship.

audience 1. one needs love. 2. the dreamer hopes that a loved one gets appropriate tribute.

audition 1. a test of some sort: physical, mental, emotional or a combination of the three. 2. a test that one has devised or set for oneself. 3. a hint to react in waking life the way one did—if one did—in the dream.

August one is depressed (psychotherapists are on vacation).

aunt 1. if the aunt is favored, one needs some sort of mother figure to come into one's life. 2. if the aunt is not favored, one might feel that she has come by to pronounce a judgment of some sort.

aurora borealis 1. spiritually in tune with God. 2. feeling peace and love in one's life.

authority one is facing a situation where one will be evaluated.

autopsy one's life is opened up fully for all the world to see.

avalanche 1. fear of an impending disaster. 2. feeling trapped, unable to escape. 3. fear that others will be trapped by some event.

avenue depending on its condition, one's path will be difficult or simple.

aviary one feels trapped.

ax 1. tool to chop away excess material in one's life. 2. weapon. 3. take care of what is being done; a poor cut could result. 4. disguised hint to "ask" a certain question.

axle take care to focus on what's important to make sure something will work.

azure desire to take a vacation near the sea (where the water is a beautiful azure color).

B

baby 1. happiness. 2. rebirth, innocence. 3. a period of vulnerability, trustfulness. 4. feeling neglected (crying baby). 5. regression to an earlier stage of development, especially to escape responsibility. 6. a creative or artistic endeavor. 7. nurturing important ideas, projects. 8. fun surprises are in the offing.

baby carriage 1. urges for a family, to have a baby. 2. a need or desire to care for the child within.

babysitter feelings of protection, guardianship or supervision over another.

bachelor 1. freedom, freewheeling adventure. 2. a repressed desire to be unencumbered. 3. great prosperity (a young bachelor). 4. if a woman dreams of a bachelor, a relationship will be fruitful.

back 1. vulnerability. 2. level of responsibility (dreaming of pain). 3. opposition, difficulties (someone else's back).

backbiting 1. family problems. 2. actions may have potential to hurt others.

backbone 1. means of support—usually social, often emotional. 2. courage and determination. 3. the "flow" of emotions and feelings, possibly communication.

back door 1. change is on the way. 2. family arguments (family members entering). 3. secrets, especially lovers.

backflip 1. ability to adapt to changing circumstances. 2. being tested, pushed beyond reason—often by an individual, often in work-related affairs.

backgammon 1. moral or character challenges. 2. a feeling that good fortune is in the offing, wealth (to win). 3. dubious characters afoot, misfortune, sometimes in love (to lose).

backpack 1. level of self-sufficiency, independence. 2. burden or responsibility. 3. unfinished business or memories rising to the surface, emotional "baggage."

backseat 1. feelings of being out of control, at the mercy of fate or the person driving. 2. feelings of unimportance, being secondary. 3. feelings of being picked on, dominated (as in "backseat driver").

backward 1. a feeling that efforts are leading nowhere. 2. a need or desire to remove oneself or to "back off" from a situation or relationship. 3. difficulties in communication, misunderstanding.

backyard 1. aspects of self, thoughts and emotions not usually revealed to others. 2. childhood, nostalgia.

bacon 1. financial security, prosperity (as in "bringing home the bacon"). 2. health issues arise (if bacon is spoiled or not properly cooked). 3. nutritional concerns should be addressed.

badge 1. a possible brush with the law in the offing. 2. social standing, authority.

badger 1. success is achieved after struggles and hard work. 2. irritation to the point of harassment—usually caused by others, sometimes internal. 3. extreme stubbornness, perseverance.

bag 1. resources and ingenuity (as in "bag of tricks"). 2. success and abundance (note condition of bag). 3. important aspects of self, often hobbies and interests. 4. responsibilities, burdens.

bagel 1. a feeling of incompleteness (as in an "empty hole"). 2. nourishment, usually spiritual, sometimes cultural.

baggage 1. repressed emotions or recollections that need to be addressed. 2. to feel overwhelmed with responsibilities, obligations. 3. self or self-worth.

bagpipe 1. solemn occasions, moments in phase of life. 2. good luck is on the way (to hear a bagpipe). 3. use caution in financial matters.

bail 1. a release, letting go of trapped feelings. 2. use extreme caution when entering into new partnerships; warning. 3. to abandon a situation or project that seems shady or somehow dishonest (to "bail out").

bailiff 1. security; money and finances, usually a good sign. 2. great efforts are rewarded; advancement, usually in business. 3. attention needs to be paid to ethical standards.

bait 1. vulnerability or feeling trapped. 2. searching, attraction, a desire to "lure" (to use bait). 3. a test of cleverness or intelligence.

bakery 1. good things are in the works, especially in business. 2. possible pregnancy. 3. prosperity in the offing.

baldness 1. fears of a loss of sexual potency. 2. fear of advancing age. 3. feeling well-loved (completely bald). 4. a measure of virility.

ball 1. perfection (shape). 2. to put to a vote (blackball). 3. good news in the offing (baseball). 4. feelings of uneasiness (football). 5. child's birth is imminent (rubber ball). 6. eternity.

ball (social event) 1. an inheritance, usually of money or something else of value, in the offing. 2. feelings of success (dancing with spouse). 3. a sense of betrayal by friends (single person dancing with a married person).

ballerina obstacles are gracefully taken on and overcome in style.

ballet 1. order, balance and grace in life are being restored. 2. infidelity. 3. troubles in the offing (dreamed by a woman).

balloon 1. creative thoughts, aspirations. 2. parties and/or commemorative celebrations (birthdays, weddings, etc.). 3. arrogance (as in "inflated ego"). 4. disappointment (riding in a balloon).

ballroom 1. usually a good omen, often to do with inheritance and legacies. 2. social standing and financial status. 3. a measure of friendships and social activities. 4. communication, intuition in social activities.

banana 1. a phallic symbol. 2. great effort yields little "fruit." 3. good luck. 4. bad luck (banana peel).

bandage 1. good news is on the way. 2. a need for protection, healing. 3. concealing a pain or injury, usually emotional.

banishment 1. a situation is changing for the better. 2. opportunities expand in a new environment, usually in terms of financial security.

banjo 1. happiness (to hear a banjo). 2. an end to worries and a renewed pleasantry is in the offing. 3. sorrow.

bank 1. sudden loss of money. 2. semen. 3. emotional or spiritual reserve or resources. 4. security, usually financial.

bankrupt 1. a need for spiritual and emotional renewal. 2. caution in financial affairs; issues of protection need to be addressed. 3. a need or desire to be more creative in finding solutions to problems. 4. a need to reassess moral principles.

banner 1. a need or desire for attention. 2. representation, declaration of self, assertiveness. 3. attempting to communicate a message, advertisement.

banquet 1. abundance, often of a social or domestic nature. 2. use caution against overindulgence. 3. an emotional hunger is revealed (note types of food).

baptism 1. a form of cleansing, as often emotional as spiritual. 2. a new project is in the beginning stages (to attend a baptism). 3. to dedicate or narrow one's way of thinking.

bar 1. depression. 2. facilitating depression in self or others (if serving). 3. escape from serious matters or situation.

barbecue 1. a need or desire to make something more basic, primal even. 2. social aspects of self, possible difficulties. 3. feelings of being drained, emotionally imposed upon (to see a whole animal roasted).

barbed wire 1. use caution in communicating in close relationships; avoid harsh words. 2. feelings of being restricted, often in relationships. 3. feelings of restricted or censored communication.

barber 1. fear of castration. 2. prosperity, accomplishment through hard work. 3. a need or desire for proper grooming. 4. spiritual needs may have to be addressed.

barefoot 1. recalling youthful, carefree times (summertime). 2. impaired mobility. 3. putting off success.

barn 1. wealth and happiness, prosperity from hard work (full barn). 2. possible bad luck (open, empty barn). 3. a repository or holding place of unconscious thoughts and feelings.

barometer 1. change is coming soon, possibly some "stormy" affairs. 2. business can be gauged according to what the barometer says.

barricade 1. an emotional block or defensive mechanism that needs to be addressed. 2. obstacles and difficulties, usually in life, sometimes in intellect. 3. a need or desire to remove oneself from a potentially harmful situation or circumstance.

barrier 1. severely limiting obstacles, often in life or circumstances. 2. feelings of territory or a need or desire for boundaries, usually protective. 3. possible emotional block, usually for protective reasons.

baseball 1. a symbol or measure of prosperity and domestic happiness. 2. competition, achievement—often in life, usually in sexual relationships.

basement 1. the unconscious mind. 2. confusion (messy, in need of organization). 3. therapeutic purge, loss of old behaviors (spring cleaning, reorganization).

basin 1. financial security (based on how full the basin is). 2. a need or desire for emotional cleansing. 3. reversal: an empty basin means happiness and a full one can mean disappointment.

basket 1. good business, wealth (full basket). 2. poverty (empty basket). 3. skill and versatility. 4. feelings of emotional instability, turmoil (as in "basket case" or "to hell in a handbasket").

basketball 1. goals and achievement acquired through teamwork and focus. 2. ability to work with others.

bass 1. foundation, grounding, an anchor, often socially (voice). 2. rhythm of daily life (bass guitar).

bat 1. darkness and obscurity (as in "creature of the night"). 2. fear and misfortune. 3. twilight or end of situation. 4. recovery from illness (white bat). 5. happiness and long life (China). 6. uncleanliness.

bat (baseball) 1. a phallic symbol. 2. powerlessness.

bath 1. the womb, motherhood. 2. a kind of cleansing, usually emotional, after difficult challenges. 3. a new beginning (as in "baptism"). 4. a need to rethink a plan or project if the water is either too hot or too cold. 5. financial or professional success, based on the clarity or condition of the water.

bathrobe 1. may indicate the need to address issues regarding intimacy. 2. a need or desire for time off, time away from routines in the outside world, usually for healing.

bathroom 1. a need or desire for cleansing, often emotional. 2. a need or desire to express a worrisome or painful emotion. 3. private or embarrassing difficulties may be growing too public (public bathroom). 4. a physical need is encroaching on the dreamer.

battery 1. personal energy, usually emotional. 2. possible health issue. 3. feelings of injury or "assault."

battle 1. a serious internal conflict, likely over something not dealt with in the past. 2. a measure of attitudes regarding achievements, successes or failures. 3. dangers or difficulties in business. 4. arguments in the offing.

bay 1. intellectual clarity, reason (note condition and clarity of water). 2. a desire or need for emotional distance (as in to "keep at bay"). 3. travel and prosperity (note the level of the tide).

bayonet 1. a phallic symbol. 2. fighting ahead (as in "pointed arguments").

beach 1. point where the emotional (water) and the logical (shore) meet. 2. ability to adapt to change (depending on the state of the water, i.e., calm, stormy, etc.).

beads 1. circular, with no beginning or end (as in necklace). 2. joy and contentment (counting). 3. to lose reputation (dropping or scattering).

beak 1. an annoyance; a pest or domineering individual. 2. may denote feelings of intrusion (as in to "stick your beak in").

bean 1. little or no value (as in "doesn't know beans"). 2. a phallus (green beans). 3. magic power (as in "Jack and the Beanstalk"). 4. feelings of financial uncertainty. 5. fertility.

bear 1. strong but gentle in nature. 2. a leader, especially military; a warrior. 3. out-of-control unconscious elements, usually dangerous. 4. to become berserk; transformation.

beard 1. masculinity and sovereignty. 2. wisdom and insight. 3. shame (shaving it off). 4. unwanted development (a woman dreaming).

beat 1. revenge or retribution. 2. severe domestic problems need to be addressed. 3. deep regret, self-punishment over a past act (to be beaten).

beauty 1. pleasant and agreeable lifestyle. 2. happiness in love and business.

beaver 1. hard work brings success, monetary gains. 2. natural obstacles to a goal; consider rethinking a plan.

bed 1. an escape from the outside world, usually emotional. 2. a womb. 3. sexual discovery. 4. business project or partnership (to be in bed with someone not a lover). 5. sense of security. 6. a sense that sickness or injury is in the offing.

bedbug 1. difficulty resting, unease. 2. period of extreme irritation, annoyance, often due to a relationship. 3. a feeling of violation, invasion, possibly from bad news.

bedspread 1. prosperity and success. 2. sexuality and how it is presented to others.

beef 1. financial security and well-being are in the future. 2. possible illness (spoiled, raw or not properly cooked). 3. a need for discretion (raw or undercooked).

beehive 1. industry, teamwork on the job. 2. prosperity and good fortune. 3. caution in business affairs (empty hive). 4. caution in love affairs (empty hive).

beer 1. social life is usually good and happy. 2. loss of security. 3. inspiration, meditation, harmony. 4. treachery (if the beer is flat).

bees 1. industry and profit. 2. obsession, sometimes distracting from important issues. 3. bad luck, vulnerability (to be stung). 4. possible or potentially dangerous situation (a swarm). 5. happiness and a satisfying love life.

beetle 1. financial success. 2. eternal life. 3. a slow-forming, emerging problem, previously unnoticed. 4. good fortune (to kill beetles or see them dead).

beets 1. abundance; successful, lucrative projects. 2. possible illness of kidneys or urinary tract. 3. successful in affairs of the heart (to eat beets).

beggar 1. use caution in business affairs. 2. reverse: good fortune and abundance. 3. a subconscious search for something missing, often aspect of self or personality. 4. poor self-esteem, self-value.

beheading 1. reverse: a period of happiness and security in the offing. 2. completion, often in business affairs. 3. fear of castration. 4. lack of connectedness (as in "losing one's head").

beige 1. neutrality. 2. often used to represent the color of some flesh tones. 3. basic color used to enhance others in decoration.

bell 1. celebration, freedom and joy. 2. an alarm or alert (as in "call to arms," or just a doorbell). 3. time to wake up (alarm clock bell). 4. creative power (sexual connotation of bell and clapper or tongue). 5. impotence (no clapper).

bellows (fireplace) hard work means struggles will be overcome.

bellows (to yell or shout) 1. a need for release, usually from long unexpressed anger, frustration. 2. a feeling of a need to be heard. 3. serenity will come after a period of worry, upheaval.

belly 1. repository or holding place for unexpressed emotions. 2. intuition. 3. possible illness (if the belly is sore). 4. good omen, health and joy (seeing one's own belly). 5. pregnancy.

belt 1. ancient symbol of authority, victory. 2. austerity ("tighten our belts"). 3. punishment. 4. constriction between subconscious feelings (stomach) and conscious intellect (head) if the belt is too tight. 5. wealth (loosening).

bench 1. be diligent in work and business affairs. 2. avoid procrastination, putting off important matters.

bend 1. a measure of adaptability, flexibility. 2. the ability to adapt to various situations and social activities. 3. to succumb to the demands of others, obligations (as in to "bend over backward").

bereavement 1. a need or desire to express disappointment. 2. reverse: good tidings are in the offing, possible pregnancy.

berry 1. industry and endeavors (as in the "fruit of labors"). 2. sexuality. 3. important, good news is in the offing, likely regarding social events or activities.

bet 1. a risk is being undertaken; use caution in business affairs. 2. good luck is in the offing (to win). 3. to gamble with something held dear—possibly a relationship, often an aspect of personality or reputation.

betrayal 1. a strong sense of vulnerability; insecurity regarding projects and major endeavors. 2. someone is being deceptive, possibly harmful. 3. reverse: great things in the offing.

beverage 1. a spiritual quest or "thirst." 2. an idea or concept and the ability to understand or absorb it.

Bible 1. possible family difficulties. 2. a need to express truth, loyalty or faithfulness (as in to make an oath or swear allegiance). 3. the authoritative or final "word" on a subject or project. 4. a moral problem or dilemma needs to be addressed (note what passage is being read or referred to).

bicycle 1. adolescent sexual energy, intercourse. 2. desire for balance between work and recreation. 3. important decision coming. 4. fear of independence.

bigamy 1. entering a new phase of life (especially for a man). 2. a need for discretion. 3. a division of loyalties or devotions (if the "arrangement" is not approved of or is met with alarm). 4. a sign of drain, loss of strength.

bikini 1. a healthy lack of inhibition (little or nothing to hide). 2. exposure, emotional vulnerability.

billboard 1. personal goals and ambitions. 2. possible message is being conveyed from one level of consciousness to another.

billiards 1. competition. 2. emotions, especially those of others, should be looked at more seriously. 3. financial losses possible. 4. feelings of misfortune (as in "behind the eight ball").

binoculars 1. a need to focus, often on a situation. 2. a need to see further ahead; consider goals and ambitions more carefully.

birdcage 1. a feeling of being dominated, trapped and displayed. 2. a struggle; severe difficulties with identity, self and self-expression.

birds 1. freedom of spirit, imagination. 2. prosperity (in flight). 3. elevation of status, economic or social (taking flight). 4. domestic security, happiness (nesting). 5. transcending adversity, especially emotional or spiritual.

birdseed 1. nourishment, sustenance—likely spiritual, possibly emotional. 2. a feeling of great effort with little in the way of rewards.

birth 1. joy. 2. anxiety (if the dreamer is pregnant). 3. good fortune (depending on the marital status of the woman giving birth). 4. a new project or concept emerges into the consciousness. 5. advancing from one phase of life to the next. 6. a new spiritual principle emerges.

birthday 1. financial success. 2. self-acceptance. 3. rebirth, new beginnings.

birthmark 1. questions or confusion regarding personal identity, especially how others perceive it. 2. regrettable deeds or activities from the past. 3. a distinguishing, identifying feature.

biscuits 1. good health, prosperity likely. 2. domestic affairs, possible quarrels.

bisexual 1. sexual confusion or previously unrecognized attractions. 2. sexual repression, difficulties with sexual expression. 3. a need or desire to address either masculine or feminine aspects of self or integrate them.

bishop 1. father figure, wisdom. 2. a feeling of trouble with the law or high officials. 3. good business news ahead.

bison 1. prosperity, wealth and sustenance. 2. life's journey or path, forward movement.

bitch 1. complaints, dissatisfaction with life and endeavors. 2. feminine aspects of self, likely with an element of hostility.

bite 1. use caution around associates or friends who may have repressed hostility (someone biting the dreamer). 2. anger, possibly unjustified, at another (to bite someone). 3. pressures are building up and need to be reduced, often in others. 4. a feeling of invasion; loss or secrets in danger of being revealed (animal or insect bite).

black 1. sorrow and mourning. 2. absorbing energy (black absorbs light, producing heat, energy). 3. sober, austere (like the clothing of a minister or priest).

blackberries 1. unconscious sexual desires emerge. 2. a need to use more vigilance in affairs, business or emotional. 3. possible reversal of fortune.

blackbird 1. possible misfortune. 2. good fortune (especially if it is flying).

blackboard 1. a message is coming—likely from the past, possibly a repressed memory. 2. a "lesson" is being communicated.

blacksmith 1. hard work "forges" permanent benefits. 2. a lack of self-confidence creates obstacles. 3. strength and the ability to endure arduous undertakings.

black widow 1. insecurities, often regarding relationships. 2. feminine power, often hostile in nature.

bladder 1. use caution in physical activities; possible illness. 2. seat of anger, frustration, especially caused by others. 3. cleansing, personal expression (relieving the bladder, urinating).

blade 1. harsh or sharp words, thoughts or deeds. 2. decisiveness and courage, especially during difficult times.

blanket 1. protection, safety and comfort. 2. love and care, especially to cover or be covered by someone.

blasphemy 1. bad luck (if the dreamer uses it). 2. goals are achieved (if used by another).

bleach 1. change, transformation. 2. cleansing, sterilizing; starting afresh. 3. an effort to cover something up, hide misdeeds or imperfections.

bleachers 1. youthful or school memories, reminiscences, often positive. 2. a measure of wealth and prosperity, advancement in life's goals and ambitions (note how close one sits to the court or field).

bleeding 1. emotionally draining. 2. losing physical vitality; tired. 3. castration (male). 4. onset of menstruation (female). 5. opposition or contempt (bloodied nose).

blending 1. a symbol or measure of the ability to manage or "blend" aspects of self or life together. 2. feelings of confusion, being overwhelmed—usually by life, often by emotions, sometimes by groups of people. 3. the ability to "blend" together sometimes conflicting thoughts and feelings.

blind (person) 1. deliberate ignorance. 2. fears of castration.

blindfold 1. a desire not to "see" something, usually a negative aspect in others. 2. a need to reevaluate reasons or motives for actions or current attitudes. 3. disappointments in the offing.

blindness 1. a lack of awareness (a "blind eye"). 2. denial. 3. feelings of ignorance. 4. codependence (leading the blind). 5. adventures to come (also leading the blind).

blink 1. the ability to see, or see well—possibly a situation or a pattern of behaviors. 2. intentionally missing a point or problem.

blister 1. long-running, annoying problems. 2. may indicate more attention or effort is required toward problems or projects. 3. a need to address repressed anger or rage.

blizzard 1. difficulties in expressing emotion, feelings of exclusion ("left out in the cold"), often in domestic situations. 2. feelings of being overwhelmed with activities. 3. difficulty or inability to "see" situations clearly.

blond 1. perceived superfluity, frivolity. 2. a need to take life less seriously.

blood 1. energy, life force (also, see "bleeding"). 2. passion, love. 3. castration. 4. guilt (on hands), usually over extreme anger. 5. bitter confrontation. 6. renewed energy (to drink blood). 7. fertility (menstruation).

blossom 1. sexuality. 2. happiness, satisfaction. 3. period of prosperity is in the offing, usually emotional.

blows 1. repressed rage, often to the point of harming self. 2. inner conflict needs an outlet. 3. improvement in luck on the way. 4. reverse: reconciliation is in the offing.

blue 1. depression, sadness and the ability to express it. 2. freedom from worries and concerns. 3. promotes healing, creativity, often spiritual and/or intellectual. 4. the risqué.

blue jay 1. a message is trying to be communicated, often of a gossipy nature. 2. warning to avoid cockiness or overconfidence.

blueprint 1. plans, details and preparations for any project or activity. 2. a need or desire for better planning regarding an upcoming project. 3. the schematic or structure, the skeleton, usually of self and personality.

blur 1. a feeling that someone is attempting to confuse, deceive. 2. confusion, a lack of clarity and vision, sometimes with boundaries, personal or otherwise. 3. accomplishing something quickly. 4. possible health issue.

blushing 1. a desire or need to explain—sometimes behavior, frequently emotions. 2. recent gossip should be stopped or discouraged. 3. feeling under the weather; not feeling one's best (to put on blush).

boa constrictor 1. a phallic symbol. 2. repressed enjoyment of sexuality. 3. a feeling of suffocation, often in an intimate relationship. 4. possible difficult, tight or "constricting" times ahead.

boardinghouse 1. concerns about prosperity, security. 2. current difficulties, often emotional, are temporary. 3. emotional state, well-being.

boardwalk 1. friendships and social aspects of life. 2. a symbol for life's journey, chosen path. 3. prosperity, financial security.

boat 1. traveling through emotions. 2. life goals will be achieved. 3. many difficulties ahead (rough water).

body 1. happiness, good business ventures. 2. internal self and well-being (note condition of body).

bog 1. feeling overwhelmed, trapped, lost. 2. an undertaking or project grows more difficult and time-consuming than originally thought. 3. reverse: obstacles are surprisingly easy to overcome.

boiler 1. source of energy—usually physically, sometimes emotionally (note the condition of the unit). 2. a reservoir of repressed anger.

boils 1. repressed anger. 2. extreme annoyance, possibly heated quarrels. 3. a need to release negative or "toxic" feelings.

bolts 1. the ability to overcome obstacles (note whether bolted in, bolted out or breaking bolts). 2. the main components of a task or project (as in "nuts and bolts"). 3. to make a new start (to open a bolt). 4. a need or desire to simplify a problem.

bomb 1. explosive situation in life. 2. repressed emotions. 3. feelings of impending disaster. 4. bad news ("drop a bomb").

bondage 1. difficulty with self-expression, communication. 2. emotional control and "restraint"—often regarding situations, sometimes in general.

bone 1. mortality (human bones, especially a skull). 2. secrets (as in "skeletons in the closet"). 3. the simplest, most basic form, sometimes of a situation. 4. difficulty in business (broken bones or meat bones). 5. possible illness.

bonfire 1. communication, the ability to ask for help. 2. aspirations and goals. 3. companionship, friendships.

bonnet 1. a narrow, old-fashioned way of thinking. 2. a desire to be sheltered, often by tradition. 3. flirtation, gossip.

boo 1. self-criticism, possibly self-loathing. 2. the value placed on the opinions of others. 3. a fear of disapproval.

book 1. serenity, contentment. 2. unexpected experience. 3. intellect, symbol of education combined with experience. 4. information; record-keeping used as guidance for future reference.

bookcase 1. levels of knowledge, understanding. 2. professional endeavors (note whether the case is full or empty). 3. success (empty bookcase). 4. reverse: success (full bookcase).

bookkeeper 1. responsibility and "accountability"; keeping aspects of life moving forward. 2. balance, harmony in life.

bookstore 1. intellectual confusion, overwhelmed and overstimulated. 2. a need to acquire knowledge or pass it from one level of understanding to the next.

boomerang 1. fear or understanding that actions or behaviors toward others return (as in "what goes around comes around"). 2. use caution around people suspected of dishonesty.

boot 1. bold mobility. 2. sexual attractiveness. 3. making a stand.

borrow 1. caution in financial matters. 2. sorrow and loss. 3. help will be available (if loaning something).

boss 1. internal authority, usually behaviorally and emotionally. 2. internal accountability and responsibility, often regarding work and business affairs. 3. difficulties with authority or authority figures. 4. a need or desire to be more independent, self-sufficient.

bottle 1. the womb. 2. emotional repression (as in "bottling up" feelings). 3. prosperity (full bottle). 4. misfortune (empty or broken bottle).

boulder 1. strength and power. 2. obstacles. 3. severe, seemingly insurmountable difficulties are in the offing.

bouquet 1. to receive honors or approval. 2. a time for celebration. 3. possible illness (a withered bouquet). 4. a period of healing is in the offing.

bow and arrow 1. power, assertiveness. 2. sexual intercourse. 3. a measure of luck depending on whether or not the target is hit, usually in business affairs. 4. the emergence of love (as in "Cupid's arrow").

bowel 1. a positive omen (to have a bowel movement). 2. a need or desire to "eliminate" old patterns of thinking or behavior. 3. communication, usually of feelings and painful issues.

box 1. long journey (to open a box). 2. containing emotions or aspects of personality (as in "keep a lid on it," "boxed in" or "Pandora's box"). 3. death (as in coffin). 4. womb.

boxer (prizefighter) 1. a struggle for success, opportunities. 2. an inner struggle, often between two conflicting points of view. 3. a feeling that difficulties are out of control.

boyfriend 1. longing for an earlier time or relationship. 2. masculine side of self.

bra 1. temptation is in the offing. 2. maternal protection, support and nurturing. 3. need for spiritual boost.

brace(s) 1. certain things, likely communications issues, need to be "straightened out" (to dream of dental braces). 2. a feeling that something or someone is unable to stand alone, likely a relationship. 3. feeling possible self-consciousness, image difficulties.

bracelet 1. will make a good match. 2. lucky business deal, joy (gold bracelet).

brain 1. to gain or achieve knowledge, wisdom. 2. creativity, artistic abilities (right side of the brain). 3. reason, judgment (left side of the brain). 4. preoccupation, obsession (as in "on my mind"). 5. a need for inspiration (as in "brainstorm").

brakes 1. ability to control situations, forward movement. 2. emotional security, control.

bramble 1. feelings of being trapped, lost, usually emotionally. 2. happiness is achieved after a difficult journey, "thorny" paths.

branch 1. growth—often personal, frequently social or family-related. 2. petty arguments; a little bad luck (to cut down branches). 3. difficulty in communication, often related to business affairs (broken branches). 4. strength, power and protection, often representing an important person in the dreamer's life (oak or similar strong wood).

brandy 1. materialism, possibly too much focus on the trappings of wealth. 2. sign of impending financial good luck.

brass 1. change in fortune in the offing. 2. use caution regarding business affairs, especially where colleagues, perhaps new ones, are concerned. 3. emotional distance, coldness (as in "brass monkeys").

bread 1. wealth, honor. 2. basic necessities, nourishment of life. 3. success in life.

breakfast 1. the beginning of a new phase of life or project. 2. desire to do something a little crazy; use caution in affairs. 3. an affair is growing more serious (not eating breakfast alone).

breath 1. possible illness, difficulties (to feel "out of breath"). 2. feelings of great contentment; satisfaction with life and affairs. 3. anxiety, apprehension (as in "to hold one's breath"). 4. symbol of life energy, the spirit.

brew 1. hard work and careful consideration yield good results. 2. peace comes after a period of difficulties and concerns. 3. a need for assistance; a mixture of elements combine to overcome problems.

briars 1. a situation is more difficult than originally thought (to be stuck or caught in briars). 2. someone may have barely hidden hostility toward the dreamer. 3. a period of difficulties, annoyances.

brick 1. steadfast and reliable, if somewhat "dense"—usually a friend or acquaintance, sometimes self. 2. representing a small part of the body, cells or components (a brick house). 3. changes possible in the near future.

bride 1. start of a new phase of life. 2. new appreciation or acceptance of self. 3. receptivity, feminine—usually qualities of self.

bridge 1. transitional phase. 2. overcoming obstacles (especially if the bridge crosses water). 3. facing a decision or change (note condition of bridge).

bridle 1. the ability to cope, "handle" situations. 2. a worrisome but profitable project is beginning.

bridle bit 1. influence and control. 2. anticipation (as in to "champ at the bit").

briefcase 1. work, professional attitudes and preparedness (note condition of portfolio). 2. a body of work, life's creative achievement. 3. possible project in the offing, more responsibilities.

bronchitis 1. delays, obstacles need to be overcome. 2. possible illness. 3. discouragement due to obstacles. 4. prosperity in the offing (if recovering from bronchitis).

bronze 1. outward attractiveness. 2. something is more valuable than originally thought and must be cared for accordingly.

brood 1. feeling overwhelmed, too much to do. 2. financial or professional success. 3. many offspring, often ideas, sometimes children. 4. good luck in ventures (many chickens in a brood, but "don't count them before they hatch"!).

Brooks, Garth 1. desire to be a successful stage performer. 2. words sung are significant in one's life.

broom 1. to clean out old, undesirable memories, putting the past in perspective. 2. sometimes magic, especially female "magic" or power and the ability to "fly" away. 3. a domestic situation needs to be straightened out or "tidied." 4. money is coming soon (new broom).

broth 1. a very good omen, prosperity. 2. a situation brought to a basic consistency, simplified, yet complete (as in "boiled down"). 3. sincerity of others. 4. possible illness.

brothel 1. domestic situation improves. 2. sexual issues need to be addressed. 3. domestic issues need to be addressed.

brother 1. masculine characteristics of self (especially if a woman is dreaming). 2. authority or repression (older brother). 3. conflicts (if arguing).

brown 1. good fortune in the offing, often in financial affairs. 2. practical matters. 3. waste and decay.

bruise 1. emotional injury, usually from long ago. 2. possible health issues. 3. denial of difficulties, often in relationships (to try to hide a bruise). 4. concern with outward appearances.

brush 1. sorting, cleaning and straightening out difficulties. 2. a need to address emotions or feelings otherwise ignored or taken lightly, likely in someone else. 3. an aspect of life needs attention. 4. desires will be addressed.

buckle 1. potential loss of reputation through indiscretions (unfastened buckle). 2. self-control in social situations. 3. serious commitments, maybe marriage in the offing (unfastening another's buckle).

buffalo 1. wealth and prosperity in business (to see a buffalo). 2. fortunes will decline, especially in business (if buffalo is injured). 3. great security, serenity and good fortune for the family (a herd of buffalo).

bugle 1. a warning, call to arms. 2. good news is coming. 3. new beginnings (as in "reveille"). 4. endings, putting to rest a situation or way of believing (as in "taps").

bugs 1. problems, worries. 2. inconveniences, annoyances. 3. consuming interest in a person or activity (as in "bitten by the bug"). 4. wealth beyond expectations (infestations).

buildings 1. the self, the body. 2. symbol of achievement, success. 3. a need to assess attitudes—possibly toward relationships, likely toward situations.

bull 1. power, potency, strength and persistence. 2. obstinate (as in "bullheaded"). 3. fertility and strength. 4. will soon receive a gift (chased by a bull).

bulldog 1. a need or desire for protection. 2. issues may arise concerning law. 3. advancement, prosperity.

bundle 1. invitation coming soon. 2. various aspects of self, personality. 3. a particularly complex, sensitive phase of life or situation.

burden 1. feeling a lack of independence. 2. success after bearing many responsibilities. 3. a need to reduce the number of responsibilities (as in to "lighten the load").

burglar 1. an inner aspect of self. 2. feelings of invasion, lack of safety. 3. a feeling of troubles, even treachery, afoot. 4. a preoccupation with material things.

burial 1. end to a difficult problem or situation, often bad habits. 2. inheritance. 3. overbearing, possessive mother.

burning 1. consuming passion. 2. worries and fears (house or other structure burning). 3. release, cleansing, a form of catharsis— often emotional, frequently sexual.

burns 1. a good omen for social affairs and friendships. 2. a cleansing. 3. accomplishment and success. 4. feeling overwhelmed.

burr 1. feelings of being trapped, stuck. 2. possible change of environment or situation.

butcher 1. use caution in emotional affairs (as in emotions may be "raw"). 2. use caution in business affairs. 3. possible illness.

butter 1. a good future, good health and well-being. 2. coolness, smoothness and ease. 3. a flatterer (as in to "butter up").

butterfly 1. desire to enhance one's image or impression (not exclusively by a female). 2. reluctance to commit, settle down. 3. creativity. 4. frivolity. 5. transformation, metamorphosis (shedding a chrysalis).

button 1. emotions kept in check ("buttoned up"). 2. intimately revealing self to others, sexually or emotionally (opening buttons). 3. a sense that someone harbors angry feelings (losing buttons).

buying (purchase) 1. acceptance of a situation, how it is presented. 2. financial caution is needed (purchases for self). 3. good fortune ahead (purchases for others).

buzzard 1. feelings of loss and doom. 2. an undesirable aspect of self. 3. cleansing, removal of undesirable, unpleasant behavior or attitudes. 4. a sense of death, decay and rot, often in a situation or business affair.

C

cab 1. hiring someone to take one away from it all. 2. if others are in the cab, a discussion is being conducted on something. 3. if the dreamer is driving the cab, he/she is in a dead-end job.

cabaret have a good time, but don't become profligate (as did the people in the play *Cabaret*).

cabbage 1. overly involved in minor matters. 2. concern about one's health.

cabin 1. one is very independent. 2. one prefers the simpler things in life.

cabinet 1. one is keeping secrets. 2. female body, particularly the womb.

cable 1. phallic symbol. 2. need to communicate with someone.

caboose 1. sexual image (behind). 2. one does not feel as important as others ("bringing up the rear").

cactus 1. need to keep others away for various reasons. 2. feeling old. 3. feeling odd.

caddie one needs help in carrying certain burdens.

café 1. questions or concerns about one's diet. 2. longing to have a good time.

cafeteria a variety of things to consider before making a decision.

cage 1. feeling restricted, confined in the expression of feelings ("bird in a cage"). 2. if putting a wild animal in a cage, an attempt to control one's emotions.

cake 1. one feels he/she should get a reward for a job well done. 2. being selfish.

calculator 1. a hint to think things through thoroughly before making a move. 2. someone is calculating against one. 3. more precision needed in one's life.

calendar 1. conscious of time passing. 2. worry about life going by. 3. worried about a big date, either in terms of business or romance.

calendula go into some area where it's sunny.

calf 1. a feeling of being helpless. 2. lovable. 3. fundamental tragedy of life.

camcorder feeling threatened to the point where a defense featuring a filmic record will be required.

camel 1. responsible. 2. faithful. 3. durable. 4. unhealthful (smoking "Camels" or some other cigarette). 5. forbearing. 6. able to store up resources for surviving leaner times.

cameo 1. love. 2. anything small.

camera 1. need to hold on to the past. 2. hint that a situation should be examined more closely.

camouflage 1. need to hide one's feelings. 2. fear of revealing one's true personality.

camp 1. desire to stay young. 2. willingness to spend a long time to achieve something.

camper 1. the need to move on. 2. worry over something temporary.

campfire 1. need for friends. 2. need to open oneself for others to see.

campus 1. need for more knowledge or schooling. 2. need to challenge oneself mentally. 3. longing to return to school environment.

can 1. worry about food. 2. can (verb) achieve.

canal 1. vagina. 2. pregnancy. 3. desire to take a trip.

cancer 1. feeling depressed. 2. indication that negative emotions should be changed. 3. suspicion that someone is plotting against someone. 4. problem is eating away at a person, perhaps lowering resistance.

candle 1. if blowing out, the end of an emotional relationship. 2. hope.

cane 1. phallic symbol. 2. chastisement. 3. need for support. 4. need to carry something to protect oneself against some threat.

canned goods hard times are at hand.

cannibal 1. rough sex. 2. selfishness. 3. sense that one is going to be devoured. 4. one wants to "eat" someone else (sexual act).

cannon 1. phallic symbol. 2. strength, ability to defend oneself.

canoe 1. autopsy. 2. smooth. 3. get away from it all.

can opener need help to unlock something emotional.

canopy 1. desire to be sheltered. 2. desire to take a risk (parachute canopy).

canteen 1. soldier. 2. thirsty. 3. good times.

canyon hint that a lot of valuable information exists in one's mind.

cap 1. old-fashioned. 2. someone losing or keeping zest for life (cap on soda bottle).

cape 1. mysterious. 2. scary. 3. take a trip.

Capricorn a mirror of oneself (people under this sign are ambitious, progressive, politically astute and have an off beat sense of humor).

capsized in emotional difficulty.

captain 1. leader of the group, whatever it may be. 2. one feels he or she is in charge of things. 3. if someone other than the dreamer looks like a captain, the dreamer feels answerable to the captain.

car 1. ambition. 2. sexuality. 3. if in the backseat, one's life is out of control. 4. if in the front (passenger seat), one is retreating into the safety of the womb. 5. if car is parked, represents some deceased person. 6. personal mobility (either driving too fast, not fast enough or just right). 7. an extension of self. 8. status. 9. ambition. 10. sexual self-image.

car (trunk of) 1. if loading, related to sex life. 2. secret a person may want to keep.

cardinal 1. beauty. 2. religious. 3. major sin.

cards 1. investing too much emotion in a relationship with someone. 2. worry about gambling habits. 3. concern over a business proposition.

caretaker feeling that in a romantic relationship he/she is the caretaker.

carnation 1. one wants to stay a bachelor. 2. lighthearted. 3. condensed milk.

carnival 1. desire to return to childhood. 2. beware, what looks worthwhile and solid may be a come-on. 3. if one has the opportunity to go to a carnival and misses it, one may be avoiding an opportunity that only comes along every so often.

carp (fish or action) one needs to be more understanding of others.

carpe diem seize the day; focus on one's life.

carpenter 1. able to overcome obstacles. 2. carefully view one's life with a critical eye (how did one build it?).

carpet 1. desire to slow down and soften the way one is living. 2. desire for a better life.

carriage 1. one needs to be helped along in some situation. 2. one wants to have a baby.

carrion one should focus on ridding oneself of certain serious problems, emotional or relational.

carrot 1. take care—someone may be trying to lead someone somewhere. 2. look carefully at things before doing something.

carry 1. if the dreamer is being carried, he/she feels like an emotional burden to the carrier. 2. if the dreamer is carrying someone, the person carried may or may not be viewed as a burden.

cartoons 1. omnipotence. 2. desire to return to childhood. 3. in need of relief from stresses of life.

cartridge 1. phallic symbol. 2. hostility toward someone.

cash 1. quick money needed. 2. one does not trust certain financial interests or investors.

cashier 1. tallying up one's life. 2. be careful.

casino 1. risky enterprise. 2. drawn by false promises of success.

casserole 1. one would like one's helpmate to make more complicated foods, but there are other things not being addressed in the relationship. 2. pregnancy (baking). 3. new ideas.

cassette there are some things one doesn't know about someone close to him/her.

castle 1. if one is living in the castle, one has been rewarded for something. 2. one is dreaming of glory.

castration 1. fear of impotence. 2. overall fear of sexual inadequacy. 3. fear that someone—usually a female love interest—seeks to emasculate one. 4. fear of failing at work. 5. fear of failing in sports. 6. fear that another male will show that he's more potent sexually. 7. one feels that one has lost a sense of self. 8. one feels one is in a relationship that results in the loss of sense of self.

cat 1. someone or something is clever. 2. aloof. 3. quick.

cataract (eye) one needs help to see something clearly.

catcall expressing what one really feels about something.

caterpillar 1. need to enhance one's identity. 2. recognition that one has potential. 3. desire to sharpen one's image. 4. desire to sharpen one's approach to things.

caverns 1. the body. 2. one's self. 3. vagina.

cedar in Native American lore, a wood burned to ward off bad dreams.

ceilings 1. limitations of the person or persons standing under a ceiling. 2. freedom to grow (high ceiling). 3. growth inhibited (low ceiling).

cellar 1. trying to excavate material from the unconscious mind. 2. fear of the unknown.

cello 1. one prefers sophisticated entertainment. 2. one desires to impress someone. 3. if playing well, one is impressed with oneself.

cemetery 1. if well kept, indicates happiness on the horizon. 2. if in poor condition, troubles ahead. 3. if placing flowers, indecisive.

centaur 1. a monster. 2. a man in one's life.

centurion need for an old-fashioned hero.

cereal considering a more healthy lifestyle.

chair quick way to get to a higher place.

chalk lines 1. death. 2. to learn to play the game more fairly.

chambermaid 1. subservient. 2. scheming behind employer's back. 3. sexually loose.

chamomile looking for a tranquil, healing environment.

chapel concerns about religion.

chasm unexpected difficulty has suddenly appeared.

cheat 1. one considers some person untrustworthy. 2. one considers oneself untrustworthy. 3. if a romantic partner is seen cheating, may indicate one is insecure about one's sexual potency. 4. if a partner is seen cheating, and the dreamer is aroused, indicates a deep-seated need to have masochistic sex where one is dominated, perhaps defiled.

check 1. there is some situation to be checked. 2. there is a question of trust when someone bounces a check.

checkout clerk 1. being "checked out," i.e., taking stock of oneself. 2. if you are the clerk, one is suspicious of some person or persons.

Cheerios one needs a change of diet.

chess 1. one is involved in a conflict with a clever opponent. 2. take great care when dealing with someone.

chicken 1. fertility. 2. nourishment.

chiffon 1. delicate. 2. beautiful.

chimney 1. phallus. 2. if operating (spewing smoke), one needs to let off steam.

Christ 1. very important message, whatever it is. 2. live one's life like Christ.

Christmas 1. if one is a little depressed at a Christmas scene, it is a sign to not be so optimistic about a project. 2. if Christmas is joyful, it reflects optimism about a project.

cigar 1. a striving for prosperity. 2. penis.

cigarette 1. unconscious pleading for someone to give up smoking habit. 2. worry about illness. 3. if someone is smoking, liking or disliking the person for being out of the mainstream of behavior, whatever that may be.

circular (leaflet, ad) one must send word out on something immediately.

circumcised one follows rules and regulations.

circus great fun.

city 1. complex dilemma that one can figure out the solution to. 2. situation where things are moving too quickly.

clam 1. vagina. 2. primitive sustenance.

class 1. desire to go back to school for additional education. 2. feeling good ("classy").

cleanliness 1. lead a moral life according to solid standards. 2. clean up one's life.

climbing 1. if difficult, means you are having difficulty achieving life's ambitions. 2. if climbing is easy, goals are being achieved easily.

clock 1. time is significant in something one is doing. 2. hostility toward someone.

clogs (obstacles) things are getting in the way of one's progress.

clover one is going to have good luck and fortune.

club 1. if one feels accepted into the club, one feels accepted by family and friends. 2. if one is thrown out of the club, one has done something that one feels guilty about. 3. a measure of how one feels in terms of expressing individuality, i.e., feeling dominated by or dominating the club one is in.

coast place one is aiming for where one will be safe.

coasting one's life is going smoothly.

coat 1. one needs emotional sustenance. 2. one needs to provide extra protection for oneself.

coconut 1. one wants to go on a long trip. 2. someone is being hardheaded about something.

coffee the best way to handle a current situation is in a friendly, open way.

coffin 1. marriage imminent. 2. property purchase imminent. 3. elaborate coffin indicates end of a partnership, either business or romantic. 4. fear of death.

coin money is a part of a new deal.

collapsing 1. sexual culmination. 2. one has given one's all in a particular situation.

collection agency 1. someone is harassing one. 2. one needs help.

collector, ticket one wants to go on a trip, get away from it all.

Colombia 1. danger. 2. law and order are not in effect. 3. drugs.

columns 1. body parts. 2. phallic symbols.

comb, hair 1. concern with appearance. 2. insecurity.

comedian 1. possibly pretending to be happy but, in fact, sad. 2. if lines are cutting, one is expressing hostility. 3. actually happy.

comet brief, meteoric success at something.

commune 1. a reflection of how one feels working together with a group where one's sacrifices are appreciated, or one feels exploited. 2. a message that one should do more work for the community.

Communist don't worry about things that don't matter.

compass 1. trouble ahead. 2. take care when going into a particular situation.

composer use one's creative side.

computer suggestion to expand horizons.

condom 1. reservations about getting involved with a particular woman. 2. reluctance to get involved sexually with anyone. 3. afraid to have a baby.

conductor, bus 1. foreign travel imminent. 2. willingness to take on large responsibility.

conductor, orchestra 1. success ahead. 2. desire to control a situation. 3. one recognizes that he/she can't achieve a task alone.

conference 1. listen to the advice and counsel of other people. 2. be more flexible in one's thinking; consider a variety of possibilities before reaching a conclusion.

congratulations 1. if received, one is going to require help. 2. if given, dreamer will help someone else.

conservatory aspiration.

contortionist one is willing to do anything to achieve one's goals.

cook 1. the dreamer is overprotective of someone. 2. need for love and affection. 3. willingness to take on responsibility or care for others.

cop 1. provide more order in one's life. 2. getting order in one's life may be more difficult than anticipated and require extraordinary measures.

cope one may not be able to defeat something, but one is capable of coping with it.

coral something is beautiful—but dangerous.

cord 1. time to tie up loose ends. 2. connected by an umbilical cord.

cord, cut 1. desire to break family ties—particularly maternal one—and become an adult. 2. loss of something. 3. feeling free of someone.

corkscrew 1. something that is useful in life but its usefulness is not immediately apparent. 2. one is being deceptive about something.

corn 1. someone is telling one untruths. 2. one is telling untruths.

corners 1. totality. 2. four points of the world.

cornflower someone is clairvoyant, psychic, able to know things automatically.

costumes 1. disguise, deception. 2. one feels need to assume other roles. 3. one does not feel comfortable presenting one's own image.

countersink one wants something secure but hidden.

counting suggestion that one must be more orderly in one's life.

courtroom 1. a serious matter has presented itself. 2. one has just been through a "trying" time.

cow 1. if a single cow, maternal instinct. 2. herd of cows signifies paying too much attention to others. 3. victim.

coyote 1. one is dealing with someone who is not completely trustworthy. 2. cleverness.

crab 1. suggestion that one tends to complain too much. 2. try to move a little faster.

cradle one needs nurturing.

crane 1. longevity. 2. magic. 3. one may be facing the lifting of a heavy burden.

credit 1. one owes something to oneself, such as time off. 2. a relative, friend or associate owes one emotional consideration. 3. one owes some consideration of some sort to friends, relatives, associates.

crib 1. desire to return to babyhood where it's totally safe. 2. home.

criminal 1. one is dealing with someone who is not to be trusted. 2. one is engaged in activities which are wrong in some way.

cripple 1. one does not feel adequate to deal with a particular problem. 2. one feels that someone else is not capable of performing a certain task.

crocodile 1. danger lurks. 2. false emotion ("crocodile tears").

croissant one is hungry for a particular kind of affection.

cross 1. to a believer, an affirmation of one's faith. 2. to an agnostic, a question as to whether one should believe or not. 3. to an atheist, a symbol of one's disbelief in God and religion. 4. a hint that though one does not believe in God, one might someday. 5. if one pictures oneself being crucified, one is making a huge sacrifice for someone else.

crossword 1. some sort of problem that must be figured out. 2. hint that one is overcomplicating particular problems, that one should simplify and use plain emotional insights rather than intellectualizing. 3. if there are filled-out sections of a crossword, these often have separate messages.

crow 1. bad omen. 2. something magical is coming. 3. intelligence. 4. removal of unwanted feelings, as the crow consumes carrion.

crown 1. one feels he/she is master of a particular situation. 2. one feels that he/she deserves the highest reward available.

crumbs one feels left out.

crust 1. one feels left out, on the outside of what's important. 2. one is too sassy (has "too much crust").

crystal ball psychic abilities may be present in one to better foresee the future.

cuckoo 1. someone who is a stranger is trying to sneak into your life. 2. something undesirable has entered one's emotional life, and is not about to go away.

current, currant 1. be concerned with current matters. 2. fear of being swept away. 3. something may be sweet (when currant means jam).

curry 1. one needs spice added to one's life. 2. one should try to curry favor with someone. 3. Indian (who eats curry).

curtains 1. not feeling up to facing a problem. 2. one feels he/she may be facing oblivion. 3. one does not want other people to know about one's life. 4. one does not want others to know something specific about one's life.

cushion 1. one is trying to protect oneself. 2. relaxing on a cushion signifies feeling good in a relationship.

custard cut out that type of food or cut down on it.

cutlery using cutlery that is inappropriate (such as eating soup with a fork), may indicate one is behaving wrongly when it comes to emotion.

cymbal crashing a cymbal may indicate one is taking oneself too seriously.

D

daffodil 1. renewal, new beginnings or phase of life (daffodils bloom in early spring). 2. romantic bliss. 3. concerns over or fear of criticism.

dagger 1. use caution in business affairs. 2. bad associations can cause problems. 3. news is coming from afar.

daisy 1. newness, innocence. 2. success and happiness are in the offing. 3. finality, loss—often emotionally, like a relationship (as in "pushing up daisies").

dam 1. emotional repression, blockage. 2. feelings of being overwhelmed (a leaking or bursting dam). 3. use caution against snap decisions, usually in financial matters.

damage 1. in need of work or repairs, usually on aspects of self or personality. 2. feelings of loss, violation (inflicted damage). 3. a need to make amends for regrettable words or deeds.

damned 1. feelings of being trapped, often self-imposed. 2. feelings of persecution. 3. extreme annoyance or irritation.

dance 1. social ritual, routine (as in "keeping in step" with the world). 2. a feeling of joy about life coming to the surface. 3. spiritual transcendence. 4. good fortune in love.

dandelion 1. extreme joy and contentment is in the offing—often in intimate relationships, often in friendships. 2. lucky in love. 3. possible illness (to eat dandelion).

dandruff 1. nerves and nervous habits; expresses a need to relax. 2. tension is in need of healthy release. 3. a feeling that one is losing one's mind.

danger 1. caution is needed in some aspect of life. 2. potential for serious disappointment. 3. attention to signs will lead to a position of honor and prestige.

darkness 1. fear of the unknown, ignorance. 2. pessimism, fear of failure. 3. depression, despair (lost in darkness). 4. chaos of emotions.

darts 1. use caution; avoid barbed and hurtful criticism. 2. arguments or attitudes are on "target." 3. a feeling someone harbors hostility.

date (social engagement) 1. a desire for self-awareness. 2. social anxieties.

date (fruit) 1. prosperity, abundance. 2. unions or partnerships form, though not necessarily with the dreamer. 3. success in professional matters.

daughter 1. the feminine side of self. 2. domestic harmony.

dawn 1. new beginnings, start of another stage of life. 2. entering a new stage of spirituality or understanding. 3. help is coming.

day 1. times of day represent stages in life: morning, noon and evening. 2. emotional clarity (sunny). 3. feelings of loss (cloudy, overcast).

dead (person) 1. an aspect of personality as represented by the dead person. 2. a need to resolve old issues—likely in relationships, often behavioral—and finally lay them to rest. 3. an overwhelming fear of loss. 4. positive changes are in the offing. 5. a level of the unconscious is attempting to communicate with the conscious.

deafness 1. isolation and seclusion. 2. feeling withdrawn from people or activities, possible neglect in relationships. 3. good fortune is in the offing.

death 1. feelings of renewal after loss, changes. 2. release of undesirable personality traits (death of self). 3. repressed hostility (another person). 4. reverse: good health (death of self).

debate 1. a feeling that unresolved conflicts will work themselves out. 2. guilt over some morally questionable activity or deed, usually an "internal debate."

debt 1. usually emotional, sometimes financial debt (anxiety or even anger over inability to repay). 2. implies a good nature. 3. a need for balance in life.

December 1. the end of a project or phase of life. 2. financial success at the expense of friendship. 3. holiday spirit or holiday depression.

decompose 1. emotional regeneration, renewal after difficult times. 2. a situation is in decline, degrading into difficulty. 3. a stagnant, possibly "rotten" attitude or situation that needs attention.

decorate 1. superficial makeover of difficulties—sometimes financial situations, often personality problems. 2. good times are in the offing, often business related. 3. reverse: difficulties in business, possible losses.

deer 1. a spirit guide. 2. a good omen, especially for friendships, relationships. 3. symbol of speed, agility and defense of family. 4. to consider something or someone especially important, with great affection, cherished (wordplay on "dear").

defecation 1. relief or elimination of burdens. 2. unloading unexpressed fears and anxieties. 3. low self-worth, self-esteem (to be defecated on).

defend 1. to be placed on the defensive—usually over a situation, often concerning behavior. 2. loyalty, trust. 3. reverse: a sense or feeling of betrayal.

deformity 1. parts of self may require attention. 2. an aspect of personality is improperly "shaped," perhaps even stunted. 3. unexpressed feelings of shame.

déjà vu 1. a message is trying to get through (repeat of a previous dream or recurring dreams). 2. a repetition of dream themes revolving around unresolved issues.

delay 1. a period of disappointment, possible disagreements. 2. possible financial setbacks or difficulties (delayed trains or planes). 3. plans for projects should be reviewed for possible obstacles.

delight 1. extreme contentment, happiness. 2. a good omen; good, pleasing times in the offing.

demand 1. possible feelings of being overwhelmed (if things are demanded of the dreamer). 2. repressed needs begin to rise to the surface—usually in intimate relationships, often in friendships. 3. an aspect of self is "demanding attention." 4. someone, possibly a family member, has needs that remain ignored.

demolish 1. completion, an ending. 2. a need or desire to eliminate old patterns of behavior or ways of thinking. 3. repressed anger or rage that needs to be addressed. 4. use caution against harsh words in relationships.

demons 1. self-doubt or contempt. 2. negative or self-defeating forces at work in decision-making or judgment. 3. need to loosen up a little, have a little fun.

dentist 1. a need for help with expressing oneself, usually after a hard time. 2. anxiety, fear of pain. 3. betrayal, possibly of a good friend. 4. possible dental health concerns.

derrick 1. difficulties on the path to goals. 2. major emotional healing is accomplished from the ground up, like a careful construction project.

desert 1. isolation, retreat. 2. a need for solitude and space, cleansing. 3. loneliness. 4. sorrow and shame.

desk 1. emotions are hard at work on an aspect of self or personality, or possibly a situation. 2. possible disappointment or bad luck in business matters. 3. self-importance or self-esteem (note condition of desk).

despair 1. reverse: true happiness is understood only through knowing despair. 2. changes for the better are in the offing.

detective 1. difficulties or problems need thoughtful attention (as in "detective work"). 2. guilt over words or deeds regarding relationships or possibly business matters. 3. issues of loyalty arise.

detention 1. feelings of guilt or shame, likely from an adolescent activity. 2. feelings of personal loss, loss of identity, dignity.

detergent 1. an extreme need to clean up, clean out—often old experiences, likely bad modes of behavior. 2. outward appearance, either physical, attitudinal or behavioral, needs to be improved.

detonate 1. conflict in the offing. 2. repressed anger or rage. 3. feelings that a situation or relationship is being manipulated.

detour 1. obstacles require an alternate route to established destinations—possibly in business, usually in personal goals. 2. a new path is necessary to the usual place—likely emotionally, often in relationships.

devil 1. wealth and good fortune. 2. portions of personality— usually negative or mischievous, sometimes sexual. 3. falseness, deception, sometimes self-deception (as in the "devil assumes a pleasing shape"). 4. repressed guilt.

devotion 1. abundance and plenty (to show spiritual devotion). 2. a need or desire for spiritual enhancement, activities. 3. contentment, joy (to show devotion in a relationship). 4. caution in business matters as if something is not what it seems.

dew 1. new ideas "dawn" and appear. 2. blessings, honor and abundance. 3. possible illness or fever.

diadem 1. "crowning" achievements, glory. 2. weighty responsibilities are about to increase.

diamond 1. self; the right combination of properties to create the feeling of wholeness. 2. recognition, appreciation, often in relationships. 3. a very positive symbol of endurance, purity and invulnerability. 4. desire for wealth and security. 5. marriage proposal likely to result in great happiness, contentment.

dice 1. use caution in risky projects or undertakings (as in "crap shoot"). 2. change of fortune in the offing. 3. use caution in unusual or unlikely relationships. 4. too much reliance on fate or luck; a lack of self-confidence.

diet 1. self-discipline, attention to consumption—often regarding food, usually emotional. 2. punishment. 3. need to take control, usually positive.

digging 1. secret revealed, usually about self. 2. unrestrained, possibly detrimental self-examination. 3. gossip (as in "dig up dirt").

dinner 1. use caution in relationships, especially domestic or possibly social (to eat dinner alone). 2. desires and goals need to be reassessed. 3. reverse: the more abundant the meal, the greater the difficulties in achieving goals.

directions 1. route to a personal goal. 2. ability to accept criticism. 3. uncertain of direction in life, disorientation. 4. a sense of purpose.

dirt 1. fertility. 2. enthusiasm, lost youth, childhood. 3. guilt. 4. catching contagious disease in the offing (dirt on clothes).

disappear 1. serious insecurities, usually involving loved ones, sometimes material possessions. 2. reverse: money or possessions will come easily. 3. unreliability, usually of an individual.

disaster 1. anxiety, often related to travel or temporary separation from loved ones. 2. reverse: an improvement of circumstances on the way. 3. fears or concerns regarding path in life or goals (travel disaster, especially involving a train).

discovery 1. start of a new phase of life or situation. 2. seeking credit for something accomplished.

disease 1. fear or lack of trust in social situations, encounters (a communicable disease). 2. possible illness. 3. reverse: good times are in the offing.

disfigurement 1. injured personality. 2. inner happiness and contentment.

disgrace 1. reemergence of childhood anxieties or traumas, usually social. 2. a need for moral reassessment of behavior in business or social affairs or intimate relationships. 3. use caution, reputation is in jeopardy. 4. unrealistic expectations of others.

disguise 1. inner view of self (mask). 2. reluctance to face reality. 3. reluctance to face someone. 4. an aspect of personality keeps people away, but can be changed.

dish 1. a measure of good fortune, sometimes financial security, depending on how full the plate is. 2. domestic difficulties (broken dishes). 3. feelings of being overwhelmed—usually with powerful emotions, often responsibilities. 4. repressed feelings of sexual attraction to another (old-fashioned word-play on "dish"). 5. domestic bliss (washing dishes).

disinherited 1. loss, feeling out of touch with life. 2. use caution in business or social affairs. 3. reverse: good fortune is on the way, changes for the better.

dismemberment 1. feeling a loss of control over situation or problem (as in "everything is falling apart"). 2. feeling great loss, usually over an aspect of self or personality. 3. note body parts that are lost: loss of mobility (loss of legs) or dexterity (loss of hands or fingers), etc.

dispute 1. use caution to avoid an extreme loss of temper; try listening carefully to others. 2. reverse: happiness. 3. an expression of internal conflict, confusion.

distance 1. feeling out of touch or untouchable (as in "emotionally distant"). 2. difficulties or disappointments ahead, possibly related to travels.

distress 1. difficulties are not as bad as originally thought. 2. a feeling that good fortune is in the offing. 3. feelings of great grief or sadness, foreboding.

ditch 1. need to avoid a situation or person. 2. stagnant or unprocessed emotions (poor drainage, pooled water).

dividend 1. profit from endeavors. 2. rewards, payoffs, usually emotional, sometimes in relationships. 3. a reminder that "what goes around comes around."

diving 1. a journey into deep emotions or exploration of the unconscious. 2. sexual intercourse. 3. caution is needed (if conditions are dangerous).

division 1. self, inner conflict. 2. feelings of being overwhelmed, drained. 3. conflict in domestic affairs.

divorce 1. shunning a deep part of self, not necessarily eliminating it. 2. transitional phase or time of life. 3. mistaken choice.

dizziness 1. disorientation in life, need of direction. 2. a lot of toil with little result.

dock 1. feelings of loneliness, loss and possibly grief which require attention (alone on the dock). 2. financial success (to stand on a busy dock). 3. use extreme caution in love affairs.

doctor 1. illness, strife, often spiritual in nature (going to see a doctor). 2. mastery of skills. 3. good health, prosperity (seeing a doctor in a social setting).

dog 1. forgotten skills. 2. ability to learn, humility. 3. loyalty and protection. 4. treachery and betrayal (a black dog, or being bitten by a dog). 5. bad reputation (being chased by a dog).

doll 1. escapism, to remove oneself from a situation (childhood fantasies). 2. idyllic home life, great happiness. 3. rehearsal for an adult stage of life. 4. stand-in for the dreamer or another individual, their personality traits or behaviors.

dolphins 1. intellectual accomplishments. 2. a spirit guide. 3. the ability to communicate between one level of understanding or consciousness to the next.

dome 1. obstacles are on the path to success. 2. honors, even blessings, are bestowed (to be inside a dome).

dominoes 1. use caution with any kind of speculation or risky affairs. 2. problems and situations grow to feel overwhelming and a desire for help evolves, often emotional (as in the "domino effect"). 3. troubles will be overcome, more so if the dreamer wins the game.

donkey 1. risky behavior backfires, often publicly (if the donkey is misbehaving, as in "jackass"). 2. stubbornness, endurance. 3. intimate relationships (note donkey's behavior, i.e., kicking or braying).

doomsday 1. big life changes are happening, likely emotional, possibly behavioral or attitudinal. 2. a need for less questionable or risky behavior, steadiness. 3. reverse: good times are ahead after a difficult phase of life.

door 1. access from one realm to another (intellectual to the spiritual). 2. money and fortune are on the way. 3. moving from one stage of life to another. 4. desire to remove oneself from a situation or stage of life (closing and/or locking a door).

doorbell 1. a message is trying to get through from one level of consciousness to another. 2. pleasant, exciting news is on the way; may be business- or family-related. 3. new and exciting experiences or people are about to be encountered.

doorway 1. spiritual change. 2. new prospects. 3. moving from one level of understanding to another. 4. fortune or wealth is at hand. 5. view of society (door opening out). 6. view of inner self (door opens in).

dormitory 1. the unconscious mind. 2. intellect, knowledge. 3. the collective unconscious or social currents.

doughnut 1. feelings of comfort and security. 2. self, personal nurturance. 3. possible travel in the offing.

dove 1. a good harvest. 2. a message, usually of a spiritual nature. 3. peace, often domestic in nature.

dowry 1. use caution; imbalance and insecurity underlie and harm intimate relationships. 2. a deserved legacy is coming. 3. dependency or lack of it—sometimes emotional, often financial—means harder work (to not receive a dowry).

dragon 1. extreme passion, carried away. 2. expression of extreme anger (breathing fire). 3. good fortune, great riches. 4. an extremely annoying, destructive individual. 5. symbol of evil.

dragonfly 1. changes in the offing. 2. some aspect of life or situation may have elements of fantasy, illusion. 3. news comes from far away; a messenger.

drama 1. someone may be addicted to "drama," gravitate toward difficult situations. 2. possible reunion with friends (attending or viewing a drama). 3. beware of being financially or emotionally overwhelmed; use caution in all kinds of affairs.

drawer 1. a good omen regarding love and happiness (an open drawer). 2. opportunities and good fortune in affairs. 3. difficulties in the offing.

drawing 1. artistic expression. 2. a need or desire to communicate nonverbally. 3. the ability to see things simply, in black and white.

dreaming 1. difficulty in taking emotions seriously. 2. urge to control the unconscious mind (as in "setting the stage" where the dreamer creates the dream). 3. express a desire to obtain seemingly impossible things. 4. worries and sorrow.

dress 1. social pleasure, fortunate love life and financial success (to have many dresses or a beautiful dress). 2. symbol of feminine self, self-perception (note color and style of dress). 3. possible guilt, a desire to present oneself as innocent and pure (to wear a white dress).

dressing 1. difficulties ahead, often social (dressing badly or inappropriately). 2. severe preoccupation, usually with a hurtful person or situation (to have difficulty).

drill 1. a change of path is in the offing; a new direction opens up. 2. some activities are not fruitful.

drinking 1. a spiritual or intellectual "thirst." 2. misfortune (to drink bad or dirty water). 3. beware of accidents caused by carelessness or alcoholic drinking (to drink liquor). 4. celebrations in the offing (social alcoholic drinking). 5. possible alcoholism, loss of reputation (drinking too much alcohol).

driver's license 1. identity. 2. mobility, independence. 3. achieving a new level of growth, dignity.

driving 1. life's journey. 2. mobility, personal control (if the dreamer is driving). 3. feeling a lack of control, letting others set your path. 4. finding lost valuables.

driving lessons 1. a need to reassess ethics, morality in professional affairs. 2. a lack of confidence. 3. a need for discipline.

drool 1. overindulgence—often in sensual pleasures, sometimes with alcohol or other intoxicants. 2. feelings of humiliation. 3. a need or desire to take life with a bit more humor and lightheartedness.

dropping 1. letting go of unnecessary things, possibly past experiences or unhelpful attitudes. 2. clumsiness, perhaps in relationships. 3. projects or responsibilities are slipping away (as in "to drop the ball").

drought 1. a dry period—likely creatively or intellectually, possibly in relationships. 2. a short stretch of difficult or lean times followed by better times.

drowning 1. to be overwhelmed, usually emotionally. 2. feelings of loss of self, identity. 3. problems with mother or motherlike person. 4. problems in an intimate relationship, often with communication and identity.

drugs 1. possible health issues. 2. possible or potential addiction. 3. a desire to fix a problem quickly, not necessarily well. 4. avoidance, escapism, usually from emotional problems (to take drugs recreationally or illegally).

drugstore 1. changes are in order, beneficial. 2. possible illness, need for relief. 3. avoidance is somehow being aided and abetted.

drum 1. feelings of being out of rhythm or out of step—often with life, sometimes socially. 2. success and pleasure achieved by a strong and assured personality. 3. an alarm or call for help, possibly from a loved one. 4. the heartbeat, possible illness, anxiety or excitement (as in "heart beating like a drum").

drumstick a very self-assured individual.

drunk 1. irresponsible behavior leads to financial difficulties. 2. control issues, fear of a loss of control. 3. need to lose control.

duck 1. good news and happiness. 2. possible avoidance issues (as in "duck out"). 3. great fortune in romance (to see two ducks together). 4. to become ineffectual, reduced in importance (as in "lame duck").

duel 1. formerly mild rivalries are starting to cause real problems. 2. unresolved inner conflicts, confusion. 3. a need for compromise—usually inner conflicts, often outward conflict. 4. someone is interested in causing a little trouble.

duet 1. highly successful love relationship, domestic bliss. 2. some activity, task or project needs a partner to be successful (as in "two to tango"). 3. rivalry in relationships, usually in business.

dumb 1. a need to keep affairs private, keep opinions to oneself. 2. difficulty with emotional expression. 3. possible arguments in the making—possibly domestic, sometimes social.

dummy 1. feelings of powerlessness, being ineffectual. 2. an important relationship is starting to feel one-sided. 3. an aspect of self feels useless.

dump (landfill, garbage dump) 1. a need or desire to let go of unhelpful emotions, burdens. 2. sadness, perhaps depression (as in "down in the dumps").

dumped (rejection in a relationship) 1. fear of rejection. 2. feelings of alienation, social awkwardness, low self-esteem. 3. extreme fear of rejection (to "dump" someone).

dunes 1. flexibility, ability to change. 2. protection or obstacle to spiritual life.

dungeon 1. feelings of being trapped or imprisoned by difficulties or obstacles. 2. the dreamer's ability to overcome obstacles.

dusk 1. feelings of accomplishment, completion. 2. end of a successful project. 3. waning or end of a stage of life.

dust 1. immobility, inertia, often in life goals. 2. a period of petty problems and irritations. 3. feelings that others have failed the dreamer. 4. concealing questionable activities (to dust a room). 5. to clear up past problems (to dust a room).

dwarf 1. recalling childhood fantasies (where dwarfs are strong, reliable, yet magical beings). 2. many pleasures in the offing (friends are dwarfs). 3. smallness, unimportance (if feelings are negative).

dye 1. to change an outward, superficial appearance; avoidance of looking inward. 2. advancement or insecurities in business affairs, depending on color (to dye hair). 3. a measure of success in social affairs, depending on color (to dye fabric or clothing).

dying 1. fear of separation, loss. 2. use caution in making or receiving promises—they are likely to be impossible to fulfill. 3. passing from one phase of life to another.

dynamite 1. repressed anger, rage. 2. rapid changes in situations in the offing.

dynamo 1. spiritual, emotional and physical energy; ability to regenerate. 2. time to slow down and take care (broken or slowing dynamo). 3. professional ambitions and abilities.

E

eagle 1. victory. 2. heroic character. 3. if in a cage, the dreamer believes he or she has eaglelike qualities but is being suppressed. 4. if in a nest of eagles high on a mountain, a dreamer sees him/herself as part of an elite group. 5. if the dreamer kills an eagle, it is a measure of his/her ruthlessness. 6. supernatural ability and power.

earnest 1. sincere. 2. sad, suicidal (Ernest Hemingway).

earrings 1. drawing attention to oneself. 2. drawing attention to one's ears, suggesting that one should listen to what is being said by others.

ears 1. the need to be more receptive to the ideas of others. 2. if cleaning one's ears, the person is trying to be receptive.

earth 1. fertility. 2. if fertile, bodes well for a project. 3. if arid or barren, bodes ill for a project. 4. it's time to get back to basics.

earthquake 1. fear of impending disaster. 2. fear of a major "shake-up" that will change one's life. 3. if one survives a quake, it indicates inner strength. 4. insecure about being able to handle something. 5. premonition or feeling that while things are stable now they could become unstable.

east 1. political affiliation (liberal). 2. if traveling west, headed in the "right" (i.e., conservative) direction.

Easter 1. one has arisen again after a period of being "down." 2. the opportunity to strut one's stuff in clothing, which symbolizes personal achievement. 3. being born again spiritually.

Eastwood, Clint desire to be unafraid of and able to handle anything.

eating 1. eating alone equals depression, or being engulfed by a feeling of rejection. 2. one is being "eaten up" by something. 3. the desire to break off a relationship. 4. overeating indicates anxiety or concern over something. 5. food equals emotional sustenance.

eBay looking for quick way to riches.

ebony 1. concern about something relating to black people. 2. desire to have people live in harmony (piano keys).

echo something very important in one's life.

Eckerd (drugstore) concern about health.

eclipse 1. a serious threat in one's life, perhaps literally. 2. eclipse of the moon signifies that some part of one's personality is being hidden.

ecstasy addicted to drugs.

eczema 1. feeling something negative but not too serious, such as embarrassment. 2. reaction to stress. 3. returning to the safety of childhood.

Eden take care before getting involved in something that is outwardly very attractive.

education the desire to be better than those around one.

eel 1. phallic symbol. 2. something hidden and dangerous. 3. not sure which way to go. 4. difficult to trap. 5. concept that is difficult to understand.

eggs 1. the desire to have a child. 2. creative potential. 3. sexuality. 4. broken eggs reflect one's fragile state, feeling vulnerable. 5. colored eggs call one back to childhood. 6. a cracked egg indicates failure or disappointment.

egoistic insecure.

elbows making one's way despite opposition.

elderly 1. feeble. 2. wise. 3. seek out someone who's experienced to get help with a problem.

election 1. need to make a choice on a course of action. 2. hope.

electoral (college) behind the times (i.e., an out-of-tune system).

electric guitar 1. a measure of one's conviction or passion about an issue. 2. rebelliousness.

electricity 1. energy, drive. 2. something powerful that must be handled with care because it's dangerous.

electric plug/sockets 1. sexual act. 2. get "turned on."

electrocution fear of punishment.

elegance 1. desire to dress and act better so one can be a member of society. 2. desire to get more respect.

element (iron, etc.) go back to the basics.

elephant 1. be sure to remember someone who has done one a favor. 2. someone is dangerously overweight.

elevator 1. making great strides in one's endeavors. 2. life's challenges and opportunities, which are controlled by which floor the dreamer presses. 3. if elevator is stopped, it indicates one is interfering with one's own success. 4. if elevator is descending, then so is the dreamer. 5. uplifting experience.

elf indicates that one should not take life so seriously.

elk 1. toughness, endurance. 2. freedom. 3. desire to leave city life.

elm tree dignity and strength.

eloping 1. leaving with one's love object means that one must have that person at all costs. 2. yearning to be free—and happy.

eloquence one may be encountering someone who is in authority soon.

e-mail 1. need to communicate quickly with someone about something. 2. one is spending too much time using the computer.

embankment difficult part of one's journey is still to come.

embarrassed 1. negative feelings about something released or shown in a dream. 2. lack of self-confidence. 3. sexual insecurity.

embassy 1. one will face someone in authority soon. 2. one wants to go on a trip abroad.

embroidery 1. creativity. 2. need to give a project a little extra something to make it acceptable.

embryo 1. a new beginning. 2. a new idea. 3. if pregnant, hoping that the baby passes scrutiny, comes out okay.

emerald 1. strong and durable. 2. beautiful. 3. honest.

emigrate desire escape.

Emmy dreams of glory in showbiz.

emotionless 1. afraid to commit in a relationship. 2. not acknowledging feelings.

emperor authority figure.

employer authority figure.

employment 1. worry about one's job. 2. if unhappy with the company, one is likely unhappy with one's job.

empress authority figure.

EMT 1. one is in serious need of emotional support (arrival of). 2. one's romantic relationship needs "life support."

enclosure if inside an enclosure, one feels trapped or suspicious.

encyclopedia desire to be smarter, more well-rounded in terms of what one knows.

enemy 1. an overt enemy that exists in life. 2. negative force in unconscious mind. 3. fighting with enemies indicates one is trying to deal with problems.

engagement longing for a marital engagement means trying to deal with loneliness.

engine 1. power. 2. force driving something. 3. broken engine means one feels lack of power.

engineer 1. taking control of one's life. 2. one is analyzing a situation.

entertainer one feels that he/she is making others happy.

entertainment happy.

entrails 1. willingness to make a sacrifice to achieve a certain end. 2. one's life is a convoluted mess. 3. read the future.

entrance how open the entrance is indicates how open the dreamer is.

envelope 1. expecting good or bad news. 2. desire to keep a secret. 3. about to reveal a secret to someone. 4. sense of being "sealed off " or isolated. 5. fear of unknown. 6. desire to push oneself to achieve a difficult goal. 7. unopened envelope indicates an unsolved problem of some sort.

envy reflection of one's own sense of inadequacy.

epic if one feels involved in such a story, then he/she feels similarly in waking life.

epidemic fear that one's life can turn bad.

epilepsy 1. fear that one will be considered abnormal by others. 2. suppressing one's feelings.

epitaph the words one reads indicate what he/she feels his/her image is to others.

equation looking to find a solution to a problem in life that should be working out but isn't.

equator willingness to go into undiscovered country to achieve one's ends.

eraser 1. means are available to erase mistakes. 2. mistakes need to be cleared up.

erection 1. power, energy. 2. exercise control. 3. desire for someone.

ermine if wearing, desire to be well-off.

errands 1. willingness to help others. 2. if the dreamer is running the errands, a good marriage.

ersatz don't make a mountain out of a molehill.

escalator 1. moving up an escalator means a steady dealing with something, either business or emotions. 2. going down an escalator means that one has successfully dealt with something.

escape 1. the need to escape from one's situation in life. 2. the inability to face a particular situation.

ESP desire to achieve a psychic solution to a problem.

establishment one wants to challenge some authority figure but is afraid that undue hardships may result.

estate 1. fear of death. 2. worry about whether one will inherit something.

estrogen controversial.

Ethiopia one is worrying about one's future.

eucalyptus health oriented.

euro 1. desire to visit Europe. 2. desire to expand knowledge of the world.

Europe 1. commencing an action that will result in money. 2. if an American, desire to return to the simpler things in life. 3. need to escape from a particular situation.

euthanasia kindness, mercy.

evacuation 1. inability to move in one's dream signifies an inability to let one's emotions go. 2. being in an empty town indicates one has a feeling that he/she will be deserted.

Eve 1. longing for religion, God. 2. one is doing something sinful.

even if an object appears even, "all's right with the world."

evening 1. the tail end of something, perhaps one's life. 2. one's dreams did not come true.

eviction 1. rejected by others because one feels worthless. 2. one does not belong to a group. 3. one does not feel capable of coping with a particular situation. 4. desire to rid oneself of a certain personality characteristic. 5. desire to rid oneself of a person or relationship. 6. desire to rid oneself of a person who symbolizes an undesirable characteristic of the dreamer's.

evil 1. the evil that one perceives in others is actually in oneself, but it is projected. 2. a generalized term for hatred.

exam insecurity about oneself.

excavating 1. trying to dig up facts. 2. trying to get to the fundamental cause of something. 3. need to work on oneself.

exchange need to give back something or someone.

excrement 1. death. 2. decay. 3. defilement. 4. trying to dispose of something.

excursion one wants to make a change.

execution 1. fear of punishment. 2. guilt over something.

executive what one aspires to.

exercise 1. if doing exercises, raises the question as to whether more real-life exercise is needed. 2. indicates more mental exercising is required. 3. be more cautious, tactful. 4. if exercising with weights, indicates the need to lose or gain weight in life.

exhale not worried about something anymore.

exhaust remember that every action has a reaction.

exhausted 1. a sign that someone has given his/her all. 2. tired of a particular situation or person.

exile 1. not rightfully belonging to a group. 2. fear of being fired.

exit (sign) desire to get out of a particular situation.

exorcism 1. one feels sinful, in need of cleansing. 2. someone is mentally ill.

expedition one is about to embark on a difficult journey and needs help.

expense no action will be without some cost.

explorer one is not afraid to seek out a new career.

explosions 1. sexual climax. 2. if long objects, phallic symbols.

expo one is considering a variety of new ways to improve his/her life.

expose one fears one's secrets will be exposed.

exposure insecurity in certain areas.

express 1. a quick trip to success. 2. a quick trip to failure.

extension one must go a little further to achieve success.

exterminator something is undesirable where one works.

extinguisher ability to calm things down.

extortionist one doesn't trust someone who has access to one's money.

extravagance excessive outlay of money indicates a need to make up for one's insecurity, to enhance one's image of oneself.

eyebright herb indicating clarity of vision and thought.

eyeglasses 1. if one puts on eyeglasses, it suggests one wants to see a situation more clearly. 2. if one takes off glasses, the situation is unpalatable. 3. if glasses are broken, something may be wrong with one's view of life.

eyes 1. dirt in the eye indicates something is in the way of being successful. 2. if one can only see out of one eye, it indicates a rigidity of thinking. 3. a third eye in the middle of the forehead indicates an attempt to evaluate a situation spiritually. 4. someone looking at the dreamer may be friendly or hostile, depending on the expression.

eyesore one has done something one is not proud of.

F

fable 1. think carefully before acting; avoid impulses (to hear a fable). 2. a very creative mind that inclines toward fantasy instead of reality. 3. a great and important event is planned.

fabric 1. the grand design, destiny, fate. 2. a need or desire to hide something, possibly an aspect of self.

face 1. the mask shown to the world. 2. wealth and happiness are at hand (a smiling face). 3. regret and repentance (to be washing face). 4. ability to cope and deal, or "face," one's problems. 5. to be overwhelmed with emotions, eruptions of feelings (to break out in acne). 6. reputation.

face-lift 1. change of social image. 2. recent changes may be superficial.

factory 1. drudgery of routine. 2. productivity, ability to complete tasks.

failure 1. reverse: success is at hand. 2. anxiety over project or dilemma. 3. review plans and activities for potential problems. 4. feelings of inadequacy and low self-esteem.

fainting 1. possible illness or risk to health. 2. avoidance of emotions or effort to repress them. 3. avoidance of obligations or confrontations. 4. a feeling of being overwhelmed.

fair 1. happiness in affairs—likely socially, usually in business. 2. to postpone business for a pleasant diversion. 3. a need or desire for diversity of activities.

fairground 1. diversions (state of mind). 2. overcome obstacles, change for the better. 3. positive, productive social activities.

fairy 1. satisfaction, contentment in life. 2. a desire for wishes, often from childhood, to be fulfilled. 3. message from one level of consciousness to another, often pertaining to the solution to problems. 4. desire or need for a little childlike fantasy or "magic" in life.

faithful 1. rivalry and jealousy. 2. a desire or need for spiritual cultivation or enhancement. 3. contentment in love relationships (faithful spouse).

faithless 1. reverse: what seems faithless is in fact worthy of faith. 2. unhappiness in love relationships (faithless spouse).

fake 1. a strong sense that something is not what it seems—often regarding business affairs, sometimes relationships. 2. reverse: a sense or measure of sincerity, truth.

falcon 1. prosperity and security, to the envy of others. 2. an urge to "hunt" wants and desires. 3. beginnings and endings. 4. use caution in business affairs (if falcon is injured or the hunted).

fall 1. failure to achieve goals. 2. loss of status ("fall from grace") in the eyes of another. 3. overcoming adversities.

fame 1. use caution against disappointment; goals and ambitions are set very high. 2. very reliant on the opinions of others. 3. a brush with authorities may be in the offing.

familiar 1. a feeling of déjà vu, having experienced something before—possibly in a relationship, possibly a set of behaviors. 2. communication or a message with another level of consciousness. 3. feelings of connectedness with a higher power, a "spiritual realm" (as in a "witch's familiar").

family 1. concern over family matters or worries. 2. self, male and female attributes and roles in personality; self-nurturing. 3. good fortune, better circumstances in the offing (to dream of animal families).

famine 1. use caution in business. 2. reassess financial security. 3. triumph over famine means comfort and prosperity will follow. 4. possible health issues.

fan 1. pleasant news or activities, especially regarding relationships. 2. a need to "cool off," likely in a relationship. 3. an intensification of emotions, likely in a relationship (as in "fanning the flames").

fang 1. feelings of danger or need of defense. 2. a sense that serious difficulties or troubles are in the offing. 3. use caution to avoid harsh or hurtful words.

farewell 1. a need to tone things down, control emotions and excitement regarding situations (to be bidden farewell). 2. new acquaintances, possible friendships are in the offing. 3. a feeling that bad news is on the way.

farm 1. need for nourishment, cultivation and/or growth. 2. longing for youth or bygone era. 3. hard work will be rewarded, bring a great harvest.

farmer 1. opinions or feelings regarding work. 2. success in business.

fart 1. indirect or badly directed anger. 2. to use time badly (as in "fart around"). 3. to reveal inner self or secrets.

fat 1. preoccupation with body weight or appearance. 2. abundance, excess, overindulgence (possible fear of or concern over). 3. wealth and prosperity. 4. fertility; ability to produce or reproduce.

fate 1. difficulties in accepting responsibility for actions. 2. feelings of powerlessness, bad luck, need for self-determination. 3. reverse: good fortune is in the offing.

father 1. highest authority, moral commandments. 2. protection, security. 3. self-reliance, independence. 4. business-related activities.

father-in-law 1. disagreements, uncomfortable family situations requiring delicacy and tact. 2. positive events happening. 3. pleasant family relations (if father-in-law is happy).

fatigue 1. possible health issues. 2. abundance and success are achieved.

faucet 1. flow of emotions. 2. sexual difficulties (leaky faucet). 3. emotional control, need for caution (beer on tap).

favor 1. a sense of loss, if asked for favors. 2. gains, if asking for favors. 3. loss of friends, if doing a favor. 4. loss of money, if receiving a favor.

fawn 1. great compassion and gentleness. 2. disappointment if the fawn is hurt or trapped. 3. to see someone "fawning" indicates false friends and sycophants.

fax 1. important message on the way—likely from the subconscious, possibly from an outside source. 2. communication is sought, but from a distance.

FBI 1. a possible brush with the law. 2. guilt over a morally ambiguous activity. 3. a feeling of being spied on or followed.

fear 1. doubts about self. 2. reverse: immense courage. 3. anxieties about tasks and projects.

feather 1. the soul or spirit of an individual, the measure of freedom it possesses. 2. a need or desire for a lightening of burdens. 3. success, wealth, business and self-fulfillment. 4. decorative, pretty feathers indicate happiness in social affairs. 5. comfort, warmth and pleasure.

February 1. emotional midwinter, fatigue. 2. possible health issues or illness. 3. a good month for business affairs, lucky if the sun shines.

feces 1. expressing or "dumping" useless or toxic feelings. 2. to unload or relieve oneself of excess responsibilities and obligations. 3. overwhelming feelings of negativity, possibly even poor self-image, shame. 4. financial success, material gain.

feeble 1. reverse: longevity and fitness. 2. physical weakness, possibly from bad habits or work activities. 3. feelings of emotional powerlessness and ineffectuality.

feed 1. financial security, gains. 2. use caution in issues where trust is concerned.

feet 1. independence, personal mobility. 2. stability (as in "both feet on the ground"). 3. regret over communication or deed (as in "foot in mouth"). 4. illness in another part of the body.

fellatio 1. unselfish, uninhibited in giving or receiving pleasure. 2. creativity, especially artistic. 3. wish fulfillment.

female 1. the feminine side of self. 2. intuition, gut feelings.

fence 1. obstacle. 2. containment or restriction, often of expression. 3. protection from uncontrollable or primitive feelings. 4. wealth and security (to build). 5. to be in over one's head (to fall from).

fence (swordplay) 1. adventuresome and romantic. 2. bad love affairs. 3. level of prestige.

fern 1. intellectual fascination, attraction. 2. a good omen regarding most affairs. 3. possible illness (if the ferns are wilted). 4. secret affairs or feelings of love, a need for discretion.

ferret 1. a certain outlook on life (ferrets are cunning, smart, brave yet playful). 2. use extreme caution regarding nosiness and hurtful gossip.

ferry 1. a journey from one level to another—usually a level of consciousness, sometimes a level of existence (as in "crossing the river Styx"). 2. benefits are the result of hard work. 3. a possible visit from one long absent. 4. the outcome of plans, activities or projects, depending upon the condition of the water.

festival 1. joy, pleasantries and congeniality—usually socially, likely of the spirit. 2. avoidance of or disregard for life's difficulties or specific problems. 3. a possible dependence on others for pleasure and entertainment.

fetus 1. start of a new idea or concept. 2. a creative approach to a dilemma.

fever 1. possible illness. 2. a rise in passions or anger, loss of control, feeling consumed. 3. fearful but small concerns and anxieties grow disproportionate, overwhelming.

fiancé(e) 1. commitment in a relationship, a belief or principle. 2. reverse: fear or hesitation regarding a situation or circumstance.

fiddle 1. life changes coming soon. 2. domestic satisfaction, happiness. 3. to idly manipulate or tinker with someone or something.

field 1. happiness (note condition of field, whether there is much growth). 2. sexuality and fertility (farm fields). 3. the need for hard work is on the way (farm fields). 4. feelings of a lack of emotional fulfillment (barren fields).

fiend 1. another, darker aspect or side of self. 2. repressed feelings of guilt over a past misdeed. 3. happiness in and longevity of intimate relationships, marriage. 4. a need to reassess morals and principles in affairs, business or personal relationships.

fifteen 1. good luck and prosperity. 2. the ability to realize dreams and ambitions.

fight 1. mounting conflict, usually of an inner nature, between parts of self. 2. conflicts in waking life getting out of control; explore more creative resolutions. 3. bad luck in relationships.

file (paperwork) 1. putting the mind in order, organization of thoughts. 2. encountering very difficult obstacles.

film 1. emotional detachment. 2. detached analysis of situation or aspect of life.

find 1. reverse: feelings of loss—usually material, often in business matters. 2. communication between aspects of self or level of consciousness. 3. entering a new phase of a relationship, a period of growth.

fingernails 1. an indicator of social standing, appearances; social disgrace or respect and esteem. 2. intellectual gifts, ability to learn and acquire new skills (well-groomed nails). 3. a difficult, seemingly impossible situation (to bite nails). 4. deceptive or false appearances (fake or polished nails).

fingerprint 1. guilt or regret, likely over a past activity. 2. difficulties in financial matters. 3. a permanent mark.

fingers 1. phallic symbol. 2. an important method of nonverbal communication. 3. arguments or loss of money (cut or bleeding fingers). 4. accusations (as in "fingering"). 5. livelihood, labor and dexterity. 6. inheritance, loss or gain (unusual number of fingers).

> **thumb** 1. direction, or direction in life. 2. indicator of life or death (as in gladiator games). 3. mobility.

> **forefinger** 1. direction, authority and judgment. 2. a point or message trying to get across, possibly from one level of

consciousness to the next. 3. a sense of accusations and harsh judgment.

middle finger 1. a phallic symbol, sexuality. 2. extreme disapproval, insult or anger.

ring finger 1. union, marriage or commitment. 2. sexual availability. 3. success in social affairs and activities.

pinky finger 1. honor, loyalty and trustworthiness. 2. weakness. 3. an oath or promise. 4. the intellect; ability to communicate.

fir 1. tremendous good luck—usually regarding financial affairs, often social. 2. difficulties in business, often due to one's own doing (to cut a fir tree down).

fire 1. passion, desire; consuming. 2. cleansing and purification. 3. libido, forbidden passions. 4. symbol of home and domesticity. 5. nurturing. 6. ultimate form of destruction. 7. bad-tempered.

firearms 1. a phallic symbol. 2. repressed hostility or fear toward an individual. 3. issues regarding personal safety. 4. goals and ambitions (target practice).

firefighter 1. higher self; quelling or balancing passions. 2. danger in the offing. 3. expression of a need for rescue, often emotional.

firecracker use caution with anger; relieve anger constructively.

fire engine 1. a continuing high state of anxiety, alarm (especially if the truck fails to reach its destination). 2. good fortune comes after scary times. 3. may be guilty of unpleasant behavior (especially if riding the truck).

fireflies 1. secrets may be brought to light. 2. new and exciting ideas are emerging from the unconscious. 3. messages are moving from one level of consciousness to another.

fireplace 1. hearth, representing center of domesticity. 2. domestic troubles (if fire is not present or dying). 3. disappointment, apathy (not present or dying). 4. love and happiness.

fireworks 1. celebrations in the offing, possible pregnancy. 2. important plans need to be reassessed for potential problems or flaws. 3. creativity; artistic expression displayed for all to see.

fish 1. speed, cleverness, evasiveness, yet graceful; quick to change direction. 2. wealth, power and very good fortune (note the health of fish). 3. difficulties in relationship should be addressed (inability to hold a fish). 4. alienation, feelings of not being able to fit in (as in "fish out of water").

fisherman 1. good news and fortune; prosperity. 2. a powerful religious, spiritual symbol, emphasizing teachings of peace.

fishing 1. deep emotions are brought to the surface. 2. loss of friendship or disappointment in the offing. 3. ability to catch an idea or concept. 4. a need or desire to relax.

fishnet 1. love affairs. 2. disappointments (a ripped net). 3. weather changes. 4. sexual attraction, pleasures and good fortune (fishnet stockings).

fishpond 1. luck and prosperity (note if the pond is clear or dirty). 2. possible illness (muddy water). 3. love will be reciprocated (to fall into a clear pond). 4. the unconscious, a "reflection of self" (note quality of water: clear or muddy).

fits 1. disagreements, conflicts. 2. career frustrations, disappointment.

five 1. humanity, "humanness"; note the five senses and five digits on each hand and foot. 2. a person of intelligence and communication, expression, eloquence and charm.

flag 1. phallic symbol, potency. 2. honors in the offing.

flame 1. inspiration, concepts and ideas. 2. passion, intensity in relationships, often surrounding conflicts. 3. need or desire for sexual release.

flamingo 1. new and possibly exotic experiences in the offing. 2. a sense or feeling of community (a flock of flamingos).

flat 1. unemotional, detached and distant. 2. something easily understood.

flay 1. a need or desire to get to the heart of a problem, likely emotional. 2. fear of confrontation, of another's disapproval.

fleas 1. there is some cheating afoot, manipulation. 2. especially hurtful gossip is going around. 3. worries and unhappiness.

fleet 1. hope. 2. changes in business. 3. news coming from someone dear. 4. feelings of being overwhelmed, overstimulated, possibly romantically.

flesh 1. overindulgences, possible extremes of behavior, usually sexual in nature. 2. the substance, fabric or "meat" of a problem.

flies 1. irritated by friends, bad behavior and petty conflicts. 2. fear or anxiety over communicable disease, concerns over cleanliness. 3. need to reassess plans for faults or potential problems.

flight 1. basic instincts under stress (as in "fight or flight" response). 2. a desire to run away or distance self from a problem or difficulty.

flirtation 1. desire for intimacy, love and attention. 2. good fortune and happiness.

floating 1. indicates balance, a feeling of lightness, unburdened and unencumbered—often a journey through the unconscious, sometimes a spiritual one. 2. freedom, obstacles can be overcome with less worry (note condition of water).

flood 1. emotionally overwhelmed. 2. sexual release (rushing water).

floor 1. foundation (as in the "floor beneath your feet"). 2. separation between parts of the mind, conscious and unconscious. 3. use caution in business ventures (sweeping).

flour 1. wealth and prosperity through hard work, thriftiness and care. 2. domestic happiness. 3. thoughts or concerns over the basic ingredients of life, usually emotional.

flower 1. youth. 2. beauty and innocence. 3. female sexuality. 4. sadness (white flowers). 5. disappointment (wilted). 6. respect and admiration (bouquet).

fluffy 1. comfort, consolation. 2. triviality, insignificance, unimportance. 3. feelings of whimsy, frivolity, possibly immature but pleasant diversions.

fluorescent 1. the ability to understand ideas and concepts with clarity. 2. a new understanding—usually intellectual, sometimes spiritual.

flute 1. a good omen regarding financial matters. 2. domestic contentment, satisfaction. 3. ability to communicate over distance.

flying 1. freedom, transcendence. 2. desire for freedom, no restrictions. 3. desire for dominance. 4. good news is on the way.

flypaper 1. unhealthy conditions in the environment, possible health risk. 2. feelings of unseemliness; feeling soiled, usually emotionally, and sometimes with feelings of guilt. 3. stuck or trapped in a situation.

foal 1. new but exciting work in the offing. 2. a possible pregnancy in the offing. 3. a new adventure is about to begin.

foam 1. a good omen regarding friends and social circle. 2. confusion, bewilderment (sea foam).

fog 1. lack of clarity, obscurity. 2. confusion. 3. the point between the real and the unreal. 4. troubles and worry.

food 1. nourishment—often emotional, more frequently spiritual. 2. fortune in love affairs (feeding others). 3. repressed sexual desire (eating).

footstep 1. legacy, inheritance. 2. a good omen of success. 3. good news is in the offing.

forefinger 1. direction, authority and judgment. 2. a point or message trying to get across, possibly from one level of consciousness to the next. 3. accusations and harsh judgment.

forehead 1. power and influence. 2. independence, self-reliance. 3. maturity, wisdom and experience (to see a wrinkled forehead).

foreigners 1. misunderstanding, usually due to inability or awkwardness in communication. 2. retrieving something lost. 3. aspect of personality never seen before.

forest 1. place of fear, unknown dangers. 2. time of change, exploration, usually of unconscious. 3. someone loves and cares for the dreamer (thick forest).

fork 1. an important turning point in life or ways of thinking (as in a "fork in the road"). 2. a release from concerns. 3. an extension of self, the ability to "grasp" things and process them. 4. negative feelings, anger and bitterness (a pitchfork).

formula 1. plans and ideas. 2. a good omen for romance and intimate affairs. 3. the knowledge of what must be done to correct a problem or difficulty.

fortress 1. emotional protection. 2. emotional withdrawal. 3. the body. 4. illness (if under siege). 5. strong sexual desire (if attacking a fortress).

fossil 1. respect or awe for the past, longevity. 2. possible illness in the offing. 3. outdated, no longer useful emotions, sometimes patterns of behavior.

fountain 1. emotional expression, sensitivity. 2. transition from the subconscious to the conscious. 3. pleasure, joy. 4. success comes from devotion.

four 1. balance, harmony. 2. free will, choice (as in the "four directions"). 3. fairness, evenness and justice. 4. stability and independence. 5. change, a new beginning in the offing.

fourteen 1. humility, the ability to "listen and learn." 2. independence, self-reliance and confidence.

fowl 1. a good omen of a prosperous life. 2. a rise in social status. 3. any problems, such as illness, will be short-lived.

fox 1. a fox possesses cleverness, discretion and cunning and is therefore the intellect and quick wits. 2. use caution; deceitful rivals or even friends involved in a seemingly threatening situation. 3. problems and obstacles may be overcome with careful thought.

foyer a new beginning, a new phase of life.

fraternity 1. brotherhood. 2. puerile, bad, adolescent behavior.

fraud 1. a sense or feeling of treachery, if being defrauded. 2. use caution in business matters or relationships; moral or principled reassessment of activities.

freckles 1. indicator of sexual attractiveness; many freckles mean a lot of love. 2. unpleasant events occur or are recalled from adolescence.

free 1. release—likely from emotional difficulties, often from a bad situation. 2. happiness is at hand, likely in relationships.

freeway 1. the flow of forward progress, the ability to realize goals and ambitions. 2. a lack of inhibitions, sense of "freedom."

freight 1. weight, a burden or obligation, usually emotional. 2. a feeling that positive change is in the offing, often in professional or business affairs.

French 1. passion and sensuality (person or language). 2. love (language, speaking French). 3. misunderstanding the nature of a relationship (not understanding the language).

freshmen 1. youth and inexperience. 2. entering a new phase of life, a new beginning.

friend 1. aspects of the personality. 2. happy news, welcome news. 3. regression or childishness (childhood friend). 4. difficulty letting go of the past (childhood friend).

frogs 1. surprising gifts are on their way. 2. renewal, fertility. 3. transformation and growth, indicating a period of change. 4. difficulty accepting situations or individuals for what they are (as in "to change a frog into a prince"). 5. male genitals.

frost 1. emotional distancing, usually of one individual to another, often involving anger. 2. use caution in business and personal affairs (frostbite or frost damage, especially to food crops). 3. advancement or travel in the offing.

frozen 1. an aspect of self or personality has halted, been put on hold ("frozen in time"). 2. emotional aloofness, detachment, often to the point of cruelty. 3. kindness and affection will be rewarded (to be freezing).

fruit 1. pleasure and productivity. 2. spiritual knowledge and growth. 3. a moderate degree of prosperity. 4. possible pregnancy. 5. temptation.

frustration 1. feelings of long-repressed anger coming to the surface. 2. a feeling that dreams and desires are unattainable, especially if the frustration is sexual. 3. plans have gone awry.

fuchsia 1. taste and refinement, culture. 2. emotional tranquility or a measure of it. 3. awareness, connectedness to the environment or spirituality.

full moon 1. avoidance of responsibilities, obligations, possibly bad behavior (as in "blame it on the moon"). 2. magic, mystery and romance.

funeral 1. ending a situation or relationship. 2. lucky in love. 3. a need to let go of some aspect of self and move on.

fun house 1. irony under difficult circumstances. 2. a strong sense that difficulties will be overcome; worry and fear are no longer necessary.

furnace 1. a good omen whether lit or not, usually regarding financial matters and security. 2. source of energy, warmth— usually spiritually, often physically.

furniture 1. perception of domestic arrangements, family. 2. economic status.

furs 1. honors, wealth and prosperity. 2. animal instincts, often sexual. 3. luxury and sensuality.

future visualization of hopes and fears.

fuzzy 1. emergence of repressed memories. 2. difficulty in understanding concepts or situations clearly. 3. softness, comfort and consolation (to touch something fuzzy).

G

gag 1. unable to say what one means. 2. a warning to keep quiet.

galaxy 1. creativity. 2. concern about eternal questions. 3. symbol of beauty.

gale 1. caught in a difficult problem that can't be avoided. 2. being blown away into greater problems.

gallows 1. betrayed by someone. 2. an empty gallows is a warning that something bad is occurring, and one should examine one's life. 3. if the dreamer is complicit in a hanging, then he/she has betrayed the person being hanged.

gambling 1. to dream of winning at gambling suggests that the opposite could be true—one will lose. 2. willingness to take a chance on everything from business to romance. 3. the dreamer is involved in some venture involving great risk.

game 1. gambling with some aspect of one's life. 2. vying with an adversary. 3. the principle or rules one plays by. 4. playing a game signifies being competitive with someone. 5. freedom of expression. 6. need to control or manipulate. 7. feeling of power.

game (wild animal) the willingness and ability to track and trap a wild animal indicates one has great confidence and courage.

gang 1. family concern or problem. 2. need to gather allies in a coming encounter. 3. unable to ward off attacks.

gangrene 1. indicates bad times are brewing for the dreamer, including loss of loved ones. 2. one is afflicted with a physical or mental condition that can kill unless dealt with. 3. the need to cut out a way of life that is damaging.

garage 1. cemetery, graveyard. 2. the underworld. 3. the unconscious. 4. staying in a garage signifies being unable to galvanize one's own efforts in one's behalf. 5. driving out of a garage means taking action. 6. parking car in garage refers to returning to safety after a difficult time.

garb pomposity.

garbage 1. if disposing of (taking out) garbage, one is actively engaged in cleaning up one's life in some way, perhaps by discarding acquaintances who pull the dreamer down. 2. landscape littered with garbage could indicate that one is very unhappy with one's life.

garden 1. if the garden is in poor condition, it means one should take steps to correct whatever is in bad shape in one's life, usually of a romantic nature. 2. passion. 3. spirit. 4. origin of "roots."

gardening 1. planting ideas (planting seeds). 2. learning from experience (picking fruit). 3. pruning roses relates to love or sex life. 4. ridding oneself of any excess. 5. satisfied with one's life. 6. growing healthier psychologically.

gargle attempt to wash bad taste from one's mouth based on unpleasant encounter with someone.

gargoyle 1. fear that a monster will pursue one. 2. inner, secret view of self. 3. hidden fears of someone. 4. considering going to church, returning to religion.

garland one is proud of one's achievement.

garlic 1. if eating garlic, one is looking to achieve better health. 2. eating garlic also might indicate a feeling that one needs to repel others (pungent breath).

garnet concern about a home improvement (sandpaper).

garret if the dreamer imagines living in a garret, he or she has aspirations toward art.

garter 1. a female picturing herself wearing a garter on her upper leg is worried about being discovered for "loose" sexual habits. 2. if a man pictures a woman with a garter, he is sexually drawn to her. 3. a lost garter indicates a lost romance. 4. desire to get married.

gas, natural 1. smelling natural gas is a warning that a situation is dangerous and should be dealt with immediately. 2. if one smells gas and deals with it by lighting a pilot light, it indicates that the problem is solved.

gasoline running on empty reflects one's running out of physical or emotional gasoline.

gas station 1. place where one can go to reenergize oneself, perhaps symbolizing a vacation spa. 2. place where one thinks others can reenergize themselves.

gate 1. entry to a new phase of one's life. 2. new opportunity. 3. if gate can't be opened, something is stopping the dreamer's ability to go forward.

gathering 1. if part of the group, indication that one gets along well with others. 2. if one is willing to become part of group, indicates one is willing to be reasonable.

gavel 1. justice. 2. authority. 3. a problem that one needs to deal with.

gear 1. depending on what the gear is, one will want to engage in the activity it represents. 2. if gear is on a car, one will want to take a trip. 3. if putting a car in gear, one is going forward. 4. if putting car in reverse, one is militating against one's own progress.

gecko 1. cuteness. 2. agreement. 3. car insurance.

geese 1. domesticity. 2. messiness (because of droppings); dumb. 3. fidelity. 4. loyalty.

geisha 1. beautiful but tragic. 2. submissive.

Gemini as in the zodiac, represents vivacity, youthfulness, alertness and versatility.

gemstone one wearing a gemstone is extra special.

genie 1. the dreamer believes in magic. 2. creativity.

genitals attitude toward sexual activities: puritanical, open, etc.

genius 1. one's image of oneself. 2. what one aspires to be.

geography desire to travel.

gentleman 1. hoping to meet someone with the qualities a gentleman embodies. 2. need someone gentle in one's life.

geographer trying to find one's way to a new place, actual or emotional.

German shepherd 1. toughness. 2. nobility. 3. training a shepherd marks the trainer as a strong person.

geometric an attempt to control the world by redesigning it into geometric sections.

Gershwin one wants romance to come into one's life.

geyser 1. expression of sexual outburst. 2. expression of emotional outburst, particularly anger.

ghetto 1. feeling that perhaps it would be better to be separate from someone, or some group. 2. feeling proud to be part of a particular group.

ghost 1. unspecified fear in waking life. 2. unidentified but upsetting memory. 3. need for emotional sustenance of some sort.

ghoul 1. oddball characteristics. 2. different from others.

giant 1. battle between the dreamer and some adversary. 2. a problem that looks impossible to solve.

gift 1. giving something to others is giving something of oneself. 2. trying to express a feeling. 3. receiving a gift shows that people around one admire one.

gigolo 1. if visiting, one is sexually hungry. 2. a need for sexual variety in one's life. 3. one wants to attract.

gin need to relax, play a game.

ginger one's life needs spice added.

ginseng the desire for healthy sexual activity.

giraffe 1. imagining oneself as a giraffe is to think of oneself as odd. 2. one should take a broad, overall view of things. 3. to have a giraffe as a pet signals a person wanting to be separate from a crowd.

girder 1. one is going to be called on to support someone. 2. the dreamer is the key supporting element in some undertaking.

girdle feeling restricted, emotionally and/or intellectually.

girlfriend if one's girlfriend appears one has the opportunity to express true feelings about her.

girls desire to express the feminine side of one's personality.

glacier realize that the greatest part of people is beneath the surface.

glass 1. if glass is broken, one has made a mistake, and it will be difficult or impossible to correct it. 2. if glass is half full of liquid, then one looks at life optimistically. 3. if one imagines glass is half empty, then life is perceived negatively. 4. if one observes a glass or glasses sparkling, this also states that one has an optimistic view of life.

glasses one needs to see things better.

glass house the dreamer suspects he/she is being observed.

glass slipper one has hope for future success.

globe 1. world view. 2. one controls one's own world.

gloves unwillingness to get closely involved with a situation by touching it with bare hands; type of gloves (work, rubber, etc.) hints at the type of job.

glow a glow around an object indicates a respect for the item.

glue 1. fear of involvement. 2. fear that a situation may break and need repair.

glutton 1. suggestion to slow down in one's life. 2. one should go on a diet.

goal one has achieved something aspired to ("score a goal").

goat 1. lower down on the social scale than most groups. 2. ability to absorb great indignities. 3. stupid and gullible. 4. no compassion (from Steinbeck's reference in *East of Eden*: "She had eyes like a goat, flat, no depth, devoid of human compassion").

God 1. father figure. 2. creation. 3. striving for an unreachable perfection. 4. one's spiritual feelings. 5. deep need for emotional relief.

goddess secret love.

godfather 1. someone to be feared. 2. someone to ask the aid of. 3. rely more on one's family.

Godzilla 1. desire to be a great baseball player (à la Hideki Matsui of the New York Yankees). 2. if one imagines oneself as Godzilla, one thinks of him/herself as very powerful. 3. if

Godzilla is an enemy, one deeply fears whomever the character represents in life. 4. fear of some great evil. 5. facing Godzilla means facing one's fears. 6. fears are out of control.

gold 1. if common household items, such as spoons, forks and bowls, are made of gold, it means that one values his/her present existence. 2. if one sees gold jewelry, it indicates free spending is occurring. 3. stacked bars of gold indicate careful money management. 4. security. 5. power.

goldfish bowl 1. boredom with one's life, career or relationships. 2. innocence.

golf 1. need to relax. 2. one's opponent may represent another side of one's character. 3. one's score—good or bad—is a way of measuring one's achievements.

gondola 1. the need to get away from it all. 2. longing for romance.

goose maternal love and caring.

goose bumps one is afraid of someone or something.

gorge unexpected difficulty has suddenly appeared.

gorilla 1. symbol of one's primitive nature. 2. fear of someone very powerful and daunting.

gorse hope for the future.

gossip 1. engaging in gossip indicates anger ("being catty") at someone. 2. device for making one feel better about oneself.

goulash someone of foreign extraction is in one's life and must be watched.

gourd 1. the womb. 2. abundance.

government 1. a feeling of being overpowered, unable to "fight city hall." 2. something powerful.

graduate 1. suggestion one has paid dues in a particular field and should go on to something else. 2. implied suggestion that the dreamer look forward to the future.

grafting 1. making connections with others for mutual benefit. 2. trying to repair a relationship.

grammar studying it indicates the dreamer is trying to do the right thing.

grandchild 1. a need to see the world as pure and innocent. 2. a need to escape from stresses of life.

grandmother need for unqualified love or other characteristics that are reflected in one's grandmother.

grandparents 1. need for love and guidance or other qualities that one's grandparents embody. 2. need to return to childhood. 3. need to be safe. 4. need for nurturing and security. 5. a search for grandparents means the dreamer is searching for love and protection. 6. a dreamer who dreams of him/herself as a grandparent sees self as a nurturer.

grandstand get a better view of something.

granite someone or something is indomitable.

grant 1. looking for monetary help. 2. looking for religious help.

grapefruit 1. hostility toward someone (from the James Cagney movie where he pushes a grapefruit into his girlfriend's face). 2. need to go on a diet.

grapes 1. trying to see the potential in someone or something. 2. one aspires to be wealthy. 3. the lush life.

grasp 1. hang on tightly to something one values greatly. 2. a dream of attaining something.

grass 1. if cutting, the need to hone or trim back something in one's life. 2. refers to some aspect of a vacation. 3. if the grass is lush and green, one's life is full and peaceful. 4. if grass is burned, brown or ragged, it means that one views one's life as unsuccessful. 5. planting grass seed or laying sod means that one is trying to renew one's life. 6. the need to be relaxed (lie down, play golf, etc.). 7. slang expression for marijuana.

grasshopper 1. a force hostile to the dreamer. 2. pointing out a grasshopper to others indicates indiscreet behavior on their part.

grave 1. visit to a grave may be a sign that the visitor needs to examine issues, perhaps unconscious, that were purportedly put to rest. 2. ready for a new start. 3. digging a grave may signify trying to unearth something that is bothering one.

gravel 1. concern with one's home. 2. concern with throat (gravelly sound).

gravestone signal to change the characteristics in oneself that are reflected in the character of the deceased person.

graveyard 1. fear of the unknown. 2. visiting issues put to rest. 3. observing discarded portions of one's personality. 4. an attempt to deal with a loss.

gravity 1. one wants to fly, to be free. 2. achieve something significant.

gravy 1. money to come. 2. something to make life more palatable, tastier.

gray 1. feeling depressed. 2. sickly.

grease 1. want to smooth the way of something. 2. if covered with grease, it indicates one has been working very hard at something. 3. to achieve an end one may have to get dirty.

greasepaint an attempt to disguise insecurities.

Greek 1. ability to read Greek for a nonnative means that the person values learning. 2. acceptance of new ideas.

green (color) 1. virginity. 2. birth. 3. dissatisfaction. 4. a new experience or fear of new experiences. 5. one feels at home in a healthy outdoor environment. 6. "green light" to go ahead on some project. 7. someone is feeling "green with envy" at the achievements of someone else.

greenhouse 1. one is trying to change, to grow, but in a controlled way. 2. one is too controlling.

greeting 1. if shaking hands with someone warmly, one is ready to take on a new project. 2. if one refuses to shake a hand, one is not ready for a project.

greeting card 1. one expects to be surprised. 2. if sending the card to someone, the dreamer has high regard for that person. 3. if receiving a card, the sender is expressing his/her regard.

Grenada looking to get away from it all.

grenade 1. danger is on the way (unexploded). 2. one has some sort of hostility toward someone. 3. one has been badly surprised by something.

greyhound 1. sleek, strong, but a meaningless life. 2. sweet, friendly.

grief mourning the loss of something.

grill one is feeling pressure.

Grim Reaper 1. fear of death. 2. embodiment of parts of personality that the dreamer keeps hidden from him/herself. 3. the end of something.

Grinch 1. one is going down the wrong road. 2. sign that you must have compassion and concern for yourself.

grinder pay more attention to one's teeth.

grindstone 1. willingness to make things perfect. 2. sharpening tools indicates that, if needed, friends will be there to help.

grit 1. toughness. 2. something is bothering one in a small but annoying way.

groans the dreamer is groaning, losing a battle to enemies.

grocer caretaker.

groceries 1. the dreamer has the capacity to survive. 2. symbol of a secure household.

grope 1. confused, trying to find something. 2. sexual encounter.

group 1. if a group is observed that is controlled, not threatening in any way, the dreamer feels like he/she is accepted into the group. 2. if the group is disorderly and threatening, the dreamer feels like an outsider. 3. if the dreamer is separated from the group without any feeling of not being part of it, then the dreamer perceives him/herself as an independent thinker. 4. if there is a yearning to be part of the group, it means that one is yearning for acceptance.

grovel what one feels he/she is doing to obtain something.

grub 1. an irritation in one's life. 2. one has to borrow something from someone.

guard 1. the appearance of a guard usually means one is being warned to be wary. 2. one is alerted that someone else may need guarding.

guerrilla one is waging a private battle with someone and has to be very crafty to win.

guest 1. one is launching a new project, familiar or unfamiliar. 2. one does not want to face up to something. 3. someone requires special attention. 4. a stranger coming signifies a quest for new adventures, interests or work. 5. a wish to adopt desirable personality characteristics of the guest.

guide one requires the help of someone.

guillotine 1. one is planning to dispense with or cut off something. 2. fear of punishment for something one has done in life.

guilt 1. fear of punishment. 2. lack of confidence in oneself.

guinea pig 1. the ability to learn from one's mistakes. 2. a helpless victim.

guitar 1. sexuality. 2. need to express feelings.

gull bridge between the worlds of sleeping and waking.

gulls if flying, freedom.

gun 1. perception of a problem where only a very difficult solution will solve it. 2. a feeling of being threatened. 3. worry about the neighborhood one lives in. 4. if one is loading a gun, anger is building. 5. hidden aggressiveness. 6. hidden power.

gunfire situation is going to result in a fight.

gunplay serious combatants.

gunpowder 1. one is hostile toward someone. 2. one is outraged.

gymnast 1. desire to be free. 2. idealized self-image. 3. yearning to be courageous.

gypsy 1. longing to be free—and responsibility-free. 2. expression of secret thieving instincts.

H

haggard 1. possible illness. 2. extreme fatigue, usually from some situation. 3. worries and fears concerning a love relationship.

hail 1. a sense of difficult times ahead. 2. disappointments.

hair 1. strength and virility. 2. fear of castration (to cut). 3. fear of impotency (hair loss). 4. infidelity (if shaved on a woman). 5. lies (red hair).

haircut 1. loss of strength, sense of power. 2. financial gains. 3. fear of losing sexuality.

hairdresser 1. exerting control over others. 2. self or self-image needs attention. 3. success will have to wait.

hairy 1. the animal or "beastly" side of self. 2. annoyances or difficulties that just do not seem to go away. 3. a particularly frightening event or situation (as in a "hairy situation" or a "close shave"). 4. intrigue and manipulation.

hall 1. community relationships. 2. start of a path. 3. passage, spiritual or emotional. 4. vagina. 5. two-faced individual.

Halloween 1. a need or desire to change identity, possibly to "mask" a wrongdoing or pranksterism. 2. a need or desire to relax, be less "grave" for a while. 3. repressed feelings of fear and anxiety regarding the unknown, possibly death.

hallucination 1. the dreamer will not accept feelings or memories that need to be addressed. 2. a situation or a relationship is not what it appears.

halo 1. divine attributes, power. 2. difficulties lead to good fortune. 3. human aura (note color). 4. quick success in endeavors (solar halo). 5. quest for perfection.

halter 1. a need or desire to maintain control—usually in life, often of emotions. 2. an attempt to influence people or situations. 3. obstacles will be overcome, things put in order (halter on a woman). 4. love and business will work out as desired.

ham 1. happiness and success, usually in business or professional life. 2. a problematic attention-seeker (as in "ham it up" or a "big ham"). 3. festivities, celebration of good fortune. 4. emotional difficulty.

hammer 1. strength and virility. 2. construction and building. 3. fertility and growth. 4. a need or desire to be listened to or understood.

hamster 1. a need or desire for time alone and undisturbed. 2. new, emerging feelings, not yet fully formed. 3. anger and frustration with current social circle.

hand 1. strength, power and protection. 2. tool, construction; ability to complete tasks. 3. blessings, healing. 4. creating debts (cut). 5. to lend aid (as in "helping hand"). 6. communication.

handcuffs 1. feelings of powerlessness; feeling trapped or restrained. 2. strong feelings of guilt—usually over a lost temper, often over past misdeeds. 3. reverse: obstacles will be overcome, prosperity achieved. 4. a possible brush with the law is in the offing.

handkerchiefs 1. overwhelming feelings of sadness—possibly grief and loss, possibly over a love relationship. 2. serious arguments, possibly irreconcilable (a bloodstained handkerchief). 3. social embarrassment, downfall, sometimes due to indiscretions, flirtations.

handshake 1. completion and renewal, beginnings and endings— often in relationships, sometimes in situations. 2. having a good reputation, a high social position.

handwriting 1. self-expression; dignity and self-honor. 2. to relay messages from one aspect of self to another. 3. the truth is revealed regarding a situation or relationship (as in the "handwriting on the wall").

hanging 1. unfinished business or relationship (as in "left hanging"). 2. period of uncertainty, insecurity. 3. a period of change.

happy 1. a need or desire to be relieved of worries and concerns. 2. a good omen regarding feelings about the future. 3. relief, contentment regarding a situation or circumstance.

harbor 1. safety zone, out of the storm, often from a relationship. 2. sheltered personality, possibly in a relationship. 3. a sense of difficult times ahead.

hardware store 1. a need or desire to fix things up, set them straight—often to repair or adjust attitudes and modes of behavior, usually to improve emotional quality of life. 2. possible feelings of sexual inadequacy, need for improvements. 3. difficulties in relationships, a need for repairs (as in to "patch things up").

harem 1. a desire for or appreciation of abundance and luxury. 2. multiple opportunities for romantic involvement. 3. repressed sexuality, shyness of sensual pleasures.

harlot 1. disapproval of one's own actions; self-scorn. 2. recent pursuits may seem unwise, unsafe. 3. possible loss of reputation.

harmonica 1. social relationships, happiness. 2. a need or desire for more social interaction, pleasantries and good company. 3. wordplay on a need or desire for greater balance and harmony in life.

harp 1. heavenly or spiritual pursuits, harmony and balance. 2. sadness over the misfortunes of others, difficulties, loss or illness (to hear sad harp music). 3. the inability to "let something go" like a mistake or a misdeed (as in "harping on it").

harvest 1. a measure of success and prosperity (note how good the harvest is). 2. will only gain insofar as one gives (as in "to reap what one sows"). 3. more work needs to be done before goals and ambitions are fully achieved, usually professionally.

hassock 1. a feeling of triumph over problems or problem people (to put one's feet up on a hassock). 2. a feeling or desire for greater humility, spiritual enhancement or divine assistance (to pray while kneeling on a hassock).

hat 1. authority, power. 2. concealment. 3. social status. 4. healing, recovery (woman's hat).

hatch 1. projects or plans will soon be realized. 2. negative ways of thinking or patterns of behavior are about to be replaced.

hatchet 1. tremendous emotional discomfort, fear and anxiety. 2. to defame or libel an individual or reputation (as in a "hatchet job"). 3. reconciliations are possible.

hate 1. long-repressed anger, never dealt with, needs to be addressed. 2. need to examine thoughts and feelings toward others, possible misjudgment. 3. emotionally draining relationship.

haunting 1. past fears, often from a traumatic event, require attention. 2. regrets from the past need to be resolved or "laid to rest."

hawk 1. motives are questioned related to activities. 2. caution needed in business deals. 3. clear insight and ability to rise above it all with a noble attitude.

hay 1. prosperity, love life and freedom. 2. reverse: finances may need looking after, or work is more involved, harder than initially thought. 3. opportunities are in the offing (as in "making hay"). 4. thoughts are turning to love-making (as in a "roll in the hay"). 5. wordplay on "hey" in an effort to draw attention to something overlooked.

head 1. the conscious mind, the intellect. 2. fortunes and fortunate love relationships are in the offing. 3. slang for oral sex. 4. a need for control, calm in difficult or desperate circumstances (as in "to keep one's head").

headache 1. a need or desire to improve, nourish, liberate the intellect. 2. small annoyances have gotten out of hand. 3. possible illness. 4. difficulties of identity, ability to accept self.

headmaster 1. a need or desire to seek assistance from a knowledgeable individual. 2. lessons needed to be learned. 3. a tendency to be too hard on oneself.

headphones 1. a message is being conveyed to the wearer alone. 2. a need or desire to focus, to exclude other diversions. 3. feeling and intuition, being in tune with one's instincts.

headstone 1. aspect of self set aside, repressed until now. 2. a message from the subconscious, usually about direction in life (inscription). 3. long life ahead.

heal 1. something damaged or in need of repair, often emotional. 2. possible health issues. 3. a need or desire to make right what is wrong, make amends.

health 1. a good omen for most things. 2. difficulties in business, a need to avoid risk-taking (especially if the dream involved recovering health).

hear 1. the ability to take in new feelings and situations, often in relationships (note the quality of hearing). 2. feelings of insignificance (to not be heard). 3. a need or desire to focus, pay greater attention, often in a relationship (near-deafness or the appearance of a hearing aid).

hearse entering a new phase of life leaving old worries and cares behind.

heart 1. seat of compassion and tolerance. 2. opposite of intellect (head). 3. truth, courage (lionheart). 4. central part of a situation (as in "heart of the matter"). 5. lack of tolerance.

heart attack 1. loss of something with great emotional attachment. 2. possible separation in intimate relationship. 3. feelings of insecurity, desire to feel accepted and loved.

heartbeat 1. powerful feelings, often love, either growing or in need of attention. 2. possible health issues. 3. primal fear or threat is perceived (rapid, adrenaline-induced heart rate).

hearth 1. the center of domestic life. 2. a good omen in most things. 3. prosperity and a happy home life.

heat 1. sexual strength and passion. 2. feelings of being overwhelmed by embarrassment, possibly a little shame; a blush. 3. a need to express intense emotion (as in the "heat of the moment"). 4. expressions of anger (as in "hot-tempered"). 5. energy and creativity.

heater 1. emotional care and nurturing (note how hot the heater is). 2. a good omen in business affairs (a cold furnace). 3. a tendency toward anger or much repressed anger.

heaven 1. great joy and happiness. 2. spirit realm. 3. seat or home of divinity. 4. restoration of hope, optimism.

heavy 1. burden and responsibility. 2. a measure of wealth. 3. emotional burdens, sadness or grief.

hedge 1. barrier or obstacle. 2. emotional boundary (often positive if the hedge is cared for and trimmed).

hedgehog 1. sensitivity, seriousness, possible defensiveness. 2. a grave or moral decision in the offing.

heel 1. an often negative omen. 2. domestic or social difficulties in the offing (a sore or injured heel). 3. feelings of being repressed, put upon.

height 1. the inner self, the spirit of an individual. 2. goals and ambitions, gauged by the ability to reach objectives. 3. concern over knowing what to do with success (fear of heights).

helicopter 1. the realization of ambitions, a measure of goals. 2. a broad and informed point of view. 3. use caution in business and financial matters.

hell 1. change of circumstance. 2. seemingly inescapable situation. 3. repressed feelings of guilt, punishment.

helmet 1. fear of frustration, often of being misunderstood. 2. keeping thoughts private, guarded.

help 1. feelings of being lost, overwhelmed—often emotionally, usually in business or life. 2. help will soon be required; a message not to be afraid to ask for it. 3. understanding, compromise, usually in social situations.

hemp 1. to postpone success (to smoke hemp). 2. difficulty in facing reality (to smoke hemp). 3. the path to success (a hemp rope).

herbs 1. expresses a need to use new ideas for old problems. 2. balance and satisfaction are in the offing (an herb garden). 3. use caution around rough situations and possibly malicious people (poisonous plants and herbs). 4. a knowledge and appreciation of good friendships, pleasure and warmth (pleasant aromatic herbs). 5. being well-loved.

hermit 1. to hide oneself or an aspect of self away. 2. a desire or need to withdraw from the fray for a while; time alone. 3. fear or shyness about trying something new, taking risks. 4. serenity and peace can come from self-knowledge and quiet contemplation.

hero 1. internal fortitude, personal power. 2. reverse: behavior warrants reassessment; moral questions or conflicts. 3. a hopeful proposition or change in attitude in the offing.

heroin 1. a need or desire to detach, escape. 2. difficult times, serious worries are in the offing. 3. possible wordplay on "heroine," to idolize a woman.

heron 1. balance and serenity in life. 2. need for patient, careful planning that covers the depth of a potential problem.

herring 1. a good omen for upcoming projects, adventures or journeys. 2. a need for good nutrition for the hungry mind (as in "brain food"). 3. use caution for possible deceptions or misunderstandings, usually emotional (as in a "red herring").

hidden 1. secrets or aspects of self kept hidden for protection. 2. feelings of guilt or regret (as in to "hide out").

hide 1. difficulty in facing hard emotional situations or life choices. 2. expresses a fear of growth and change, usually a change of a life phase or mode of behavior. 3. someone has a secret he/she needs to let go of.

hieroglyphs 1. confusion, difficulties with communication. 2. obstacles related to communication or journeys, possibly life journeys. 3. understanding concepts and ideas lies just out of reach.

high heels 1. feminine appeal, sexuality. 2. constricted in social roles, limited mobility. 3. vulnerability to pain (pinching, discomfort).

high school 1. passionate friendships. 2. conflicts are temporary. 3. need to take goals and ambitions more seriously. 4. return to old ways of thinking, old worries and fears.

high tide 1. a knowledge that positive things will happen shortly. 2. a swelling up or "high tide" of emotions. 3. projects and plans are progressing well. 4. a time of change, renewal, possibly in environment.

hijack 1. fears and anxieties—usually over loss of emotional control, often over loss of control of a situation. 2. anger or feelings of futility that one has no control over destiny. 3. someone has "hijacked" the dreamer's projects, activities or even relationships.

hike 1. independence, self-reliance. 2. goals and ambitions realized through hard work. 3. perseverance will bring success.

hill 1. a large undertaking or project. 2. an obstacle. 3. success (standing at the top). 4. very good luck. 5. woman's breast.

hips 1. the ability to move and adapt to a changing environment. 2. a gauge and measure of wealth (large hips indicate prosperity and small or injured hips point to losses). 3. health and well-being of domestic partnerships. 4. avoid casual relationships.

hissing 1. a sense that deceit is slowly revealing itself (to hear a hissing snake). 2. a need for caution in expressing anger inappropriately (a hissing snake). 3. progress will continue in spite of others (people hissing rudely).

history 1. reverse: to look forward to opportunities and possibilities. 2. applying outdated values or solutions to new situations and problems. 3. current activities, projects or events have a permanent importance (also note what is happening in the history).

hitchhiking 1. reckless thoughts or behavior. 2. feelings of being adrift, reliant on others for goals and ambitions. 3. taking advantage of others.

hitting 1. repressed anger seeking outlet in inappropriate ways. 2. intensifying conflict, with likely irreversible consequences.

hive (beehive) 1. the locus of industry, productivity and prosperity (note the mood of the bees and how much they are getting done because of it). 2. the center of activity and power that controls situations and events.

hives 1. irritations grow more annoying the more attention and concern they receive. 2. reverse: a good omen that things are moving along well.

hoe 1. work needs to be done before improvements happen. 2. preparations before an important project or undertaking, often emotional (to prepare a field or garden with a hoe). 3. moving beyond old limits to a greater growth. 4. slang for prostitute.

hogs 1. financial prospects depending on the condition of the hogs (as in "bringing home the bacon"). 2. symbolic of a person deemed dreadful, sometimes with poor sexual boundaries or boundaries in general (as in a "pig" or "swine"). 3. inclined toward a tendency to hoard, not share.

hole 1. feeling unsatisfied, empty. 2. a desire or need to experience new things, hobbies. 3. undesirable encounters (crawling into a hole).

holiday 1. time to break a little with routine, possible rest from responsibilities. 2. absence from responsibilities or obligations.

Holy Communion 1. counting or being aware of "blessings," looking on the positive side of affairs. 2. seeking greater spiritual enhancement or "communion." 3. reverse: a feeling of disappointment, possibly rejection, "outsider-ness."

home 1. emotional, physical and spiritual abode, center. 2. desire for family (of or in childhood home). 3. time of transition from one stage of life to another. 4. domestic security.

homeless 1. insecurity—usually spiritual and/or emotional, sometimes physical. 2. feeling uncentered, adrift.

homesick 1. reverse: comfort with present home life and setting. 2. a feeling of loss of self; emotional distance from friends, family and intimate partners. 3. feelings of personal insecurity, a lack of protection or care and affection (if childhood home is missed).

homicide 1. a possible need for a vigorous, sudden end to old habits and modes of behavior, often involuntary. 2. reverse: long life, security and safety. 3. possible feelings of anguish and humiliation. 4. an extreme state of repressed anger, hostility.

homosexual 1. need or desire to become more in touch with self. 2. attraction to member of the same sex—usually emotionally, sometimes physically. 3. anxieties regarding own sexuality (if afraid). 4. prosperity.

honey 1. purity and pleasure. 2. great success in endeavors and industry, especially with the help of others. 3. repressed need for better communication, assertiveness in expressing needs.

honeysuckle 1. a good omen for marriage and partnerships. 2. happiness regarding any kind of commitment, including those made to oneself for self-improvement, in business and social affairs.

hood 1. a sense or feeling that deception is occurring; use caution in matters of trust. 2. a need or desire for protection for a secret or simply a need to hide—usually emotionally, often socially. 3. slang for neighborhood, immediate environment. 4. short for hoodlum.

hook 1. gifts or important finds are in the offing. 2. a need for the attributes of whatever gets caught by the hook being used. 3. feelings that a preoccupation with something or someone is not a good or helpful idea (as in "get hooked"). 4. possible issues regarding intimacy or intimate relationships, trust.

hookah 1. nonchalant in the face of reality. 2. emotional repression. 3. great success in all affairs.

hoop 1. representing hope, joy and happiness at childlike behavior (to be playing with a hoop). 2. a disorganized, circuslike environment is very demanding; feelings of discouragement (as in to "jump through hoops"). 3. friendships have a greater importance than usual.

horizon 1. a new beginning (east) or end (west). 2. an attempt or desire to gain perspective on life—likely ambitions and goals, possibly emotions.

horn (musical instrument) 1. warning or "call to arms" from one level of consciousness to another. 2. a phallus. 3. a call to repent, a moral question (as in a shofar). 4. a feeling that joyful news is coming.

hornet 1. extreme anger (aggressive or stinging). 2. desire for vengeance against perceived enemies. 3. a sense that someone is jealous.

horns (animal) 1. strength, aggression; conflict. 2. mischievous ("of the devil"). 3. a phallus. 4. magic (unicorn).

horoscope 1. good and exciting, maybe romantic, things are on the way, possibly due to travels or changes. 2. a need to focus on the "here and now" and rely less on fate or destiny. 3. fears and anxieties regarding the future.

horse 1. sexual energy. 2. intelligence. 3. wildness, mystery (dark horse). 4. purity (white horse).

horseshoe 1. good luck and omens for all projects and activities. 2. a measure of success in love (to play a game of horseshoes). 3. progress is impeded (a broken or worn-out horseshoe).

hose 1. need to extinguish some strong passions or emotional conflict. 2. sexual satisfaction, completion. 3. emotional life needs cultivation and care (as in watering a garden).

hospital 1. possible illness or injury—often emotional, sometimes physical, possibly material. 2. being instrumental or playing a role in healing of another (doctor or nurse). 3. view of self or state of being; in need of healing (feeling miserable).

hostage 1. feelings of a loss of control, powerlessness in life. 2. lack of mobility.

hotel 1. state of mind. 2. pause in journey. 3. need for a getaway from demands. 4. need to remove oneself from a state of mind.

hour 1. worry over time, promptness. 2. feelings of loss, often regarding relationships. 3. secrets revealed.

hourglass 1. intense fears regarding time and its use. 2. sense of impending doom (as in "time is running out"). 3. frustration because of an upset routine, change of plans by outside forces (upside down).

house 1. the dreamer: psyche, soul and physical self. 2. financial security. 3. woman.

housekeeper 1. may indicate that help is needed with "house-keeping"; emotional upheavals or feelings of being over-whelmed, often by the past (note the condition of house). 2. the ability to cope and manage life (also note the condition of house). 3. reverse: being a housekeeper, having labors indicates that hard work can pay off.

hugging 1. security and safety. 2. a need or desire for attention, care and affection. 3. a possible change is in the offing.

humidity 1. a fertile environment, especially the intellect (to dream of a humid place or rain forest). 2. possible environment for illness. 3. indicates a sense of anxiety over understanding a situation or problem. 4. intellectual stagnation.

hummingbird 1. problems with commitment, possible fear. 2. fast success comes with focus. 3. small thoughts and concerns are actually very powerful, carry a lot of weight.

hunger 1. left unfulfilled—often sexually, usually spiritually. 2. fleeting, superficial desires left unanswered. 3. in need of affection.

hunting 1. searching, seeking—usually physical, often emotional or spiritual. 2. a feeling that good news, prosperity are in the offing. 3. a quest, most often sexual in nature. 4. a feeling that more effort is required in endeavors.

hurricane 1. powerful, repressed emotions, possibly destructive. 2. difficulties will soon be resolved. 3. major changes as some-thing is "swept away."

hurry 1. caution against avoidable accidents. 2. lack of preparedness results in difficulties. 3. desire, need to reduce stress, get rest in waking life.

hurt 1. to hurt oneself may indicate a tendency to ignore it when others are doing the hurting. 2. reverse: wealth and financial gains. 3. a need or desire to allow time for healing and recovery.

husband 1. aspects of the dreamer, possibly the male (even "fathering") side of self. 2. unconscious feelings toward actual husband. 3. the "fertility" of ideas and creativity.

hut 1. need to assess basic necessities, simplify. 2. overcoming adversity, tragedy.

hydrophobia 1. fear of emotional "drowning" or being overwhelmed, often in a relationship. 2. feminine side of self, possible difficulty in understanding or acceptance. 3. a fear of inner exploration, looking inward.

hyena 1. too many responsibilities and obligations. 2. a good, raucous sense of humor. 3. a feeling that others are taking advantage, too dependent, a drain on the dreamer.

hymn 1. a need or desire to communicate needs and aspirations, often to friends. 2. a connection, communication with the unconscious mind. 3. success and contentment over well-completed projects.

hypocrite 1. someone is being hypocritical (to be a hypocrite or to commit hypocrisy). 2. a feeling that someone may be false, or deceptive. 3. possible health issues or medical contact (as in Hippocrates and the Hippocratic oath).

I
___

Icarus one is getting involved in a foolhardy journey.

ice 1. if ice is dirty and jagged, one feels threatened. 2. if ice is clear and shapely, a diamond ring may be in one's immediate future. 3. if one is afraid of falling through the ice, then some situation in life is threatening one. 4. lacking emotion or feeling. 5. thoughts are frozen. 6. emotions are frozen. 7. if walking on ice, one is in a precarious position. 8. keep cool.

iceberg 1. danger. 2. the most important part of something is out of sight.

ice cream 1. enjoying eating ice cream means one is happy, particularly with sexual matters. 2. if the ice cream is tasteless, one is not satisfied, particularly with love life. 3. keep cool. 4. a situation one is involved in is "cool."

Iceland wherever one plans to go, don't.

iceman something is old-fashioned.

ice milk falseness.

ice pick 1. if present with ice, represents emotional opportunity to break through. 2. hostility.

ice tongs one needs special help to handle a "slippery" problem.

icicles 1. a foreboding landscape, rife with danger. 2. if icicles are melting, then problems they symbolize are also going away. 3. if icicles are very large, they represent a physical threat.

icing adding to an experience to make it more enjoyable.

icon 1. one seeks help from a powerful, religious source. 2. one is being urged to make more frequent and better use of a computer.

id for Freudian thinkers, concern about one's ego.

ID 1. to see one's ID (identification) signifies one's own self-confidence. 2. to lose ID denotes confusion about one's own identity.

Idaho a desire to return to a simpler form of living, like farming.

idealization picturing an ideal person in a dream is often a way to posit someone who is unattainable, and this enables one to avoid the terror of romantic involvement.

idiot 1. dreaming about having mentally deficient children is a message that warns against having children; you will not make a good parent. 2. fear that one's intellectual abilities are lacking. 3. a target that it's easy to express rage to without fear of reprisal. 4. if the dreamer pictures a family member as an idiot, then he/she may be thinking the family member is not understanding them.

idle 1. if the dreamer senses an individual just milling around, doing nothing, then it reflects on his/her own inaction or laziness. 2. one's career or forward progress in some endeavor is at a standstill.

idol 1. if the dreamer sees a friend, associate or relative worshipping someone the dreamer does not respect, it hints at a problem in the relationship between the dreamer and the person who's doing the adoring. 2. breaking an idol, such as a statue, means an attempt to destroy qualities that one doesn't like in oneself.

igloo 1. female sexuality. 2. strength, power. 3. longing for simpler times.

ignites trying to eliminate bad things.

ignition start oneself up.

illness 1. a feeling of despair, of inability to deal with something or someone. 2. if one dreams of being ill, it is the harbinger of a bad future. 3. if the illness is terminal, the dreamer may feel that something is incurably wrong with his/her character. 4. feeling helpless.

illumination a very bright light often refers to the door to heaven (going to the light).

image if one sees an image of oneself, some change is being suggested.

imbibe in using this term, one is trying to rationalize excessive drinking.

imitation 1. fear that something in life is false or misrepresented. 2. belief that one is easily fooled or willing to accept "second best." 3. an indication that one is not completely satisfied with one's image.

impeach take down one's boss or other authority figure.

impediment (speech) fears that one might not be able to communicate clearly.

implements (tools, damaged) 1. one is working with tools, ideas or people that are inferior. 2. frustration in thinking that goals will be difficult or impossible to attain.

implements (tools, good) 1. belief that one has the "tools" to achieve one's goals. 2. challenge to create or build.

impotence 1. one feels unable to cope with some nonsexual type of situation. 2. one feels threatened sexually.

Imus 1. vicious. 2. childish. 3. angry.

inaccurate one is striving too hard for perfection.

incarceration one is locked into something.

incense one wants to have some religion in one's life.

incidental don't get worked up about whatever one is looking at.

incipient something significant is in the offing.

inclines approaching trouble or turmoil.

income one is satisfied or concerned about it.

incurable don't try to solve a problem; move on.

indecent desire to expand one's sexual horizons.

Indian 1. need for independence and freedom. 2. admiration of someone who embodies heroic qualities.

indigent fear of losing everything.

indigestion 1. surrounded by sadness or depression. 2. unable to "stomach" something done or said to one.

indigo exotic.

indiscreet 1. having an affair. 2. making a verbal faux pas that is embarrassing to someone else and/or oneself.

industry a measurement of how well—or poorly—one is pursuing one's goals.

infant(s) 1. joy or celebration of life. 2. longing to return to the womb. 3. childhood and innocence.

infanticide desire to kill the child inside one who is interfering with emotional progress.

infantry one feels under siege by something.

infection 1. nagging or persistent problem. 2. fear of problem or situation growing worse.

inferiority depending on what shows up in the dream, one feels inadequate in that area.

infertility 1. female dreamer: not feeling sexual or desired. 2. life situation not "bearing fruit."

infidelity 1. guilt about being unfaithful or being tempted. 2. dissatisfaction with current relations. 3. adventure.

ingratitude 1. someone is not trustworthy. 2. one is not being paid properly.

inheritance 1. one has support or approval of others. 2. one has been fortunate to have loving, caring parents, friends or relatives. 3. need to make decisions or plans about the future.

injection 1. one feels sick inside. 2. sexual or phallic symbol. 3. being forced to accept ideas or situations one disagrees with or fears.

injury 1. realizing that one could be hurt by ongoing or future lifestyle or situation. 2. need to heal old wounds or correct thoughts. 3. thoughts of being vulnerable or cautious.

ink 1. spilled ink symbolizes negative feelings or being out of control. 2. desire to communicate thoughts or ideas. 3. unfulfilled plans or desires.

in-law(s) 1. warning to operate "within the law." 2. conflict or other issue with the in-law in the dream. 3. fear of being dominated or manipulated by others. 4. fear of not being able to please.

inn (broken down or dilapidated) 1. unhappy or unrewarding journey or situation. 2. need to continue or strive for new situation or places.

inn (in good condition) 1. need for rest or relaxation. 2. escape. 3. return to childhood.

inoculation 1. taking precautions about something, particularly one's sex life. 2. a warning to take care in a particular situation, sexual or otherwise.

inquest one wants to make sure that justice is being served in a particular situation.

insanity 1. fear of being unable to handle a particular situation, either emotionally or intellectually. 2. being unable to discern what is right or wrong. 3. loss of control. 4. not knowing on what course to proceed. 5. irrational fear of something.

insect 1. a group of insects indicates that something is in the way of one achieving one's goals. 2. the ability to exterminate insects indicates the ability to clear away problems.

insurance 1. lack of trust. 2. need for security. 3. fear of future events and consequences.

inter 1. bury a wish. 2. bury a long-standing quarrel.

intercom 1. readiness to help or listen to others. 2. need to communicate. 3. message from the unconscious.

interior(s) 1. the inner mind or soul. 2. things or characteristics that only the individual knows about him/herself.

interior scenes the inner mind or soul.

intermarriage 1. willingness or desire to fight for one's beliefs no matter what the consequences. 2. liberal attitude toward social standards, especially sexual relations.

Internet 1. belief in modern technology; new ideas. 2. desire to be "up to date." 3. need to make oneself heard by more people. 4. need for knowledge and ideas. 5. curiosity about the world.

interrupt(ions) 1. inability to make oneself heard or understood, especially by a superior or mate. 2. lack of confidence in completing tasks or handling situations. 3. fear of saying or doing the "wrong thing."

intersection 1. time for a decision or change in direction. 2. fear of making choices or changing course of life.

interview 1. questioning one's motives or actions. 2. one is considering a course of action. 3. feeling of being scrutinized or appraised by someone else.

in the mood ready for romance.

intoxication 1. inability to face situation or person(s). 2. wanting to "let go," have a good time and detach from current problems.

intruder 1. fear of future. 2. sexual interaction, especially with a stranger. 3. sense of being violated or manipulated by others. 4. inability to stop worrying about something. 5. a reflection of oneself.

invasion 1. if one is involved in an invasion, he/she is likely interfering in something. 2. if someone is invading the dreamer's life, interference is involved. 3. need to fight back and attack problems or other people. 4. fear of the unknown. 5. feeling of being unprepared.

inventor 1. vision of being bold and intelligent. 2. readiness to meet problems and solve them. 3. desire for "fame and fortune."

investigator 1. fear that people and situations near one are not what they appear to be. 2. fear that others are prying into one's life.

investiture 1. rejoicing in high achievement. 2. becoming part of something that is very important to one's sense of self.

investment 1. taking a chance on oneself. 2. emotional investment in something.

invisibility 1. the unborn. 2. need for protection or concealment. 3. sense of being forgotten or ignored.

invitation(s) 1. acceptance of others and their qualities and characteristics. 2. accepting an opportunity for adventure.

invoice something is owed to someone, not necessarily money.

IRA (financial) take care of one's investments.

IRA (Irish Republican Army) fear of being accosted by fanatical forces, terrorists.

iridescent false promise, worthless (like a spangled garment).

iris 1. perfection. 2. purification.

Irish longing to be carefree.

iron 1. feeling of strength, permanence. 2. someone or something harsh, unbending or ruthless.

ironing 1. preparation to do something important. 2. need to correct or "iron out" problems. 3. neatness, cleanliness or morality.

island 1. isolation. 2. romance is in the offing. 3. independence. 4. escape. 5. becoming inaccessible or unavailable.

Isvara appearance by this or any other religious leader indicates a situation of great importance.

itch(ing) 1. sexual urge. 2. contemplation or expectation of event or challenge for a long time. 3. restlessness or uneasiness.

ivory 1. strength with purity. 2. something of great value.

ivy 1. beauty. 2. one loves someone. 3. growth or aging of oneself (withered or dead). 4. disappointment about something. 5. ill health. 6. lost opportunities or broken promises. 7. sadness.

J

jackal 1. being looked after, cared for. 2. manipulation, sometimes cruelty. 3. a feeling of being taken advantage of. 4. tenacity.

jacket 1. a strong focus on outer appearances. 2. feelings of protection from emotional storms.

jackhammer 1. need to break down old ways of thinking to make room for new. 2. particularly difficult situations or relationships need greater effort and perhaps help.

jade 1. prosperity is in the offing. 2. a need or desire for protection, feelings of safety. 3. truth.

jaguar 1. chaos, often emotional. 2. adaptability, agility, often in situations. 3. prosperity, wealth and power (to dream of the car).

jail 1. feelings of confinement, punishment, sometimes over guilt for a past misdeed. 2. reverse: happiness, likely domestic. 3. a feeling someone close may not be truthful. 4. temptations should be avoided (as in "jailbait").

jailer 1. a possible loss of reputation in the offing, a need for moral reassessment. 2. an aspect of personality that may be slowing down growth or advancement. 3. feelings that an individual is confining or detaining the dreamer. 4. a feeling that someone close is up to no good.

jam 1. pleasure from creative surprises, spontaneity, usually with friends. 2. family fun and happiness. 3. small problems (as in "caught in a jam").

janitor 1. a "custodian" or caretaker who cleans up the messes of other people. 2. waste or problems of laziness in business matters (to see a janitor not cleaning).

January 1. new beginnings, a new start, often financially. 2. monetary rewards, gains. 3. feelings of loss of love or a loved one, loneliness.

jar 1. rewards and security, depending on how full the jar is— often financially, sometimes emotionally. 2. social pleasantries are on the way. 3. deep feelings of depression, possibly illness (to see a broken jar).

jaundice 1. to feel hostility, even rage, toward an individual or self. 2. possible illness. 3. situations improve after setbacks and disappointments. 4. difficulties in love matters.

javelin 1. a phallic symbol. 2. feelings of being personally unsafe, physically insecure (to be chased by someone with a javelin). 3. indicates success in matters concerning love, intimate relationships.

jaw 1. portal, gateway, most often to hell. 2. inner exploration. 3. conflict with partner (injured jaw). 4. stubbornness. 5. repressed anger (locked or tightened jaw).

jealousy 1. unconscious rivalry, jealousy, comes to the surface. 2. fear of vulnerability in important, even intimate relationships. 3. need for an improved sense of self.

jelly 1. pleasant diversions. 2. good luck and much happiness. 3. concepts or understandings begin to take shape or "gel." 4. feelings of intense insecurity, loss and uncertainty.

Jerusalem 1. social relationships take on a primary, "sacred" importance. 2. a journey, embarking on a crusade.

jester 1. a message regarding taking things too seriously. 2. a message of not taking things seriously enough. 3. a longtime riddle or a puzzle may yet be solved. 4. someone may be taking advantage of a situation.

Jesus Christ 1. seeing the divine in humanity. 2. healing, reconciliation and joy. 3. consolation and comfort in extreme adversity.

jet 1. changes are coming soon. 2. a feeling that bad news or negative changes are on the way.

jetty 1. good financial times are in the offing. 2. a need or desire for travel. 3. feelings regarding emotions or emotional phase.

jewel 1. qualities of the jewel: permanence, luster, incorruptibility. 2. unhappy affairs. 3. woman's genitals.

jewelry 1. business affairs, usually positive. 2. sense of self, identity and self-esteem. 3. sadness, disappointment (to see broken jewelry).

job 1. dissatisfied, unfulfilled sense of purpose—usually in life, sometimes emotionally (looking for a change of job). 2. an important task is coming (at work). 3. a better life is in the offing.

jockey 1. surprises from surprising places are in the offing. 2. financial gains are possible, but use caution regarding the source. 3. to misuse or overuse someone or something, often in a relationship (as in "ride it like a jockey"). 4. someone harbors bad intentions. 5. good communication skills. 6. good omens regarding relationships.

jog 1. steady forward motion, progress—usually in life, sometimes in situations. 2. to stimulate or jar suddenly (as in "jog the memory").

join 1. connections, relationships between one thing and another. 2. feeling connected, belonging.

joint 1. a period of positive change and growth is in the offing. 2. things are not progressing according to plan. 3. a measure of flexibility—often in situations, likely regarding personality.

joint (marijuana) 1. avoidance of responsibilities. 2. a need or desire for emotional quiet or distance. 3. guilt over relatively small problems.

joker 1. issues of avoidance. 2. a feeling that certain individuals are a drain or are taking advantage. 3. feelings of not being taken seriously.

journey 1. profit in the offing. 2. disappointment (unpleasant journey). 3. spiritual adventure.

joy 1. current difficulties are about to be overcome. 2. reverse: a feeling that bad news is on the way. 3. a measure of domestic bliss.

judge 1. ability or need to make good decisions at a crucial point. 2. judgment, likely guilt over emotions. 3. difficulties, regrets.

jug 1. friendship; a full jug indicates many friends or friends of good quality. 2. health and/or employment; a broken jug may indicate possible illness or work-related problems. 3. exciting new adventures (a broken jug).

juggling 1. the juggler may have "too many balls in the air at one time," have too many responsibilities or be emotionally over-whelmed. 2. ventures may have an element of risk about them (also note what objects the juggler is juggling and their potential to do harm). 3. a fear that someone is being deceptive.

July 1. use caution regarding personal financial matters. 2. pessimism or gloom emerges after a period of good times. 3. there is a cause to celebrate independence, usually emotional and likely due to a period of growth.

jump 1. risk-taking adventures, often emotional. 2. questionable judgment in love affairs. 3. avoiding danger or frightening situations.

June 1. activities are successful. 2. avoid situations that can inspire jealousy.

jungle 1. primal ways of coping, usually with relationships. 2. risky financial matters. 3. trouble dealing with the commercial world (as in "it's a jungle out there"). 4. the unconscious mind.

junior 1. a need or desire to learn more, acquire wisdom. 2. feelings of admiration and awe toward another.

juniper 1. difficult situations or circumstances will take a turn for the better. 2. bad luck, ill omens.

junk 1. feelings of worthlessness, poor self-esteem. 2. a need or desire to do away with unwanted things, usually patterns of behavior, sometimes repressed feelings.

junkyard 1. repressed rage, anxiety. 2. feeling taken advantage of; emotionally used as a "dumping ground."

jury 1. feeling of being judged by a group, possibly peers. 2. changes in the offing. 3. quick, perhaps too quick, to judge another (sitting on a jury).

K

kaleidoscope 1. situation is complex and hard to discern. 2. confusion and lack of direction. 3. diversion and/or escape from reality.

kangaroo 1. maternal figure. 2. desire for safety and comfort as symbolized by pouch. 3. something odd and playful. 4. ability to move very fast. 5. highly creative. 6. encountering unconventional opponent. 7. powerful.

Kansas longing to be in a place where life is simpler.

karaoke 1. fear or reservation about one's abilities (being unable to sing one's "song"). 2. being dependent on others. 3. desire to copy or imitate.

karate 1. need for protection. 2. need to focus on life and its problems. 3. desire to "show off" or be respected.

Karo one should add sweetness to one's personality.

kazoo don't take life so seriously.

keg 1. symbol of "good times" or frivolity. 2. if the dreamer is rolling a keg, it suggests difficulties in life. 3. broken or empty keg symbolizes desire to stop drinking.

kelp 1. fear of entanglement (going "too deep" in relationships or commitments). 2. mystery or fear about future.

Kennedy family 1. tragedy. 2. dreams gone awry.

kennel if occupied, one has things under control.

Kentucky long-buried desire to be involved with horses.

kerosene small warmth and poor side effects.

kettle 1. difficulties lie ahead (dark colored). 2. easy path ahead (light colored).

kettle (boiling on stove) 1. indicates work or problems ahead. 2. fear of being overweight.

kettle (pot) settle down with others and discuss in a relaxed way.

keyboard musical inclinations.

keyhole (looking through) 1. being suspicious of others. 2. fear of uncovering damaging secrets about others.

keys 1. the "unlocking" of the soul or truth. 2. search for knowledge or understanding.

khakis 1. part of or threatened by army. 2. sign of approaching conflict. 3. desire to impress (or scare) others, looking good in uniform.

kicking 1. hostility. 2. objecting to something.

kid (baby goat) 1. dreamer feels small and defenseless. 2. reckless or playful youth. 3. desire to be a kid again.

kidnapped 1. being abducted oneself indicates strong confidence in winning a battle with someone else. 2. witnessing someone else being abducted means that one senses bad news coming.

kidneys 1. indication of unusual tastes, not only in food. 2. worry about illness.

killer(s) 1. need to face imminent threat. 2. fear and/or excitement. 3. feeling of helplessness.

killing 1. reinforcing belief that one can defend oneself. 2. desire to eliminate or minimize certain aspects of personality, in the dreamer or others. 3. indication of need to control one's anger.

Kilroy a mystery in one's life, à la "Kilroy was here."

kin relatives from farming country.

kindness the way one wants to be treated.

kindred (spirit) one shares religious beliefs with someone else.

king 1. feeling in command. 2. feeling someone else is in command.

kink someone one knows is "bent."

kinship one feels very close to someone, but not in a romantic way.

kiss (others) 1. expression of love or approval of person kissed.

2. narcissistic self-love (kissing oneself). 3. homosexual desires, though dreamer may not be homosexual (kissing same sex).

kit one has what it takes to do a particular job, whatever that may be.

kitchen 1. hunger, both physical or emotional. 2. place of fulfillment and pleasure. 3. need for more serious approach in meeting situations or problems.

kite (in flight) 1. high goals or ambitions. 2. showing ability to handle or control difficult situations. 3. longing for return to childhood.

kitten feeling helpless.

knack feeling able to accomplish goals.

knapsack 1. excess emotional "baggage" that weighs down the carrier. 2. waking dreams and/or desires that are kept out of sight. 3. travel, freedom or adventure.

knee 1. if bent as in prayer, religious icon. 2. fear of either giving or receiving a "swift kick."

knife 1. being threatened. 2. phallic symbol. 3. sense of being frustrated by or unprepared for problems.

knight 1. a savior or protector. 2. religious icon. 3. someone admired or respected by the dreamer.

knitting 1. peace and tranquility. 2. home life and childhood. 3. desire or need for creative activity. 4. solving difficult and complex problems. 5. boredom with one's present existence. 6. desire to broaden one's horizons.

knob(s) 1. need or ability to "turn things around" by making the correct move or opening the right door. 2. need for control or moving ahead with problems or ideas. 3. mystery and/or surprise. 4. sexuality.

knocker (door) 1. asserting ideas or desires. 2. reaching for help from someone behind the door. 3. female sexual symbol.

knockers slang word for breasts.

knocking (hearing) 1. message from the unconscious. 2. opportunity ("knocking at the door"). 3. mystery or fear.

knots 1. facing problems without obvious solutions. 2. lack of direction or inspiration. 3. fear of commitment ("tying the knot").

know-it-all someone is compensating for a small ego.

knuckles 1. fear of being assaulted or punched. 2. hard work or diligence. 3. anger and aggressiveness.

Krishna 1. spirituality. 2. being wholesome and sharing knowledge with others.

L

label 1. a need to organize and control, categorize—usually parts of life, possibly social affairs. 2. good news, a surprise is in the offing. 3. change of address. 4. to call attention to something, allow others to see or know something that might ordinarily be viewed as private.

labor 1. hard, manual work indicates advancement toward goals, prosperity and bounty. 2. a measure of progress; busy workers mean good progress, idle workers mean inertia. 3. great success will come after hard work (labor pains).

laboratory 1. experimentation with or testing of inner self. 2. in the process of change.

labyrinth 1. a mystery to be addressed. 2. searching for goals, confusion. 3. complications in waking life, especially domestic.

lace 1. an abundance of sensuality, desire, love. 2. need for a little frivolity, sensual enjoyment.

ladder 1. connection between one level of consciousness and another. 2. ambition. 3. intercourse. 4. happiness, success (climbing).

ladle 1. a feeling that someone is not being completely forthcoming, possibly secretive or only giving information out by the "spoonful." 2. happiness can come from the presence of children. 3. feelings of loss (if the ladle is broken).

lady 1. a good omen regarding health and ambition. 2. a sign of maturity, refinement and thoughtfulness in aspects of life, often relationships. 3. the feminine side of self.

ladybug 1. an omen and symbol of good fortune and happiness. 2. wordplay on a woman who is annoying or "bugs" someone. 3. good work or business affairs.

lake 1. state of the unconscious mind (note condition and clarity of water). 2. important romantic relationships (large lake). 3. place of mystery and magic.

lamb 1. tranquility. 2. gentleness, innocence and purity. 3. intense sadness (eating). 4. wealth is in the offing if ethical means are used in business affairs.

lame 1. difficulty or inability in forward movement—sometimes emotionally, often in life. 2. difficulties and disappointments. 3. not readily believable, dishonest (as in "lame excuse").

lament 1. great difficulties and trials are in the offing. 2. reverse: tremendous happiness, success. 3. feelings of deep disappointment.

lamp 1. guidance. 2. spiritual essence. 3. inspiration, intellect. 4. setbacks in business.

lance 1. a phallic symbol. 2. to be resolute in opinions and beliefs, taking a stand. 3. relief comes in a pressure situation (as in "to lance a boil").

land 1. fertility and nourishment. 2. wealth, possible marriage, depending on the condition of the land. 3. expresses a need for grounding (as in "down to earth").

landlord 1. responsibility and restraint. 2. difficulties in domestic affairs. 3. positive changes are coming soon, usually in environment (to argue with a landlord).

landslide 1. emotional fortitude and stability give way under pressure. 2. fear of being overwhelmed by change.

language 1. difficulties in communication. 2. an inability to understand, awkwardness in social situations.

lantern 1. a good omen, favorable for business and friendships especially (to possess a lantern). 2. guidance and leadership. 3. family troubles (a lantern going out). 4. certain issues need "illumination."

lap 1. actions may cause hurt to others. 2. a possible loss of reputation. 3. good news is on the way, especially in terms of love relationships (to be sitting on the lap of a member of the dreamer's preferred sex).

lapdog 1. to be seen as under the influence of others. 2. good fortune in happy, solid friendships. 3. a feeling that friends are attempting to be manipulative.

laptop a need or desire to be more versatile, more mobile in communication.

lard 1. triumph over hard times and difficult people. 2. use caution around people with dubious reputations.

lark 1. a good omen if the lark is healthy and flying, usually regarding dreams and personal goals. 2. a good friend, very loyal. 3. good news and great success.

laryngitis 1. a need or desire to avoid speculation, risky proposals. 2. difficulties in communication, especially in a relationship. 3. possible health issue.

laser 1. clarity of vision and mind. 2. precision, sharpness, directness, usually in social situations.

lasso 1. the ability to initiate love relationships (note if the lassoing was done well or badly). 2. a need for some restraint, likely regarding behavior. 3. a strong sense of or urge for control, often over people; social conformity (as in "riding the herd").

Las Vegas risk-taking, adventures, gambling—possibly with emotions, likely with situations or financial matters.

Latin 1. success in business and professional matters. 2. a quest for knowledge. 3. a period of frustration, inability to understand situations and surroundings.

laughing 1. a desire for release—sensual, possibly sexual. 2. humiliation (to be laughed at). 3. knowledge or "joke" not shared by others.

laughter 1. a catharsis; release and relief. 2. reverse: unhappiness, loss. 3. a period of financial good luck (to hear children laughing).

laundry 1. emotional assessment, cleaning out usually negative things (doing laundry, needing to do laundry). 2. social contentment, pleasure.

lava 1. repressed anger, fear, coming to the surface. 2. a sense of vulnerability, possible danger. 3. excitement is in the offing, likely regarding relationships.

lavender 1. peace and serenity, emotional healing. 2. sense that sadness and difficulties will soon end. 3. intimacy, openness, communication.

lawn 1. sense of well-being. 2. concern for outward appearances. 3. prosperity (if lawn is well kept).

lawsuits 1. use caution in business matters and personal affairs. 2. one's honesty or integrity is called into question. 3. use caution in love affairs; keep a serious attitude.

lawyer 1. feelings of being trapped, of last resort, desperation. 2. guilt over past misdeeds, indiscretions. 3. possible brush with the law.

laxative 1. emotional "constipation" or repression, often regarding a specific situation. 2. a need or desire for cleansing—often health related, possibly emotional. 3. difficult work in the offing.

lazy 1. disappointment in business matters. 2. a need or desire for rest and rejuvenation. 3. difficulty in love affairs. 4. a measure of affluence and wealth.

lead (metal) 1. feelings of heaviness, discomfort, usually emotionally. 2. discontent, arguments. 3. possible health issue, lack of energy.

lead (to lead) 1. direction and guidance, self-confidence or confidence in others. 2. feelings of being controlled or manipulated (as in "being led on").

leak 1. indiscretion is creating an impact on a situation. 2. a quiet sexual need should be addressed. 3. there is slow waste in some aspect of life, likely emotional.

learning 1. a message or lesson from one level of consciousness to another. 2. a feeling that too much responsibility is being taken on. 3. a general thirst for knowledge or a desire to learn a new skill, intellectual stimulation.

leather 1. emotional resilience, toughness. 2. natural, animal instincts and intuitions in humans. 3. domestic happiness.

leave 1. feelings of detachment or separation, usually from emotional growth. 2. a need or desire for time off, a change in scene.

leaves 1. seasons, time periods or phases of life (note the stage of leaves—if they are buds, fully green, or falling, brown or yellow). 2. important, new and exciting events are coming soon. 3. abundance, prosperity and good health (green leaves). 4. change for the good is in the offing, likely behavioral (as in "turn over a new leaf").

lecture 1. ability to communicate is growing one-sided. 2. intellectual process playing itself out.

leeches 1. feelings of being drained—likely emotionally, possibly financially. 2. possible health issue. 3. severe feelings of disappointment, sadness.

left 1. sinister, opposite of right or good. 2. change toward the progressive. 3. repressed thoughts or emotions; passivity. 4. prosperity (left-handed writing).

leg 1. mobility and support. 2. independence, self-sufficiency. 3. admiration for others.

lemon 1. health and prosperity. 2. a need or desire for cleansing, possible health issue. 3. use caution in financial matters.

lens 1. point of view. 2. a need or desire to look more closely at something, often a situation, sometimes a relationship.

leopard 1. obstacles and the ability to overcome them. 2. a feeling that someone has bad intentions. 3. speed and power. 4. an inability to change.

lesbian 1. feminine power, getting in touch with one's feminine side. 2. possible fear of or confusion over sexual identity. 3. a need or desire for changes—likely minor, sometimes regarding sexuality.

lesson 1. a need or desire to acquire new knowledge. 2. feelings of being overwhelmed by problems or obstacles, often in life. 3. having failed to learn a previous lesson, often in relationships.

lethal (killing or murder) 1. a symbol or catalyst for the end of a situation or phase of life, usually for the better. 2. jealousy of another. 3. jealousy of one aspect of the personality over another.

letter 1. messages from the unconscious need attention. 2. virginity (an unopened letter). 3. news is in the offing. 4. primary stage of new emotions (letters of the alphabet).

lettuce 1. fleeting happiness. 2. a negative omen regarding financial affairs. 3. possible health issues. 4. use caution to avoid jealous arguments.

levitate 1. one is "left hanging," immobile and inert. 2. freedom and happiness. 3. feelings of being "adrift" of reality, not grounded.

library 1. internal wisdom and experience accumulated over time. 2. emotional resource. 3. rapid progress.

lice 1. abundance and good fortune. 2. a lot of small annoyances become a large problem. 3. possible cleanliness or hygiene issues. 4. unhappiness or displeasure, especially in relationships.

license 1. mobility, obtaining freedom (as in "license to drive"). 2. change in life stage and status, a rite of passage. 3. change in situation, possibly employment.

licking 1. testing or sampling before you commit. 2. adventuresome disposition. 3. good luck and wealth are in the offing (to be licked by a dog).

lifeboat 1. security, a backup plan. 2. success over difficult or trying times, possibly great adversity. 3. a project or situation is seriously wrong. 4. difficulties in the offing.

lifeguard 1. "guarding" or "guarded" feelings. 2. a need or desire to be rescued from feelings of "drowning" or being overwhelmed. 3. a need or desire to be needed, to "rescue" situations or people.

life jacket 1. feelings of security, personal safety. 2. confidence in conflicts and confrontations.

ligament 1. two elements joined together—often a relationship, frequently concepts (note health or elasticity of ligament). 2. connectedness, being a part of something.

light 1. insight, clarity. 2. happiness, success in business. 3. difficulties in love (dim or no light). 4. truth of a matter is "illuminated."

lighthouse 1. a guide through difficulties, possible dangers. 2. a need or desire for moral guidance and direction. 3. a phallic symbol. 4. happiness, contentment—usually domestic, often professional.

lightning 1. sudden inspiration, revelation. 2. feelings of sudden disaster. 3. sudden change in the offing, usually in a situation.

lilac 1. new beginnings, renewal and healing. 2. feelings of attraction, sexuality.

lime (chemical) 1. financial situations are about to improve. 2. a need or desire to be rid of something, often an aspect of self.

lime (fruit) 1. a good omen regarding prosperity and good fortune. 2. possible health issue. 3. levels of energy, vitality.

limousine 1. mobility in style, showing off. 2. great sense of self-worth. 3. sorrows may come (black limousine).

limp 1. desire for balance in waking life, sometimes emotional. 2. fear of showing vulnerability or appearing weak. 3. an old emotional injury is more profound than originally thought.

line 1. ego. 2. division, duality. 3. limitless possibilities (infinity). 4. moving beyond means ("overstepping the line"). 5. boundary ("crossing the line").

lion 1. courage, dignity, strength. 2. justice and righteousness. 3. latent passion. 4. wild, uncontrollable passion.

lips 1. sexuality and attractiveness. 2. ability to communicate. 3. happiness and prosperity.

lipstick 1. falsehoods and deception. 2. flirtation and sexual availability, possibly overt sexual behavior. 3. a good omen for business matters.

liquor 1. relaxation. 2. abandonment. 3. withdrawal. 4. used as an escape or change.

liver 1. feelings of fatigue, a drain on vitality. 2. repressed anger, bile. 3. possible health issues. 4. improving circumstances.

living room 1. part of inner self shown to the public. 2. a woman (dreamed by man). 3. core of identity.

lizard 1. feelings of loss or injury. 2. basic, primal instincts. 3. vision, creativity and creative energy. 4. genitalia.

llama 1. comfort, care and consolation. 2. feelings of too many responsibilities and obligations. 3. success, trust and happiness.

load 1. charitable in nature. 2. a burdensome secret, desire to share (to carry).

loan 1. a need or desire for assistance, to ask for help. 2. use caution to stay within financial means. 3. a need or desire to replace a loss or fill a gap, likely emotional.

lobby 1. revelation to come, usually by the dreamer. 2. potential for betrayal or treachery by friends.

lobster 1. ability to overcome difficulties, obstacles. 2. shyness and discomfort with social affairs. 3. a positive omen regarding success in endeavors.

lock 1. aspect of self, kept or locked away, perhaps even from the dreamer. 2. fear of emotional risks. 3. assured happiness (opened lock).

locker 1. secrets and/or hidden aspects of personality. 2. long hidden or repressed emotions or problems (to see a school locker). 3. a phase of uncertainty, confusion (to be unable to open a locker).

lockjaw 1. difficulty or awkwardness in communication. 2. use caution to avoid harsh words with those closest. 3. a need or desire for more discretion in affairs. 4. a feeling that someone may be deceptive.

locust 1. intellect and creativity. 2. an unusually destructive nuisance. 3. phases of life, life cycles.

log 1. a good omen regarding prosperity and abundance, sometimes regarding aspects of self. 2. a negative omen regarding financial matters (to cut up a log). 3. possible wordplay on "to sleep like a log." 4. a good family life (to see a burning log in a hearth).

longing 1. reconciliation in the offing. 2. disappointment, sadness.

loon 1. a need or desire for introspection, thoughtful self-exploration, sometimes spiritual. 2. general symbol for balance and serenity.

lost 1. a negative feeling about life. 2. difficulties in determining path or direction—usually in situations, often in life. 3. reverse: good fortune is in the offing (to lose a game).

lotion 1. the soul and spiritual pursuits. 2. spiritual comfort, pleasantness and balance. 3. sensual contact, connectedness.

lottery 1. difficulties in the offing, sometimes regarding domestic affairs. 2. good times, good fortune are in the offing (to win a lottery). 3. a need or desire for greater self-confidence and less reliance on chance or fate.

lotus 1. spiritual aspects of self, personality and behavior. 2. happiness and romance. 3. intellectual and creative growth, acquiring wisdom and knowledge.

loud 1. a strong sense that a message is being missed or ignored (loud noises or knocking). 2. inability to focus, concentrate. 3. a measure of annoyance or distraction, often in a relationship.

love 1. happiness, affection, admiration and care. 2. a measure of abundance and prosperity. 3. feelings of acceptance and approval.

love letter 1. truth and happiness. 2. a positive message from one aspect of self to another or one level of consciousness to the next.

lover 1. self-acceptance. 2. masculine or feminine side of self (opposite gender). 3. unresolved or recurring problems (old lover).

low tide 1. a fear or reluctance to change, possibly due to an unhealthy environment. 2. a feeling that troubles will soon end. 3. a time of change.

Lucifer 1. prosperity and good fortune. 2. repressed feelings of hostility toward an individual. 3. feelings of temptation or a potential "fall from grace." 4. another, darker side of self or personality.

luggage 1. possible travel in the offing. 2. coming change, often in a relationship. 3. repressed emotions or recollections. 4. sense of self, self-worth.

lumber 1. prosperity. 2. displeasure, sadness and disappointment. 3. a need or desire for "remodeling," sometimes an aspect of self. 4. wordplay representing a lack of energy, possible illness.

lunch box 1. social skills, resources. 2. a symbol of domestic balance, contentment. 3. slang for male genitals.

lungs 1. a negative sense of loss, disappointment in the offing. 2. creativity, ingenuity and adaptability. 3. possible health issues. 4. feelings regarding one's place in the world.

lust 1. suffering feelings of want, dissatisfaction. 2. acting on impulse rather than with forethought, caution.

lying 1. feeling cheated, betrayed (to be lied to). 2. self-deception, foolish and destructive behavior. 3. difficulty in accepting responsibilities, obligations.

lynch 1. guilt, regret and a need to make amends. 2. inertia, immobility. 3. feelings of persecution.

lynx 1. a sense that someone is keeping a secret. 2. a remarkable ability to adapt to change. 3. a feeling that someone harbors anger toward another individual.

M

macaroni 1. something Italian. 2. if eating, one is conscious of financial difficulties. 3. a large quantity of it means that financial problems will extend some time into the future.

Macbeth one's life has taken on some "sick" aspects, like desire for someone one is related to.

mace one is not sure about the intentions of a male date.

machine gun well-equipped for a battle.

machinery 1. if machinery is complex, it means life is complex. 2. if one feels awed by, unable to operate, machinery, then one feels overwhelmed by reality. 3. powerful. 4. smoothly running machinery means a smooth-running life.

macho one doubts one's virility, manhood.

Madame Bovary to those who understand the novel, the desire to engage in an adulterous affair.

madcap one has a light, humorous approach to life.

mad dog 1. unexpected attack from someone one doesn't know. 2. if one kills the dog, then the unknown adversary is vanquished. 3. if running from a mad dog, one is unable to cope with an adversary. 4. if someone else kills the dog, it means that the dreamer has a good friend who will come to his/her aid.

made 1. one feels he/she has accomplished (made) things. 2. fear that a criminal will come into one's life.

madness 1. illogicality despite evidence. 2. extremely worried about some aspect of one's life. 3. watching associates or friends in the throes of madness indicates that one's friends are damaged, flawed, not worth getting close to.

Madonna 1. feeling rebellious, doing it one's own way. 2. open sexuality. 3. Mother of Jesus.

Mafia 1. very afraid of something. 2. family approach is best.

magazines 1. search for inner self or identity. 2. quest for knowledge, information. 3. bettering oneself intellectually. 4. feeling sales pressure.

maggot 1. maggots feeding on flesh is an indication that something disgusts one deeply in life. 2. someone is taking advantage of one's generosity. 3. fear of death.

magic 1. desire to return to the happy-go-lucky times of childhood. 2. impressed with the skill of someone else. 3. a solution to a problem that in reality seems insoluble.

magistrate 1. feeling in command. 2. capable of rendering a decision about something. 3. authority figure.

Magnesia, Milk of 1. one is sick of oneself. 2. one is sick of someone else.

magnet 1. high regard for oneself. 2. the ability to draw good things into one's life. 3. the ability to draw bad things into one's life. 4. one is already drawing good or bad things or influences into one's life.

magnetized desire to draw someone close to one.

magnifying glass 1. tendency to magnify or distort things, making problems worse than they are—or less than they are. 2. look at something closer. 3. don't make things bigger than they are.

Magoo, Mr. unable to see what should be obvious.

magpie 1. a tendency to emotionally ventilate by talking excessively. 2. telling the wrong people secrets or proprietary information. 3. a dead magpie sends the message that excessive talk kills, or kills a relationship. 4. a caution to change one's ways re talk.

mahogany it's time for a hobby, such as woodworking.

mail 1. hope or dreams of the future. 2. message from the unconscious. 3. in female dreamers, a male object of affection.

mailbag one expects to communicate with many different people.

mailbox 1. hoping for good news. 2. if box contains mail and the door or flap is open, it indicates good news. 3. if door is closed, bad news.

mailman 1. a communicator, a bearer of ideas. 2. person entering one's life, possibly unwanted. 3. anticipation and/or anxiety about future events.

makeup 1. escape from reality. 2. sorrowful. 3. exercising imagination.

mall 1. the dreamer yearns to "keep up with the Joneses" by acquiring material goods, often unnecessary. 2. desire to meet and possibly flirt with others. 3. need to make decisions, especially financial ones.

mallard 1. affection for outdoor living. 2. duck! danger coming in.

malleable someone one is dealing with is flexible.

mallet 1. feeling threatened. 2. symbol of hard work or problems to be dealt with. 3. sexual symbol.

mallet (croquet) desire or jealousy for the life or "games" of the privileged.

malodorous trying to be diplomatic when something smells very bad.

malpractice fear of doctors.

man (old) 1. wisdom and knowledge. 2. forgiveness. 3. aging and death.

man (young) 1. flighty, capricious, daring. 2. be careful.

manager one feels capable of handling some situations.

mandrake 1. symbol of male genitalia. 2. desire to have some sort of magic come into one's life.

Manhattan dreams of glory.

mania obsession about something.

manicure 1. desire to look one's best. 2. self-attention, especially after achieving some success.

Manila (city) would like to visit faraway place.

manila 1. rope for tying things together. 2. a friend.

mannequin 1. extension of one's self, but emotionally empty or detached from reality. 2. fear of the unknown, or of revealing inner thoughts.

manners 1. if a person is well-mannered, it is a hint that he/she will be easier to deal with. 2. if a person is poorly mannered, they will be difficult to deal with.

mansion 1. symbol of personal glory, wealth and achievements. 2. envy of rich or famous people. 3. sense of being demeaned or feeling "small" in status or personality.

mantelpiece something looks important, but it is not a crucial part of the situation one is involved in.

manure 1. doing something unpleasant yet positive to make a dream grow. 2. signal that difficult means are needed to make things grow. 3. a euphemistic term in a dream that expresses one's reaction to what one is hearing. 4. desire to grow things (become a "farmer").

manuscript 1. need to "tell a story," reveal inner thoughts and memories. 2. symbol of one's persona or hidden self. 3. acceptance or rejection, depending on how manuscript is interpreted by others.

map 1. path to achieving goals. 2. expectation of travel and/or adventure. 3. affirmation of ability to change course or solve problems. 4. one has help in achieving his/her destination. 5. one is willing to get help.

maple 1. desire to move to Canada. 2. would like to return to nature.

marble 1. wealth and power. 2. timelessness and stability. 3. admiration or longing for ancient times and cultures. 4. something to be achieved. 5. if polishing, one values quality.

marbles 1. desire to be young again. 2. taking a chance.

March (month of) 1. renewal of hope about one's future and dreams. 2. uncertainty about how to approach new problems or situations.

marching 1. being part of a group or crowd. 2. ready to take on the future or current situation. 3. feeling of pride in accomplishments or ability.

Mardi Gras 1. need to lose inhibitions. 2. need reckless pleasures and adventure. 3. desire to explore other cultures and meet exotic and unknown people.

margarine something or someone is false.

marijuana 1. rebelliousness or recklessness. 2. desire to escape from reality. 3. thrill in going "beyond the law." 4. need for medication or pacification.

marine 1. someone one admires. 2. having to do with the sea.

marjoram one should have mental clarity for a long time.

market 1. searching for things missing in one's life. 2. security in finding abundance of necessities. 3. if needed items are not available, sign of emptiness, despair and lack of hope.

Marlboro stop smoking.

marmalade adding something pleasing to one's life.

marriage 1. a journey, romantic or otherwise. 2. death, either of close relation or friend. 3. commitment, either need for or fear of.

Mars fight for one's rights.

marshmallow though dark forces threaten, one will be loved and protected.

mascara 1. sadness or mourning. 2. needing help to face situation or hide physical or emotional imperfections. 3. flirtation.

mask 1. hiding one's true self. 2. trying to deceive or avoid deception by others. 3. fear of one's actions being misconstrued. 4. trying to avoid recognition by enemies or associates. 5. deception. 6. lacking sense of self, identity. 7. feeling distracted from reality or a particular situation.

mason 1. wanting to belong to an important, yet exclusive, club or organization. 2. feeling of success and wealth. 3. wanting to keep secrets from friends or loved ones. 4. desire to build something lasting.

massacre to witness a massacre in one's dream suggests that the dreamer is a follower who will follow the ideas of others without question or hesitation.

massage 1. in need of sensual or sexual stimulation. 2. nurturing. 3. signifies a message that the person receiving the massage should stop being defensive.

mast 1. phallic symbol. 2. journey.

mastectomy 1. one feels less than attractive as a female. 2. if diagnosed with cancer, worry over the condition.

master 1. one feels in control of a situation. 2. to have a master means one feels controlled by someone.

masturbation (self) 1. sexual attraction to someone in life or imagination. 2. possible contempt for person thought about while masturbating. 3. sexual insecurity. 4. sexual curiosity about others.

mat one will have to fight to achieve something (wrestling mat).

matador 1. taking on a great danger. 2. display of masculinity. 3. need to emulate the courage of the matador.

matches 1. striking a match signifies the need to put a spark in one's life. 2. looking for a romantic partner.

mathematics 1. the need to be more precise in one's life. 2. don't make decisions based only on emotion.

matron 1. one wants to be controlled. 2. one needs a mother figure in one's life.

mattress 1. the need for rest before undertaking something big. 2. about to go to a kind of war ("going to the mattresses").

mausoleum 1. difficulties ahead. 2. fear of death.

maverick one is determined not to go along with group thinking.

maze 1. overemphasizing the importance or complexity of a situation or emotion. 2. frustration and/or fear of the future.

meadow 1. peace and tranquility. 2. security and comfort. 3. reflection on one's achievements or status.

meadowsweet uplifted spirits, joy.

meals 1. one feels secure. 2. indication of spiritual or emotional hunger. 3. need for comfort or companionship. 4. self-gratification or overindulgence.

measurement one has doubts about his/her performance at something.

medal one feels deserving of some reward, perhaps a raise, for an achievement.

medicine 1. problem solving. 2. need for direction or relief from a situation, not necessarily medical.

medicine man need solution to a problem outside one's normal sphere.

melons 1. a woman's breasts. 2. fertility issues of some sort.

Memphis aspirations in show business.

menagerie one is involved in a very chaotic situation.

menopause 1. fear of the end of a sexual life. 2. some important change is coming.

menstruation 1. fear of maturing. 2. happiness at growing up.

menu 1. one faces a number of choices in a situation. 2. one is trying to get the "big picture" in a situation.

Mercury (planet) 1. message, possibly false. 2. thievery.

mercury (substance) 1. ambitious. 2. possibly dangerous. 3. very fast-moving.

mermaids 1. female element in one's unconscious. 2. "goddess" icon. 3. taking an adventure into the unknown.

merry-go-round 1. desire to return to childhood. 2. someone is leading one on a one-way trip to nowhere.

meter one is being evaluated.

Miami 1. need to go someplace warm and sunny. 2. R & R.

mice 1. disarray of one's life or thoughts. 2. need to "put the house in order." 3. playfulness or teasing, in oneself or others. 4. timidity. 5. something undesirable. 6. small-minded.

Mickey Mouse 1. longing for childhood days. 2. cheap, flimsy; of a lower grade.

microphone 1. one is not being heard. 2. someone is bothering others.

microscope take a long, hard look at something.

middle finger 1. a phallic symbol, sexuality. 2. extreme disapproval, insult or anger.

midwife 1. one needs someone involved who can make two parties come together. 2. one wants to become pregnant.

mildew a wide, deep problem that is difficult to solve.

milestone 1. one has achieved something important. 2. change is coming in one's life. 3. a sense that time is passing.

militant determined to express one's own thinking.

milk 1. mother. 2. nature. 3. need for emotional nourishment. 4. if one gives milk away, it indicates kindness. 5. if one gives milk away, it may mean one is foolishly giving his/her own resources to others. 6. if one spills milk, a mistake has been made. 7. if someone else spills milk, that person has made a mistake.

mill 1. hard work. 2. rip-off (à la "puppy mills").

millionaire desire to be secure.

mine 1. vagina. 2. one must take risks to achieve something. 3. a declaration that something important in one's life belongs to one.

mineral water time for a healthier lifestyle.

minesweeper beware, danger ahead.

mining 1. sexual interaction. 2. one is in the middle of doing something risky to achieve a certain end.

miniseries one feels one's life is out of control.

minister 1. time to turn to religion. 2. continue to be caring.

minotaur one has a dangerous instinct buried deep in one's soul.

mint 1. one's personal hygiene needs improvement. 2. rich. 3. health. 4. honesty.

miracle one needs a miracle or religious intervention to get through a very difficult situation.

Mirandize one feels oppressed by an authority that is difficult to fight.

mirror 1. worry about failure of a business or health. 2. taking a hard look at oneself to determine what, if anything, can be changed—or should be changed—about oneself, perhaps things that one has been hiding for years. 3. searching for reality. 4. baring one's soul to self or to others if they are observing.

miscarriage 1. one feels the need to end a relationship. 2. one feels the need to discard something one has long carried around.

miser suggests that one is not as giving in life as one should be.

misprint one is being misinterpreted by someone, perhaps for his/her own gain.

missile long-standing hostility toward someone.

missionary 1. willingness to take chances. 2. very determined. 3. feelings of love. 4. religious feelings. 5. helping others out with advice or spiritual leadership.

Mississippi 1. one is working too hard (from Broadway song "Old Man River"). 2. trouble (civil rights upheaval).

mist 1. obscuring the truth. 2. a mystery, puzzle. 3. the unknown.

mistress one is obsessed with something or someone, not necessarily a woman.

moat to reach one's goal is not going to be easy.

mob 1. a reflection of one's own angry personality. 2. a reflection of someone else's angry personality. 3. a reflection of public opinion, hostile or not.

Moby Dick willing to take on any challenge.

moccasin 1. desire to be fair about something (the way Native Americans deal). 2. desire to return to a simpler lifestyle.

mockingbird something good and precious (from *To Kill a Mockingbird*).

model 1. dissatisfied with oneself. 2. wanting to be like someone else.

molding one is trying to decide how to put the finishing touches on something.

mole 1. scared of life. 2. someone with a hidden agenda (à la spies). 3. damaging or destructive in a hidden way.

monarch 1. feeling in control of everything. 2. one feels controlled by someone who appears to be a monarch.

monastery 1. desire to be by oneself. 2. desire to be religious.

money 1. desire for security. 2. shallow goals. 3. finding confidence in one's ability or future. 4. if stealing, indicates jealousy or dislike of person one is taking from.

monk 1. desire to be by oneself. 2. desire to be deeply religious to help solve a problem.

monkey 1. playful. 2. need to imitate the behavior of others. 3. desire to be by oneself.

Monroe, Marilyn 1. one feels very insecure, though attractive. 2. sadness. 3. possible drug use.

monsignor 1. respect for religion. 2. disrespect for religion.

monsoon caught in a disaster that one can't do anything about.

monster 1. deep fear of something. 2. deep fear of someone.

Montessori on one's own and liking it.

monument 1. remembering someone very important in one's life. 2. phallic symbol.

moon 1. if the moon is full, it indicates that one's life is full. 2. to the degree that the moon is not full, one's life is not full. 3. if the moon is dull, partially covered with clouds, or an odd color, it symbolizes worry about some issue. 4. female icon. 5. search for eternal truths. 6. desire. 7. ascending to the heavens.

Morse code 1. need to communicate with someone. 2. need to communicate secretly.

mortgage 1. heavy monetary obligation. 2. obligation.

mortuary 1. unwillingness to let go of the past. 2. guilt over something. 3. regret.

mosaic problem has many parts.

mosquito 1. an annoyance. 2. indication that one needs to take precautions.

mother need to be nurtured.

motorcycle 1. phallic symbol (because of stereotypical easy sexuality among motorcycle gang members). 2. proof of manhood or sexual abilities. 3. anger. 4. aggression. 5. permissive female sexuality.

mountain(s) 1. problems that must be surmounted. 2. hope for the future, if one can just get over the mountains. 3. female sexuality (breasts). 4. fear of something that is large, such as elephants.

mouse 1. timid. 2. industrious. 3. vulnerable to harm.

movies need to escape into another world.

moving 1. if easy, one's life is easy. 2. if difficult, one's life is difficult. 3. desire to improve oneself.

Mss ego, i.e., one is a professional writer.

muffins 1. peaceful, tranquil life and settings. 2. need for physical and emotional nourishment.

muffins (with hole) sexual symbol.

mule 1. goes along with the crowd. 2. stupid, foolish. 3. strong, committed.

murder 1. if the dreamer murders or attempts to murder someone, it is a measure of how angry—or afraid—he/she is of someone else. 2. if the dreamer witnesses a murder, there is an indication that profound change is taking place in one's life.

music 1. the meaning of music will depend on what it is—from rock and roll to classical—and what it means in particular in the dreamer's life. 2. sexual activity. 3. inspiration. 4. retreat from reality.

mussel female sexuality.

N

nag 1. good news and events in the offing. 2. some confidants are not trustworthy. 3. feelings of repressed anger and resentment, usually regarding a relationship.

nail 1. sexual intercourse. 2. final resolution to a situation ("hit the nail on the head"). 3. failure in business or industry (bent, broken or rusted nails). 4. joining two thoughts or ideas.

naked 1. extreme sense or fear of exposure, vulnerability. 2. shame, embarrassment, possibly guilt (public nakedness). 3. desire to be more revealing about oneself.

name 1. a need to reacquaint oneself with sense of individuality (dreamer's name). 2. too many burdens (to forget a name). 3. pleasant news is on the way.

nap 1. tuning out of the environment. 2. a need for rest, short time away. 3. good fortune is in the offing.

napkin a visit will call for some social activities.

narcissus 1. a fortunate omen regarding money matters. 2. a high regard for self, self-image, vanity. 3. wordplay on narcissistic behavior or individual.

narcotics 1. emotional and/or spiritual pain. 2. a need or desire to escape, inability to face difficulties, often in social situations. 3. slowness or lethargy, disorientation, inability to respond, usually in intimate relationships.

narrow 1. a measure of difficulties along life's journey (narrow passageway or road). 2. a general feeling of claustrophobia, feelings of being nearly trapped or squeezed. 3. may be a metaphor for a way of thinking being narrow. 4. also intellectual; focus, ability to concentrate.

Native American 1. a desire or need to reacquaint oneself or commune with nature, the natural world. 2. a desire or need to remove some of the restraints of society or ways of thinking. 3. a need for greater community or family bonds.

Nativity 1. a new or surprising self-awareness, likely regarding inner strength, is emerging. 2. a new level of spirituality is achieved, likely regarding the ability to forgive or redeem the self. 3. a signal or message is moving from one level of consciousness to another.

nature 1. a need or desire to commune with nature. 2. a desire for "wildness," to lose some of the constraints of society. 3. a message from baser instincts or intuition, usually about social situations. 4. regarding behavioral traits, emotional turmoil will be lifted (as in "good-natured").

nausea 1. a feeling that a situation or dilemma has gone from bad to worse (as in "sickening"). 2. inability to accept or intense fear of a situation. 3. a need or desire to "purge" a usually emotional, sometimes behavioral, set of traits or reactions. 4. possible illness or pregnancy.

navel 1. self, core of the individual. 2. a period or phase of self-involvement, likely to the exclusion or neglect of central relationships. 3. a good omen for business or financial matters. 4. concern over parents (pain or injury to navel).

navigate 1. a general symbol for one's ability to deal with life. 2. moods and whims (note success of navigation). 3. good news, possible joy in the offing.

navy 1. a desire for adventure, likely as an escape from present circumstance. 2. use caution regarding relationships; temptation to infidelity is in the offing. 3. multitasking is growing overwhelming, confusing. 4. a need or desire for discipline and leadership from others instead of self-reliance, independence.

Nazi 1. extreme prejudice, bigotry, censorship. 2. immovable, overwhelming dread or fear of the future, severe oppression.

3. use caution in relationships; there may be a tendency to be too rigid, didactic to the point of possible cruelty (to be a Nazi).

nearsighted 1. approaching embarrassment due to "shortsighted-ness," failure to look into the future. 2. possible need for an eye exam. 3. surprise visitors in the offing.

neck 1. use caution regarding projects or situations (as in to "stick one's neck out"). 2. possible illness. 3. some friends may not be what they appear or all they say they are. 4. the path between the heart (emotion) and brain (intellect) and the point of verbal communication. 5. money.

necklace 1. circular connection, often spiritual (as in rosary or prayer beads). 2. social or official status, influence. 3. attaining requited love.

necktie 1. a need for a little more formality, seriousness regarding personal goals, possibly in social settings. 2. ability to commu-nicate and be understood or heard. 3. business matters must be completed.

necromancy 1. unresolved issues need to be addressed and laid to rest. 2. a sense of "evil" doings, danger afoot.

need 1. a good omen for happiness, success (to recognize needs, ask for help). 2. lack of money, poverty (to be in need of money).

needle 1. something needs to be mended or repaired. 2. need to penetrate a difficulty. 3. annoyance from a relationship ("needling").

negligee 1. transparency, often regarding emotions; vulnerability, usually regarding actions or intentions. 2. a desire to be noticed, admired. 3. a desire or need for intimacy.

neighbor 1. domestic pleasure, contentment. 2. dissension and fights (angry neighbor). 3. community project.

nephew 1. pleasant social situations. 2. good health and long life (if nephew is well and in good spirits).

Neptune 1. spirituality, vision and mysticism (to dream of the planet). 2. a need for greater compassion and understanding—especially socially, sometimes regarding the inner self. 3. a desire, usually spiritual/emotional, to see the ocean or large body of water (to see the god Neptune or Poseidon). 4. horses.

nerd 1. feelings of impotency, inferiority. 2. to suffer derision, likely adolescent in nature. 3. feelings of social ineptitude, teenage or teenage-like awkwardness.

nervous 1. reverse: good news, good fortune and calm. 2. a lack of self-confidence, fear of failure. 3. use caution not to spread one's resources too thinly.

nervous breakdown 1. possible signal of emotional or mental illness. 2. to relinquish responsibility for one's actions and responsibilities. 3. inability to approach a situation or relationship rationally, with clarity of judgment.

nest 1. domestic security and happiness (bird's nest). 2. problems or difficulties need space (wasp or hornet nests). 3. problems or difficulties need patience in unraveling (rat's nest).

net 1. feelings of being trapped, "netted"—usually in situations, sometimes in relationships. 2. to have security (or to lack it)—usually regarding activities, often social, sometimes projects or business (as in "working without a net"). 3. love and commitment. 4. difficulties with business dealings.

nettles 1. happiness and prosperity (to be stung by nettles). 2. a situation or relationship of extreme annoyance and irritation.

new 1. prosperity, happiness (to have new things). 2. beginning of a new phase or period in life, a change. 3. a new sense of self (a new house). 4. feelings of social awkwardness, not belonging (as in the "new kid in school").

newborn 1. a return to innocence, purity. 2. a new idea or project is generated. 3. a need for nourishment, oxygen, usually intellectual (to hear a newborn cry).

news 1. fortune and relationships; good news means good friends. 2. use caution in expressing anger or frustration, especially with children (to hear bad news). 3. reverse: good news means bad news in the offing. 4. important information is being conveyed (note content of news).

newspaper 1. a feeling or sense of harmful deceit, falsehoods afoot. 2. use caution in upcoming affairs; possible loss of reputation is in the offing. 3. a need or desire to resolve issues, problems.

news reporter 1. to suffer doubt, possible deception; a feeling of having been used. 2. varied and unusual travel is in the offing (to be a reporter).

New Year 1. time to look forward and back. 2. financial optimism, hope. 3. circumstances will soon improve.

nibble 1. something is eating away, draining emotional resources. 2. use caution in matters of trust, confidence with secrets.

nickname 1. feelings of fondness, affection (to call or think of someone by a pet name or nickname). 2. a message is being conveyed about personal attributes or upcoming dilemmas (to receive or give a nickname; note the name). 3. happiness and success.

niece difficulties and concerns crop up.

night 1. doubts. 2. feelings of ignorance, inferiority. 3. a feeling of misfortune, serious obstacles in the offing. 4. feelings of family contentment (at home at night).

nightclub 1. a measure of social life (note condition of club and people within). 2. an improvement in social affairs is about to occur; new friends. 3. aspects of life.

nightgown 1. revealing a very personal, vulnerable side of self. 2. a feeling of not being prepared for life, activities or business affairs (to be in a nightgown in public).

nightingale 1. pleasure, contentment and serenity. 2. the beginning of a good period. 3. confusion in communications; misunderstandings.

nightmare 1. bitter disappointments. 2. possible health issue. 3. out-of-control anxieties, fears.

nine 1. completion and fulfillment, earthly contentment. 2. cycles of development (as in "coming full circle"). 3. happiness (as in "cloud nine").

nipple 1. childishness, dependency. 2. feelings of sexual inadequacy.

nit 1. playing host to small annoyances. 2. incubating small problems, feeling overwhelmed by useless details. 3. a need or desire to focus on the grand scheme of things (as in "nitpicking").

nobility 1. indicates a great concern with outward appearances. 2. difficulties in business, obstacles (to be a member of nobility).

noise 1. arguments and dissension in domestic affairs (loud noises). 2. gossip is in the air.

none 1. feelings of deprivation, loss and suffering. 2. reverse: abundance, clutter. 3. feelings of nonexistence, a void, unwanted.

noodles 1. use caution regarding unusual urges or "appetites"; they may be unhealthy. 2. mysticism. 3. projects move forward as expected.

noon 1. the midpoint, the high point, usually in life's journey. 2. use restraint and care in regards to health.

noose 1. a feeling of being strangled, cut off, especially in regards to communication. 2. extreme hostility toward another person (to see someone with a noose around his/her neck). 3. persecution; fear and terror.

north 1. advancement, movement in a positive direction, usually in life. 2. success follows hard work, turbulent times. 3. a journey in the offing.

northern lights 1. indicates a wealth of energy, vitality. 2. a sudden inspiration, awareness, often in relationships.

North Pole 1. the beginning of journeys, sometimes the end. 2. plans are moving ahead well. 3. Santa's home, childhood hopes and dreams, a magical place.

nose 1. curiosity; may express a need to mind one's own business. 2. good intuition, acuity (as in a "nose for business"). 3. a penis. 4. success in activities. 5. beware of haughtiness, superiority (as in to "look down one's nose").

nosebleed 1. feelings of being taken for granted. 2. sadness, disappointment, feelings of defeat. 3. possible financial stress is in the offing.

nosegay 1. youthful innocence, purity and energy. 2. happiness and contentment in the moment. 3. use caution in financial matters, particularly borrowing.

nosey 1. curiosity regarding one's environment, social circle. 2. being overly curious and intrusive. 3. prosperity in the offing.

nostalgia 1. a need or desire to draw on the past. 2. repressed feelings or memories are trying to surface. 3. an attempt to connect a current situation to one in the past.

notary 1. possible lawsuits, encounters with the courts. 2. validation, a witness on one's behalf. 3. a fear of nosiness, gossip in the community.

notebook 1. a keen observer, meticulous record keeper. 2. a greater need for mobility, diversity in communication (especially a "notebook" computer). 3. returning to a time of learning—possibly a reminiscence of school, likely a life lesson.

notes 1. keeping up, staying ahead with aspects of life. 2. a message is trying to get through, often from one level of consciousness to another. 3. feelings of guilt, to be held in a dubious light.

novel 1. a need or desire for control in life, sometimes over specific situations or relationships. 2. difficulties in the offing. 3. a good omen regarding social activities.

November 1. happiness, especially in later life. 2. monetary gains, position and prosperity.

nuclear bomb 1. an extreme, devastating sense of helplessness, powerlessness. 2. reverse: a need to start over from scratch, a complete changeover. 3. great rage and hostility, a desire to completely annihilate or "vaporize" the object of rage.

nudity 1. feelings of public disgrace. 2. fear of exposure. 3. vulnerability.

nuisance 1. financial success or business gains in the offing. 2. possible deception afoot.

number 1. personal, individual power (note which numbers). 2. possible difficulties regarding financial or business affairs. 3. a measurement of time (as in "days are numbered").

numbness 1. a good omen for business and activities. 2. possible health or physical issues. 3. a feeling of loss, cut off from energy and life force—usually emotionally, sometimes socially. 4. avoidance of difficult or painful situations.

nun 1. escape from the world and expectations (woman dreamer). 2. repressed sexual desire (male dreamer). 3. seeking purity, chastity and obedience. 4. a teacher of harsh lessons, a lesson to be learned (teaching nun).

nunnery 1. disciplined self. 2. contemplative self. 3. feminine sexual repression.

nuptial 1. arrangements that will lead to contentment, fruitful commitments. 2. a public declaration of union, advantages in not "going it alone," usually in problematic situations.

nurse 1. compassion and healing, mental or spiritual. 2. misery, in need of care (with doctor).

nursery 1. fruitfulness, progeny. 2. an environment conducive to growth, cultivation—often of ideas, likely emotional.

nursing 1. a good omen. 2. to provide sustenance for growth, usually of an idea or project (breast-feeding). 3. contentment and harmony in affairs (breast-feeding). 4. to provide care for healing, usually emotional.

nutcracker 1. family troubles, arguments are in the offing. 2. a happy omen regarding intimate affairs. 3. wordplay regarding someone who is overbearing.

nutmeg 1. change, often in prosperity and financial matters. 2. a measure of success in social affairs, the degree to which the present company is viewed as pleasant.

nuts 1. inner character attributes, usually positive traits. 2. successful projects and activities. 3. good health and well-being. 4. wordplay meaning craziness, or to be deeply infatuated. 5. slang for testicles.

nymph 1. adolescent aspirations, fantasies of passion possibly coming to life. 2. romantic adventures. 3. the midpoint of change, metamorphosis (as in the "nymph" stage of insect growth).

nymphomania 1. an overabundance of feminine energy, a lack of balance between parts of self. 2. a lack of balance in life; use caution regarding excessive attention to certain urges or desires to the exclusion of other issues. 3. possible illness or addiction.

O

oak 1. endurance and strength. 2. wisdom and truth.

oar 1. one is able to control emotions. 2. phallic symbol. 3. need for someone to help one.

oasis 1. need to find oneself emotionally. 2. searching for peace in a stressful environment. 3. need for a vacation.

oath 1. some kind of strife exists in one's life. 2. need to prove that one is honest. 3. refusing to take an oath indicates that one is dishonest. 4. one dislikes someone intensely (blood oath, curse).

oatmeal 1. indicates control over one's life. 2. nourishment and satisfaction.

oats (horse eating) 1. security. 2. horse refusing to take oats indicates rejection of care.

obedience 1. a desire to succeed. 2. when others are obedient to the dreamer it means he/she regards him/herself as a good boss.

obelisk phallus.

obese 1. if the dreamer is overweight, a lack of esteem. 2. the desire to protect oneself from romantic involvement with others. 3. one is undisciplined. 4. one should have a healthier lifestyle.

obituary one's collection of thoughts or personality is passing away.

objection legal action is impending.

obligation 1. jealousy of someone one is obligated to. 2. guilt.

oblique be careful, someone may attack from a position one doesn't see.

oblong odd shape signifies something is not quite right in what the dreamer is observing.

oboe to achieve one's goals one will have to take a different approach.

obscene 1. disgust about something or someone. 2. emergence of innermost feelings or anger.

obscure one must dig deeper to discover the truth about something, but it is there.

obstacle be prepared for plenty of these on the way to one's goals.

obstetrician 1. if female, one wants to become pregnant. 2. if male, one wants partner to become pregnant.

occult one sees other-worldly answers to problems.

ocean 1. state of one's life, rough to tranquil. 2. traveling on an ocean means a desire to get away from it all. 3. the inner soul. 4. mother. 5. death. 6. limitless space or unconscious.

Oceania 1. going back to the womb. 2. safe.

October time of hope and joy (holiday season).

octopus 1. entangled in a problem. 2. the dreamer is trying to control someone.

odor catalyst for specific memories or issues.

odyssey getting to one's goal is going to be difficult and lengthy.

Oedipus 1. one has incestuous sexual fantasies. 2. one has kinky sexual fantasies.

off 1. want to be rid of someone. 2. someone turns one off. 3. someone gets one off.

offal someone or something is not worth getting involved with.

offense 1. "taking the offensive" to fight problems or obstacles. 2. feeling blocked or obstructed by others.

offering an attempt to be spiritual.

office 1. worried about what is going on at work. 2. proud of one's achievements at work.

officer authority figure.

ogre 1. projected fear of something in one's character. 2. deep fear of someone.

Ohio 1. mid-America. 2. saying hello to someone ("oh, hi, oh"). 3. presidential election.

ohm small but powerful.

oil 1. desire to be treated like a child (baby oil). 2. emotional upset or crisis (oil spill). 3. problems increasing uncontrollably (oil spill). 4. need for things to run smoothly (oil as lubrication). 5. wealth.

ointment needs relief from something.

old 1. need to discard something in one's life. 2. feeling one is not up to solving one's problems. 3. fear of becoming old. 4. wisdom. 5. listen to experience.

oleo false.

olives 1. contentment is the "good life." 2. desire for or feeling of immortality.

omelette 1. things are confused. 2. make do with what one has.

one (number) 1. most important. 2. the problem can be reduced to one thing.

one-eyed 1. being unable to be objective about other people's views or ideas. 2. being unable to face situations or problems.

onions 1. addressing problems with many layers, all of which require examination. 2. facing problems that may make one cry.

open one should be more open with feelings.

opening 1. a new opportunity. 2. inspiration. 3. desire to attain goals and realize new or full potential.

opera 1. desire to seek the nobler things in life. 2. need to curb emotions. 3. to succeed, one will have to sing one's song in the best way possible, but one must have backup.

opera singer someone trying to succeed on his/her own.

opinion one's position is easy to listen to because it's not presented as fact, but as opinion.

opium 1. recognition of bad habits blocking the way to progress and success. 2. need to escape from problems and reality.

opponent(s) 1. internal conflict and fear. 2. recognition of problems or opponents in real life.

Oprah 1. someone with a large ego. 2. caring. 3. wealth.

optician take another look at one's interpretation of something.

oral try to express oneself more openly.

oral sex (female) 1. deep desire to please one's partner. 2. desire for uninhibited or forbidden sex.

oral sex (male) need to return to the womb.

orange 1. bright and sunny future. 2. one needs hardware (Home Depot).

oranges 1. health and prosperity. 2. sexual object (sucking on). 3. primitive urges or desires.

orchard 1. life under assault or in decline (decaying). 2. one's future looks plentiful (in good shape). 3. emotional or intellectual blossoming.

orchestra 1. the need for orchestrated activity with one's peers to succeed at something in particular. 2. a measure of how well the particular group was doing in performing a certain activity. 3. desire to harmonize or be "part of the group." 4. admiration for "group" effort.

orchid 1. the great love of one's life. 2. special flowers for special people. 3. beauty and sensuality.

ordained one desires advice from someone spiritual.

orders 1. suggestion that one should follow those in authority better. 2. way to deal with underling(s) is with strictness.

ordnance getting ready to be assaulted by someone.

ore 1. one hopes to strike it rich. 2. if one searches hard enough, there are riches to be found.

organ 1. penis. 2. musical instrument. 3. proficiency in sex act (listening to or playing).

orgasm 1. sexual release. 2. realization of a goal.

orgy 1. desire to get involved in wild sexual adventures. 2. realization that one has a secret side. 3. feeling that one is not having sex often enough. 4. moral disarray. 5. lack of focus or discipline in one's life.

orient 1. spiritual awakening. 2. desire for the exotic and/or remote.

oriental 1. perhaps a different approach is needed to solve something. 2. one may not be able to figure something out.

oriole 1. innocence and beauty. 2. desire to play baseball.

ornament 1. way that one regards oneself or someone close. 2. happiness and rejoicing.

orphan 1. feeling of being alone and unwanted. 2. fear of being abandoned or ignored.

ostrich desire to hide unpleasantness from oneself.

otter seeking an unconventional job.

ouija board 1. unpredictability or uncertainty about the future. 2. acceptance of destiny. 3. mystery and curiosity.

outdoors desire to be free.

outed 1. one revealed as homosexual. 2. other deep secret exposed.

outer space 1. creativity. 2. contemplation of long journey. 3. the unknown.

outhouse one is about to face something very unpleasant, but it must be done to rid oneself of problems.

oval(s) 1. female sex organs (e.g., vagina, womb). 2. feminine qualities.

ovation 1. approval. 2. satisfaction with oneself. 3. attainment of goals.

oven 1. slang for the womb. 2. desire to have children. 3. not wanting to have children (empty, cold). 4. an upcoming project may be very difficult, but it can be managed.

overalls 1. preparing to take on a task or address problems. 2. need or desire for "blue collar" job or manual labor. 3. trying to hide or "cover up" faults or shortcomings. 4. desire to return to a simpler way of life.

overcoat 1. feeling unloved. 2. need to be protected against rejection and isolation. 3. mystery and curiosity.

overdose one is getting too much of something.

overflow one is getting more than he/she expected.

overspending one is creating problems in one's life.

overtaking if one keeps trying he/she will succeed, no matter how hopeless something may look.

overtime 1. one is spending too much time at work. 2. one is not being compensated adequately for work.

overture the theme of one's life is in the music.

owl listen to the counsel of others.

ox 1. strength. 2. ability to bear or carry a burden, emotionally or physically.

oxygen one needs fresh air, freedom.

oysters 1. wisdom. 2. caution. 3. danger.

P

pacifier 1. a need or desire to recall simple pleasures, usually an emotional need. 2. need to use caution against immature remarks. 3. leave off a heavy load of responsibility.

pacify 1. compromise, diplomacy and peacemaking. 2. will soon be admired for kindness and tact. 3. to keep in a state of denial and defense, usually in a relationship.

pack, packing 1. preparation for change, leaving behind possible situation, relationships or environment (note what is being packed). 2. repressed or "stuffed" emotions (note what is being packed). 3. to cling to unresolved feelings or behavioral patterns that are no longer helpful (as in to "carry too much baggage").

package 1. surprises in life are waiting. 2. secrets soon to be revealed. 3. to send off old patterns of behavior, emotional baggage.

page 1. lack of ambition (to see a blank page). 2. romantic pain; use caution to avoid a rebound or "next available" situation. 3. misfortune in business affairs (to be paged). 4. time to take things more seriously.

pageant 1. deceptive, illusionary public image. 2. insecurities about personal appearance (beauty pageant). 3. happiness, joyous spectacle.

pager 1. a message is being sent from one level of consciousness to another. 2. an individual is trying hard to communicate. 3. overwhelming feelings of demand and lack of privacy.

pagoda 1. possible exotic journey in the offing; adventures and romance. 2. a distinct and honorable aspect of self, spiritual, serene and content. 3. surprises, pleasures and happiness.

pail 1. prosperity and abundance—usually financial wealth, often social—the quality of friends. 2. situation or conditions are improving (to carry a pail). 3. use caution in financial affairs (to spill a pail).

pain 1. possible illness or unknown injury. 2. extreme unhappiness, sorrow. 3. lack of balance, usually emotional. 4. an annoyance.

painting 1. creating a false or illusory image (as in "paint a rosy picture"). 2. a long prosperous life (to have a painting). 3. object of gossip (to have paint on clothing). 4. to obtain a different or fresh perspective.

palace 1. entering a phase of happiness. 2. prospects and adventures will prove fruitful.

palette 1. to be filled with colorful human attributes and aspects; emotions, intellect, instinct and the senses (note the colors spread on the palette). 2. coping skills. 3. a need to paint or "color" emotional events.

pall 1. "legacy" or enrichment will come from changes or sorrowful loss. 2. bad news, news of changes may be in the offing.

pallbearer 1. a sign of approaching change—often for the better, usually relating to social relationships. 2. honor and distinction, especially in relationships or socially.

pallet 1. change in abode or status of relationship (as if alternate sleeping arrangements will be necessary). 2. one has "made one's bed and must now lie in it." 3. jealousy may be making a wedge in primary relationships.

palmistry 1. the future is good and prosperous. 2. a feeling that goals and ambitions will be achieved. 3. reputation grows suspect.

palm tree 1. success, hope and happiness. 2. unexpected sorrow, disappointment (to see a withered or dying palm).

palsy 1. uncertainty, instability. 2. possible illness. 3. situations and activities, or possibly individuals, may be affecting the nerves.

pancake 1. success and fortune. 2. pleasures and happiness are abundant.

pane 1. how situations or relationships are viewed, often negative. 2. use caution and patience in relationships (to clean a pane of glass). 3. trouble is ahead (to break a pane of glass). 4. obstacles (to try to communicate through a pane of glass).

panorama 1. an all-encompassing, wide view or vision of the world—likely life in general, sometimes situations. 2. a need or desire to make great changes—often in professions, likely in location or environment.

panther 1. power and leadership; victory over adversity. 2. danger or troubles ahead. 3. feminine strength.

panties 1. lucky at love. 2. a change for the better (to change into clean ones). 3. exposure, shame, embarrassment (to be caught in). 4. feminine self; an exploration of sexuality.

pantomime 1. a sense that a "charade" is afoot, deceptions are close by. 2. a need or desire to explore alternative means of communication, understanding; the usual method is lacking.

paper 1. a return to innocence, renewal—often spiritual, sometimes a new phase of life (a blank piece of paper). 2. messages are being sent from one part of the consciousness to another (note any writing on the paper). 3. flimsiness, fragility; a temporary state.

parable 1. a lesson, possibly moral, is attempting to get through from one level to the next. 2. confusion about what path to take—likely morally, possibly in financial matters.

parachute 1. to act with abandon; risky business. 2. travel between levels of understanding, consciousness. 3. to rely on someone or something else for safety—usually emotionally, often financially.

parade 1. public exposure, display. 2. happiness, celebration. 3. distractions, displays, are taking too much attention away from crucial matters.

paradise 1. a very good omen in general. 2. an indication of what forgiveness can achieve. 3. success, prosperity.

paralysis 1. loss of feeling and expression, likely emotional due to injury. 2. difficulty in accepting changes, even healthy ones. 3. feeling trapped by conflicts, sometimes domestic.

paranoia 1. overwhelmed by fears; paralyzed with anxiety, preventing action.

parasite 1. an abusive, draining relationship or situation. 2. dependence to the point of taking advantage.

parasol 1. a good omen, especially in matters of love (if open and in the sun). 2. a need or desire for assistance with difficulties.

parcel 1. a feeling that pleasant surprises are on the way. 2. a new beginning, a new way of life or belief system. 3. difficulties or hard responsibilities, choices are on the way.

parchment 1. wealth is attainable; good omens for legal entanglements. 2. possible legal entanglements (to receive documents on parchment).

pardon 1. regrets over misdeeds or secrets are beginning to work their way to the surface. 2. possible embarrassment is in the offing for questionable business affairs. 3. good times, good fortune are in the offing (to be pardoned).

parents 1. the "parenting" roles and aspects in a broad sense; nurturing, shelter, unconditional love and support. 2. relationship between the dreamer and parents. 3. approaching change, often in aspects of life or personality (if dreaming of being a parent when the dreamer is not). 4. good luck and prosperity.

park 1. escape from cares and worries. 2. peace, happiness. 3. self.

Parkinson's disease 1. possible illness. 2. a sign of losing control, usually over a situation or relationship (to dream of having Parkinson's disease).

parricide (to kill parents) 1. anger at aspects of self represented by parents (e.g., nurturing mother, overprotective father). 2. repressed anger at parents or parental figures. 3. desire for a quiet life.

parrot 1. a feeling that a relationship is growing on flattery. 2. gossip and idle chatter run rampant in the immediate environment.

3. a message is being repeated from one level of consciousness to the next, or advice from other sources is trying to get through.

parsley 1. success and recognition, especially for work well done. 2. healthy family life, environment.

parsnips 1. a good omen for professional life or business matters. 2. difficulties in love relationships, settling for less.

parting 1. unease and discomfort, as if things are falling apart. 2. annoyances get to be a little too much. 3. reverse: success and joy (to part with a spouse).

partner 1. a need or desire for help. 2. self, a mirror image. 3. disagreements, bickering.

partridge 1. many little annoyances begin to pile up. 2. capabilities, competency. 3. a good omen for business matters.

party 1. happiness, fleeting pleasures. 2. a need or desire to socialize, have fun. 3. difficulties, arguments and dissension (to throw a party).

passenger 1. leaving control, direction and drive to others, to relinquish power (note mode of transportation). 2. success is on the way (depending on mode of transportation). 3. domestic disagreements.

passport 1. safe passage, contentment. 2. sense of self and place in the world. 3. start of a new phase of life or journey.

password 1. self, inner self, private feelings. 2. a feeling of social awkwardness, of not knowing what is going on (to forget a password). 3. to give in to questionable pursuits and desires (to give away a password).

pastel 1. indicates a positive attitude and appreciation for simple pleasures, simple environment. 2. denial—usually emotional, often in relationships or in life. 3. a lack of intensity, drama or "overdoing" the obvious.

pastry 1. the sweetness of life, fleeting pleasures and sensuality. 2. beware of frivolity in business or financial matters. 3. upcoming important matters need attention.

pasture 1. success, happiness and longevity. 2. change, perhaps long in coming, a time to move on (as in "greener pastures").

patch 1. a down-to-earth, unpretentious individual (patched clothing). 2. reverse: wealth and prosperity, security (patched clothing). 3. to conceal a questionable trait or urges.

patent 1. meticulous and thorough work or projects. 2. a time for speculative or risky enterprises. 3. little annoyances, usually caused by individuals, are accumulating.

path 1. destiny. 2. progress. 3. peaceful state of mind (if path is unblocked).

paunch 1. wealth, abundance, perhaps to the point of overindulgence. 2. possible illness. 3. repressed or "stuffed" emotions. 4. reverse: possible losses.

pauper 1. reverse: wealth and security. 2. obstacles to success, often internal; poor sense of self-worth. 3. a strong sense of negativity; spiritual poverty.

pawnshop 1. indicates a poor use or misuse of resources. 2. reverse: fortunes will improve with prudent actions. 3. a sense of loss, possibly of a friend.

peaches 1. a feeling that hopes and dreams can be realized. 2. fleeting, small pleasures are in the offing. 3. positive, pleasant feelings are in the offing (as in "just peachy").

peacock 1. justifiable pride of bearing, appearance. 2. reverse: loss of status, reputation or appeal. 3. fertility, immortality.

peak 1. height of achievement, successful project. 2. fear of continued mobility, fear of a fall.

pearl 1. a treasure, a beauty often neglected—frequently a concept, usually intellectual. 2. unhappiness, financial misfortune. 3. success is at hand (obtaining pearls).

pears 1. female energy and fertility. 2. the germination of new ideas, the fertility of the intellect and creativity. 3. the unexpected could happen.

peas 1. avoidable little annoyances seem to go on forever; use caution against undermining one's own activities. 2. health, especially against communicable diseases.

pebble 1. hidden strength. 2. difficult times, troubles. 3. harsh judgments, often not justifiable (as in "people who live in glass houses should not throw stones").

pecans 1. wealth and prosperity. 2. projects and activities will bear fruit. 3. success will be achieved after some initial difficulties.

pedestal 1. ego; superiority or inferiority, depending on position. 2. sense of importance, immortality. 3. to hold in high esteem, admiration.

peel 1. revealing secrets, hidden treasures. 2. change is in the offing, a "shedding of the skin" for a period of growth. 3. change, feelings of loss or distance from friends. 4. a need or desire for greater understanding, delving beneath the surface, usually of self or another individual.

pelican 1. empathy, consideration shown toward others, nurturance. 2. mixed outcomes, commingling disappointment and success.

pen 1. the ability to communicate between the intellect and the emotions. 2. the ability to express emotions, especially anger and disappointment, in a constructive way (as in "the pen is mightier than the sword"). 3. possible message or news coming from a distance. 4. use caution in love relationships; some things may not be what they appear.

penalties 1. guilt, a need for punishment for past transgressions or patterns of behavior. 2. to feel distance from or "out of the game," out of sync with society (to be penalized for a foul). 3. reverse: success, victory is achieved through determination and honest hard work.

pencil 1. the influence of a higher road, an internal call to "do the right thing." 2. things are "erasable," temporary—possibly relationships, usually mistakes or errors in judgment. 3. wisdom of thinking before speaking (to sharpen a pencil). 4. a phallic symbol.

pendant 1. the realization of hopes and desires, especially in love. 2. selfless virtue in love, unconditional admiration. 3. a connection between individuals, understanding and empathy.

pendulum 1. extreme confusion, especially in life choices. 2. extremes of thought, ambivalence—usually regarding a situation, frequently in a relationship. 3. routine, rhythm, the pulse of life, a heartbeat.

penguin 1. a sense that situations are not as dire as they initially seemed. 2. feelings of being drawn unwillingly toward the negative side of things, usually in situations. 3. working together for a common goal, the betterment of all, usually regarding a family or community.

penis 1. male sexuality. 2. masculine power. 3. fertility symbol (note size).

penitentiary 1. the part of self reserved for regrets, guilt and punishment, usually a source of obstacles and the failure to reach potential. 2. loss of reputation, embarrassment in the offing. 3. feeling trapped. 4. difficulty in communication.

penny 1. a measure of success of money or business endeavors. 2. financial loss. 3. idle contemplation, musings (as in "a penny for your thoughts"). 4. a cheap individual, a tightwad.

pension 1. the wealth of maturity, wisdom. 2. financial security, thoughts for the future. 3. much-needed assistance is in the offing.

people 1. symbol of self, having attributes the dreamer desires or admires. 2. a measure of how one fits into society, belonging.

pepper 1. anger, likely a need to moderate the temper. 2. excitement, "flavor." 3. gossip is afoot (especially if the mouth gets burned by pepper).

peppermint 1. goals and ambitions will be achieved. 2. a difficult time in accepting or understanding a situation or part of life. 3. an interesting social life, entertainment is about to begin.

performing 1. desire for recognition. 2. happiness, community (to see others perform or performing with others). 3. great importance is placed on appearances.

perfume 1. pleasure and romance, often emotional (not necessarily in relationship). 2. a need or desire for sensual pleasure;

taking the time to enjoy it. 3. embarrassment (to receive as a gift). 4. corruption (bad perfume).

perspiration 1. suggests the possibility that anxiety has proved overwhelming, an obstacle in itself. 2. a need or desire for physical work, manual labor, as a catharsis. 3. a difficult period may be about to pass, a restoration of reputation.

pest 1. negative aspects of life are getting overwhelming, draining. 2. prosperity, social status and honor.

pet 1. love and acceptance, usually unconditional. 2. steadfast, loving affection and companionship. 3. return to simple pleasures, a more innocent time.

pewter 1. circumstances will improve; peace of mind, happiness will be achieved. 2. the importance of the past, holding on to memory perhaps to the detriment of the present. 3. social adventures in the offing.

phantom 1. troubles seem to take on a life of their own (to see a phantom). 2. a past experience causes regret, pain, in spite of its absence (as in phantom pain). 3. emotionally overwhelmed. 4. disappointment in the offing.

pheasant 1. financial security, successes and gains. 2. a good omen for social engagements and activities. 3. personal sacrifices for the benefit of others; care and nurturance.

phone 1. a message is coming through from one level to the next, possibly the unconscious to the conscious or the heart to the mind. 2. telepathic communication. 3. difficulty in trying to communicate (to make a call). 4. someone relaying an important message, guidance (to receive a call).

phosphorus, phosphoresce 1. a message is being conveyed, trying desperately, even through darkness, to get through. 2. an idea or concept coming into being. 3. use caution against risky, temporary pleasures.

photograph 1. recollections. 2. image of the world, an event or self-image, depending on the subject. 3. a feeling that a possible deception is approaching. 4. rivals may vie for the affections of dear ones.

photographer 1. to seize images, to be preoccupied with appearances and, less so, contents. 2. a reluctance to let go of sometimes false perceptions. 3. a need or desire to control or understand memories or situations, perhaps alter them in ways that make them less painful.

physician 1. to have many skills and talents, to profit by mastery over many situations and activities. 2. possible illness. 3. a need for healing and care—likely emotional, often spiritual. 4. a good omen for improving situations.

piano 1. success, pleasures and sheer joy—often socially, frequently in domestic or business affairs. 2. a need or desire for "harmony"—likely with inner self, often with friends and family (note the quality of the playing and whether or not the piano is tuned).

pickax 1. a desire to get to the bottom or the heart of a problem. 2. pressure, intensity, stress, usually sexual in nature.

pickle 1. a problem situation, trouble in the offing (as in being in "a pickle"). 2. a phallic symbol. 3. a good omen for the general state of things. 4. resolution of difficulties, "mysteries" and secrets.

pickpocket 1. the object of envy, jealousy. 2. the sense that harassment is growing out of hand, starting to do emotional and psychic damage. 3. loss and invasion.

picnic 1. signifies pleasure in life, enjoyment. 2. the ease of success, accomplishment of goals, depending on the company, weather, insects, etc. (as in "this is no picnic").

picture 1. a measure of happiness in intimate relationships (note the contents of the picture). 2. a distorted recollection (to see a faded, blurry or otherwise damaged picture). 3. overall view or perception of life or a situation or circumstance (as in "to get the big picture"). 4. small changes in the offing.

pie 1. a measure of domestic bliss, contentment (note condition or contents of pie). 2. to have a slightly negative sense of one's hopes and dreams, deem them impossible to achieve (as in "pie in the sky"). 3. entitlement (as in "a piece of the pie").

pier 1. introspection, self-examination. 2. goals will be achieved; success and prosperity. 3. the ability to communicate emotions, "off-load" emotional "cargo."

piercing 1. sexual intercourse, penetration. 2. an act of social defiance or conformity, depending on one's attitudes toward piercing. 3. regrets over harsh or "sharp" words said out of turn (to have a pierced tongue or lip).

pig 1. a general gauge of prosperity (note condition of pig). 2. avarice, greed and overindulgence. 3. uncouth behavior, inappropriate sexual attitudes and behaviors and uncleanliness. 4. intelligence, things sacred and ancient wisdom.

pigeon 1. charity, comfort and devotion. 2. a feeling of being blamed for other's transgressions. 3. homesickness, a desire to go home (as in "homing pigeon"). 4. somewhat useful chatter and gossip, messages in the air.

pilgrim 1. the traveler, a spiritual journey. 2. hospitality. 3. reverse: signifies that wealth comes from frugality, a simple life and staunch work ethic.

pill 1. harsh criticism (as in a "bitter pill to swallow"). 2. responsibilities or consequences, often of an unpleasant or disagreeable nature. 3. time to pay attention to some spiritual aspects of self.

pillow 1. to take comfort, a need for comfort, security—usually spiritual, often physical. 2. sense of luxury, life of ease. 3. a need for more rest. 4. a need or desire to have fun, cut loose a little (pillow fight).

pilot 1. the one in control, offering guidance; may be an actual person or someone who represents an aspect of personality. 2. desire for greater mobility. 3. capable of achieving dreams or desired goals and ambitions (to be a pilot or piloting a plane).

pimple 1. the surfacing of repressed anger. 2. negativity in self-image, socially awkward, adolescent discomfort. 3. personal gains, likely in silver, are in the offing. 4. worry and anxiety out of proportion to concerns is not useful.

pineapple 1. a good omen regarding relationships and domestic arrangements. 2. success in goals and ambitions, possessing a lot of self-confidence. 3. an exciting new love interest (to see pineapple growing).

pine tree 1. a good omen; resilience, endurance and immortality. 2. happiness, rebirth and renewal. 3. negative omen if furniture is made out of pine.

pink 1. a very good omen for success and health. 2. a positive omen for social activities. 3. a good omen for intimate relationships.

pinky finger 1. honor, loyalty and trustworthiness. 2. weakness. 3. an oath or promise. 4. the intellect; ability to communicate.

pins 1. disagreement, contradictions, the severity of which depends upon the number of pins and whether or not one is stuck by them. 2. anxiety and/or excitement (as in "on pins and needles"). 3. pointed, sharp comments or criticisms. 4. particularly annoying individuals (as in "a real prick").

pipe 1. a narrow view of things, focused and intent, connected to others and the flow of things (plumbing and various types of conduits; note the type of pipe). 2. masculinity, a fatherly figure, responsible and wise. 3. communication, voice (as in "to pipe up"). 4. to make peace, a spiritual ritual (as in "peace pipe").

pirate 1. not having control over one's life, destiny. 2. justifiable issues of trust in relationships, likely friendships, may arise. 3. freedom and adventure may be in the offing; use caution with questionable behavior. 4. to feel unworthy of credit for or undeserving of accomplishments or gains.

piss 1. power and strength. 2. a need to clean up after oneself. 3. a cleansing, a release of tension, sometimes sexual, pent-up emotions. 4. to anger someone (as in to "piss" someone off).

pistol 1. a negative omen regarding luck and reputation. 2. "targeted" goals and ambitions (target practice). 3. a sharp and dynamic individual. 4. repressed anger or rage or possibly fear.

pit 1. feelings of hopelessness and despair (to be at the bottom of a pit). 2. feelings of decline and bad luck. 3. being confined and trapped, restrained.

pitcher 1. fortune and contentment, hospitality. 2. a measure of fidelity—usually between lovers, sometimes between family members. 3. the ability to communicate ideas and concepts (note the condition of pitcher and its contents).

pitchfork 1. hard work, attempts to improve circumstances. 2. a tendency to overdo, overindulgence. 3. to create a mischievous environment where almost "anything goes."

placenta 1. the source of life; sustenance and air, essential for growth. 2. once necessary attributes are no longer needed, usually regarding personal growth.

plague 1. pervasive, long-ranging difficulties. 2. good news coming about money.

plain 1. an open expanse of opportunity and chance. 2. frontier spirit; adventure, desire to try something completely new in life. 3. wholesomeness, recalling an innocent, simpler way of life. 4. the adjective "plain" is usually the reverse; not ordinary, lavish, lush and full of vibrancy.

plane (airplane) 1. mobility, often vertical; achievements. 2. a journey to a higher consciousness. 3. feelings of control.

plane (tool, carpenter's) 1. successful projects are underway. 2. a desire to make things work well, "smooth" out difficulties, remove obstacles.

planets 1. personal sphere of influence. 2. sense of fate, fortune or future (horoscopes). 3. possibly difficult journey ahead (to travel among).

plank 1. a tenuous path, uncertainty and doubt (note what the plank is crossing). 2. the beginning of an adventure. 3. an integral part of a structure, an important aspect of self or personality (note the condition of plank).

plants 1. a measure of health and well-being (note condition of plants). 2. personal, emotional growth. 3. progress in affairs and plans.

plaster 1. concerns over appearances, surface or superficial aspects. 2. wordplay on drunkenness. 3. family or domestic arrangements (note condition of plaster). 4. indicates healing, often of a physical injury or an emotional injury like an insult.

plastic 1. level of function, helpfulness and pliability. 2. authenticity, how "real" something is, often a personality aspect.

plastic surgery 1. a need or desire for restructuring, enhancement of self-image, often after emotional injury, devastation. 2. avoiding "deeper issues," inner problems.

plate 1. emotional and intellectual capacity, or "how much can one take." 2. a measure of overall prosperity in life, achievements (note how full the plate is). 3. domestic disharmony, arguments (to break a plate or see broken plates). 4. a period of "famine"—likely social, sometimes emotional (an empty plate).

platinum 1. endurance, usually in relationships, including friendships. 2. personal ambition and determination, tenacity and drive—often in regards to prosperity and business affairs, frequently in relationships.

platter 1. feelings toward domestic or family relationships (note condition of platter and what or how much is on it). 2. personal expectations have gotten extreme; a lack of ambition or good fortune (to be "handed everything on a silver platter").

play 1. the cause and effect or plot of a situation, playing a role. 2. deepest desires are achieved. 3. the playing out of a deep-seated memory or emotion.

playground 1. stage of youthful dramas, competition. 2. desire for simpler times, way of life. 3. sense that a situation has taken a turn for the immature.

playing 1. need for physical movement and activity; fun. 2. to act out and release trapped emotions. 3. desire to take life less seriously.

pleasure 1. a period of pain will or must end soon. 2. gains and profits. 3. reverse: a feeling of overwhelming disappointment.

plough 1. sexuality, intercourse, fertility. 2. success will come only after hard work. 3. the intellect, creativity.

plums 1. a positive omen of youth, vitality and abundance. 2. a measure of happiness and success (note the stage of ripeness or general condition of the plum). 3. a cure for possible emotional "constipation," repression (to encounter or eat prunes).

pocket 1. a need to keep certain things, possibly aspects of self, secret or "under wraps." 2. cheap, stingy. 3. sexual attraction, interaction (as in "is that a mouse in your pocket . . .").

pocketbook 1. self, personal identity (note condition and contents of pocketbook). 2. financial good luck, prosperity (to find a pocketbook). 3. a feeling of financial misfortune (to lose a pocketbook).

poetry an important, highly emotional message is being conveyed (note the content of the poetry).

poison 1. subtle, painful injury is done—usually emotional, sometimes spiritual. 2. an obstacle that undermines growth and well-being.

poker 1. taste and distinction, good social affairs. 2. a feeling of deception going on—likely in a situation, possibly a relationship. 3. signifies a situation that may require good strategy and careful forethought.

polar bear 1. power, innocence and purity. 2. overcoming obstacles, improvements of situations and conditions. 3. solitude, rebirth and communication—usually spiritual, often emotional.

police 1. control and authority; rules of conduct. 2. feelings of safety and security. 3. warning against unsafe behavior; misfortune (being caught by police). 4. guilt, emotional or sexual repression.

polish 1. refinement, class. 2. clarity of view, an immaculate image. 3. completion, uniformity and thoroughness, as if one needed to pass an inspection.

politician 1. a feeling that the truth is being manipulated, things are not what they seem. 2. keeping bad company; use caution in choosing friends. 3. arguments, to take sides or demonstrate loyalty.

polka 1. pleasant preoccupations, social gatherings and sense of community. 2. a business affair or situation requires quick steps and a leap. 3. a need or desire to reacquaint oneself with one's ethnic roots, traditional activities.

pomegranate 1. a excellent omen for prosperity and health. 2. sexual allure and fertility. 3. difficulties lie ahead (to see a spoiled pomegranate).

pond 1. the unconscious, a "reflection of self" (note quality of water, clear or muddy). 2. close relationships (note size of pond and quality of water). 3. a need to pay attention to "stagnant" aspects of life. 4. luck and prosperity (note if the pond is clear or dirty).

pony 1. fun and play. 2. a good marriage, attractive partnering, possibly aspects of self. 3. sexuality, sexual power and sense of freedom.

poor 1. will have future wealth. 2. worry; sense of loss.

poorhouse 1. financial obstacles, a failure to live up to earning potential. 2. reverse: a feeling that prosperity is close at hand.

pope 1. "fatherly" guidance, usually spiritual. 2. preoccupation with the service of others, a need to reassess independence. 3. feelings of moral superiority, self-righteous attitude.

poplars 1. a good omen in regards to robust health and energy. 2. use caution around adventuresome friends; resist peer pressure.

poppy 1. use caution around superstitious matters; a need to be more self-confident. 2. a need or desire for more relaxing activities. 3. rising passions, a pleasurable release.

porcelain 1. wounded psyche, emotional vulnerability. 2. exotic travel is in the offing. 3. current situations or circumstances will improve.

porch 1. image of self presented to the world, accessibility to others (note condition of porch). 2. a new, positive phase of life is about to begin. 3. embarrassment or shame over circumstances (to sleep or eat on a porch).

porcupine 1. a "prickly" project or situation is underway. 2. vulnerability, defensiveness, a need to keep the world at a distance. 3. greater success will generate greater responsibilities.

pork 1. financial gains, security and success. 2. success is achieved at a great price, possibly loss of self-respect. 3. a desire for general knowledge, to understand how things work, sometimes in relationships.

pornography 1. intimacy issues. 2. a need for release, usually emotional energy. 3. need or desire to not take sexuality so seriously.

porpoise 1. great intellectual accomplishments. 2. a spirit guide. 3. the ability to communicate between one level of understanding or consciousness and the next.

porter 1. the burdens of travel or journey of life, often emotional (as in "emotional baggage"). 2. humility, self-image (to be a porter). 3. misfortune.

portfolio 1. work, professional attitudes and preparedness (note condition of portfolio). 2. a body of work, life's creative achievement. 3. emotional "investment."

portrait 1. self-image. 2. a measure of success regarding love life, intimate relationships. 3. use caution, flattery may be deceiving.

Poseidon 1. kingly, lordlike behavior; negative, misogynistic (to see the god Neptune or Poseidon). 2. a desire, usually spiritual/emotional, to see the ocean or large body of water. 3. horses.

postage 1. validated, important communications, usually from one part of self or level of consciousness to the next. 2. external guidance, often of a spiritual nature.

postman 1. a messenger of great importance—often from the unconscious, sometimes external. 2. a spiritual guide. 3. sense that news is in the offing.

post office 1. expressive of a need for communication. 2. a message is trying to get through, usually from one level of consciousness to another. 3. bad news or misfortune is in the offing. 4. good news is in the offing.

pot 1. use caution in money and professional matters (as in "haven't got a pot to piss in"). 2. use caution in business enterprises, matters of trust, especially if the pot is broken. 3. confinement (if it is a flower pot).

pot (marijuana) 1. responsibilities are being pushed aside (to smoke). 2. possible health or addiction problem. 3. ability to feel euphoria, pleasure.

potato 1. good luck. 2. success and fondest wishes come to pass.

potter 1. industry and hard work. 2. success on a project or life's journey (as in "taking shape" or "shaping up"). 3. feelings of responsibility, perhaps sole responsibility, for a project.

pottery 1. self or character (as in how one "shapes up"). 2. the beginning of a new and creative project. 3. progress in life or toward specific goals.

poultry 1. wordplay on "paltry," or unimportant, trivial matters. 2. difficulties are on the way, possibly financial.

powder 1. happiness, comfort and pleasure. 2. a "toxic" person, set of behaviors or situation, a need or desire for distance from it. 3. possible health or addiction-related problem.

power 1. success in personal aspirations. 2. reverse: loss, weakness. 3. energy and enthusiasm. 4. a lack of inspiration and guidance (if the electric power is out).

prairie 1. hopes and dreams, journeys and self-discovery. 2. luxury, creature comforts.

praying 1. to give up control over problems, situations. 2. goals achieved, plenty of happiness. 3. to cast off responsibilities or seek help with them.

preacher 1. a moral lesson is trying to get through. 2. feelings of being nagged, or "preached" to. 3. use caution in business or relationship matters, moral issues need to be addressed. 4. a need or desire for guidance, likely spiritual.

precipice 1. difficulties and problems will be solved. 2. feelings of being made fun of, ridiculed. 3. gloom or impending disaster.

pregnancy 1. a creative project in the making. 2. aspect of self, personal life is emerging. 3. better health is on the way. 4. safe delivery (if the dreamer is pregnant). 5. the high point of desires.

present (gift) 1. good fortune. 2. use caution against idle flattery; something or someone may be deceptive.

present (moment) 1. a need or desire to focus, think in the "present." 2. a feeling of connectedness, involvement in current events and affairs.

priest 1. desire for guidance, likely spiritual. 2. a need to curb indulgence, excess. 3. a need for counsel, guidance over conduct, possibly business related. 4. a challenge or change in moral code; a test of principles.

primrose 1. happy domestic affairs and arrangements. 2. exciting love life is in the offing. 3. innocence.

prince 1. a romantic ideal (as in "Prince Charming," if dreamed by a woman). 2. hero, the inner masculine self. 3. a high estimation of oneself. 4. a surprise is in the offing.

princess 1. inner female self, power. 2. use caution against indulgence. 3. a female romantic ideal (usually if dreamed by a male). 4. a desire to be rescued.

printer 1. attempt at clear, simple communication. 2. trying to get a message across (to receive or send). 3. possible secrets hidden away.

prison 1. guilt and containment. 2. confining or trapped situation. 3. repressed communication, expression, usually emotional. 4. repressed aspect of personality (someone else imprisoned).

privacy 1. feelings about relationships. 2. feelings of being repressed by overbearing individuals.

prizefight (boxing match) 1. a struggle for financial success, opportunities. 2. an inner struggle, often between two conflicting points of view. 3. a feeling that difficulties are out of control.

procession 1. formal honors in the offing, advancement. 2. succession, continuity; maintaining the order of things.

profanity 1. bad character traits are being cultivated. 2. careless behavior, disregard for the feelings of others. 3. loss of hope, misery.

professor 1. a lesson is being offered, new skills can be acquired. 2. improvements in conditions or circumstances are coming soon. 3. a serious, formal affair is in the offing.

profit 1. rewards and success are just around the corner. 2. reverse: feelings of failure, disappointment. 3. wordplay on "prophet," regarding events of a spiritual nature. 4. a time to keep affairs quiet and close to the vest.

prom 1. going from one stage of life to the next. 2. an adolescent vulnerability, awkward sexuality. 3. a tremendous reliance on the approval of others.

promenade 1. a need or desire to relax and take part in social activities. 2. guilt over a public display of affection (to promenade alone). 3. to actively pursue—usually business matters, often intimate relationships.

property 1. a measure of wealth, prosperity. 2. a need or desire for grounding. 3. a measure of success in friendships, close relationships.

prostitute 1. a poor self-image, low levels of self-respect. 2. a need or desire to loosen inhibitions, often regarding sex. 3. view of women (if dreamed by a male or seeing a male with a prostitute). 4. adjusting principles for profit.

protection 1. a lack of self-reliance, independence—usually emotional, sometimes physical. 2. a strong sense of vulnerability. 3. desire to be more relaxed over concerns.

pruning 1. period of great growth. 2. need to eliminate unnecessary, inhibiting behavior patterns or ways of thinking.

psychic 1. seeking awareness (seeing a psychic). 2. an extraordinary awareness and sensitivity (to be psychic). 3. desire for control over situation.

publisher 1. attempts at communication. 2. use caution in relying too much on "professional" advice.

pudding 1. profits, feelings of little yield for a lot of work. 2. profits are in the offing.

puddle 1. a feeling that a possibly bad or even dangerous situation is presenting itself. 2. a time to watch progress, watch steps closely, possibly relating to a situation or problem solving. 3. a need to pay attention to "stagnant" aspects of life.

pulpit 1. good social standing, good character. 2. guilt-related difficulties. 3. a sense of moral superiority, self-righteousness.

pulse 1. possible health issue. 2. the beginning of new and exciting activities, possibly romantic affairs.

pump 1. a measure of progress in business affairs. 2. sexual intercourse. 3. secondary relationships, casual social circle or co-workers, possibly neglected or overlooked.

pumpkin 1. happiness, usually in domestic relationships. 2. a bad omen regarding reputation, possible issues over revenge. 3. female sexuality. 4. the limitations of time (as in "Cinderella").

punch 1. repressed anger or rage. 2. feelings of power—sometimes the abuse of power, but always personal. 3. reverse: feelings of powerlessness. 4. deriving pleasure, especially from a variety of interests or activities (if drinking punch).

puppy 1. relationships will grow in quality and strength. 2. the ability to learn new skills. 3. a loss of control, seemingly innocent carelessness. 4. feelings of joy, a new beginning.

purple 1. an honorable standing, regal bearing, often in social settings or possibly the community. 2. repressed anger or rage. 3. blood.

purse 1. desire for privacy, likely because of secrets. 2. financial security. 3. achievement of goals (to receive or win a purse). 4. loss of control of resources (to lose a purse).

puzzle 1. revealing the interrelationships of things, connectedness of events—often emotional, usually intellectual. 2. a mystery, not having all the facts; use caution regarding decisions (missing pieces). 3. intellectual challenges.

pyramid 1. stability and longevity. 2. focus and direction toward achieving goals and dreams. 3. monumental change in the offing.

python 1. transcendence from one level of consciousness to another. 2. emotional pressure, feelings of constriction. 3. phallic symbol. 4. overt sexuality, engrossing passion. 5. plans will not go as expected, progress limited or strewn with obstacles.

Q

quadruplets something amazing.

quagmire something one is involved in is complex and difficult to solve.

quaint desire to return to a simpler way of life.

quake — see earthquake.

quarrel reflects disagreements with someone.

quarry upcoming work will be hard but rewarding.

quarter 1. part of something is better than nothing. 2. confusing (different quarters made today). 3. football.

quash stop something one doesn't like, but in a diplomatic way.

queen in control of a situation.

Queen Elizabeth hard to figure something out.

quest an attempt to achieve something very important, almost biblical in character.

question 1. one is questioning oneself about something. 2. one has raised a question about someone else.

quibble small argument with larger significance than at first apparent.

quick perhaps one is doing something too quickly.

quicksand there is a problem to be avoided.

quiet 1. one is afraid of something. 2. one is annoying someone else. 3. one is being annoyed.

quill one thinks that perhaps the best way to communicate with someone is with plain, old-fashioned language.

quilt something one faces may be more complicated than at first thought.

quit it is time to give up a fight for something.
quiver 1. afraid. 2. ready to fight fear.
quixotic one wants to change the world.
quiz one feels one is being tested.
quorum others agree with one's position.

R

rabbi 1. a good omen regardless of the dreamer's faith. 2. joy and the ability to make peace, forgiveness. 3. help is on the way toward achieving goals.

rabbit 1. fertility, lust. 2. good fortune. 3. change of direction, perhaps career. 4. steadfastness, fidelity.

rabies 1. deeply repressed rage. 2. too sensitive to touch—usually emotionally, sometimes a health-related concern. 3. use caution; some may believe that violence can solve problems.

raccoon 1. appearances may be deceptive; who or what seems attractive may be harmful. 2. new adventures or skills prove profitable (raccoon fur). 3. a feeling that thievery is afoot.

race 1. preoccupations or obsessions. 2. jealousy of others, competition. 3. need to slow down, relax.

race car 1. forward-moving attitudes and "drive." 2. rivalry and competition. 3. possible health issues related to lifestyle, a need to slow down.

racket (noise) 1. obstacles and a loss of free time, an inability to relax. 2. difficulties at home.

radio 1. an important message is trying to get through a host of others. 2. domestic bliss is on its way. 3. family arguments (if the radio is annoying).

radish 1. business affairs and financial success. 2. relationships, friends are sensitive and caring.

raffle 1. a feeling that one does not deserve success and achievements. 2. use caution in business affairs; an aspect of work has a risky feel to it. 3. a lucky phase of life is coming up.

raft 1. a time of adventure is set (note the condition of the water).

2. a period of slow leisurely travel is in the offing. 3. an overwhelming sense of drifting, losing direction—usually in life, very often in relationships.

rage 1. repressed anger is growing out of proportion, becoming emotionally draining. 2. caution needed in business or professional life. 3. a need for self-control. 4. quarrels may be in the offing.

railroad 1. the route toward goals is well thought out. 2. a period of prosperity is in the offing. 3. a feeling of having been forced into something (as in to be "railroaded").

rain 1. life-giving force, abundant growth. 2. purification, emotional cleansing. 3. sadness (cloudy skies). 4. emotionally overwhelmed (heavy or flooding rain).

rainbow 1. restoration of hope, end of troubles. 2. transfiguration. 3. connection between "earthly" matters and spiritual. 4. very good luck, especially if dreamed by lovers.

raisins 1. feelings of discouragement, loss; prospects seem to "dry" up. 2. a measure of prosperity, wealth and fortune.

rake 1. work will best be accomplished through a "hands-on" approach. 2. good, happy relationships and home life. 3. abundance (as in to "rake in the dough").

ram 1. a good omen in business matters and legal pursuits. 2. bad luck (to be chased by a ram). 3. masculine power and aggression, possible dominance by a masculine figure or masculine aspect of self.

ramble 1. a feeling that sadness is in the offing. 2. a good omen of achieved desires and good business affairs.

ramrod 1. misfortune, grief and pain. 2. a feeling of repression, almost violent in its nature, usually emotional.

ransom 1. deception and trickery. 2. a large sum of money feels unearned, undeserved. 3. strong feelings of being a hostage, almost always emotional.

rap 1. an important, highly emotional message is being conveyed, often regarding love and relationships (note the content of the song). 2. feelings of anger and disassociation may need to be communicated.

rape 1. violation of principles, beliefs. 2. assault on sense of worth, self-esteem. 3. feelings of vengeance.

rapids 1. an emotionally turbulent period is ahead. 2. a deep feeling of a loss of direction in life, a loss of control over one's destiny.

rash 1. an irritation or annoyance, frequently associated with infantile behavior. 2. emotional difficulties—usually associated with repression, often caused by unexpressed anger. 3. use caution regarding hasty decisions (as in "to act rashly").

raspberry 1. relationships and love affairs. 2. emotional roller coaster ride regarding one or more relationships. 3. disillusionment and disappointment over negative talk.

rats 1. a sense of trickery afoot, deception of someone close. 2. difficulties are on the way (many rats). 3. difficulties are on the way out (white rats). 4. feelings of upset or disturbed state of being. 5. smart and pervasive emotions or reactions are underfoot and just out of reach.

rattle 1. a return to infantile pleasures, getting attention. 2. "things" are coming apart—often emotional, sometimes in life experiences (a rattling sound of a vehicle or machine). 3. the end or "demise" of a project or situation (as in "death rattle"). 4. feelings of having had a close call, avoided danger—often emotional, frequently a bad situation (to see or hear a rattlesnake).

razor 1. dangerous risk-taking. 2. feelings of being out of control—usually emotionally, sometimes behaviorally. 3. someone speaks too harshly. 4. quarrels and arguments.

reading 1. success in tasks and projects. 2. need for stimulation, intellectual pleasures.

reception 1. a foreboding of family arguments and unhappiness. 2. a pleasant social life. 3. community status.

recluse 1. withdrawal from the world, a mistrust of human relationships, fear of intimacy, often unintentional. 2. a withdrawal for the purpose of healing—sometimes from difficult relationships, usually from intense emotional situations.

reconciliation 1. need for reconnection with part of self. 2. alleviate burdens. 3. disgrace (reconcile with spouse).

recreational vehicle 1. self-confident, high-powered life and lifestyle or character. 2. rebellion, out of step with society, unconcerned with the mundane (as in "off-road").

red 1. energy, vigor. 2. passion, love, romance. 3. anger, aggression. 4. embarrassment, even shame (blush). 5. arguments.

redhead 1. desire to act more on impulse, add some improvisation to daily life. 2. good luck. 3. vitality and passion.

reef unseen dangers just beneath the surface, often emotional.

reflection 1. a need or desire for introspection. 2. feelings regarding one's image. 3. reverse: mirror image or backward thinking. 4. wordplay on thought denoting the need to consider something more carefully.

refrigerator 1. emotional distance, usually for protective reasons (as in "put it on ice"). 2. a search for elusive goals. 3. preservation.

rehearsal 1. emotional preparedness. 2. honor and fulfillment to come.

reindeer 1. a drive for the fanciful, mystical. 2. the return of something thought lost. 3. the help friends may offer.

rejection 1. low self-worth, self-rejection. 2. refusal to accept a certain situation or aspect of another person.

relationship 1. the view or value of relationships. 2. different aspects of self. 3. the ability or desired ability to communicate in a relationship.

relative 1. domestic affairs, sometimes negative. 2. news, possibly negative, is in the offing. 3. help, security and safety, usually with financial matters.

religion 1. a possible need or desire for spiritual enlightenment or moral reassessment, especially if it is the dreamer's religion. 2. social control, restraint. 3. contentment and serenity. 4. a message is being conveyed from one level of consciousness to another (note type of religion and its tenets).

remember 1. repressed or neglected memories need to be addressed. 2. a need or desire to detach or avoid situations or problems (to forget).

remodel 1. a superficial change, cosmetic enhancement—often to behavior, often regarding relationships. 2. a need or desire to alter behavior, often regarding relationships.

remote control 1. emotional distance, fear and anxiety. 2. someone is being manipulative, overbearing and "controlling."

renovate 1. a need or desire to "redo," restructure something, often modes of behavior or ways of viewing life. 2. a "restoration"—often to health, sometimes to former status.

rent 1. finances. 2. approaching misfortune (to not be able to pay the rent). 3. approaching gains, financial boon (to collect rent).

repairs 1. a time of healing after difficult or traumatic events. 2. a need for healing emotional wounds (seeing something in need of repairs). 3. obstacles in the offing, often related to domestic life.

report 1. important information, a message likely from another level of consciousness. 2. feelings of ignorance, ineptitude and self-doubt (to prepare a bad report or not have it ready on time).

reprieve 1. the ability to overcome difficulties. 2. reverse: difficulties to come. 3. a period of good fortune is in the offing.

reptile 1. troubles ahead, usually in relationships (to be bitten by a reptile). 2. a feeling that someone near does not have good intentions. 3. subconscious hopes and fears, a vision for a better life.

rescue 1. helplessness, dependence on others for survival. 2. a close call, an avoided disaster. 3. reverse: plans for recovery need to be reviewed for faults. 4. a need to remove oneself from a situation or relationship in waking life.

reservation 1. reverse: feelings of being unprepared. 2. a need or desire to plan ahead, avoid disappointment. 3. hesitancy, doubt, possibly a healthy caution.

reservoir 1. pent-up emotions, possibly anger but likely a mix of conflicting feelings (note the condition of the water). 2. feelings of being drained of energy, extremely fatigued (to see an empty reservoir). 3. wealth and prosperity.

resign 1. a feeling that some recent decisions were regrettable. 2. reverse: a drive and determination to complete projects and plans. 3. the end of one phase of life, the beginning of another.

resort 1. a need or desire for rest, an escape from routine or situation (notice type of resort and activities offered). 2. new and exciting acquaintances in the offing, possibly romantic. 3. reverse: hard work is in the offing. 4. wordplay on "last resort."

restaurant 1. social relationships. 2. difficult decisions. 3. seeking assistance or answering needs from outside the usual relationships.

restraint 1. control issues. 2. situation or person is out of control and in need of guidance. 3. illness.

restroom 1. restoration, refreshment, often from emotional situations. 2. a need or desire for "rest." 3. reverse: difficult endeavors are in the offing.

résumé 1. a need or desire for change (to brush up the résumé). 2. a measure of self-confidence and abilities. 3. a life's work, professional history.

resurrection 1. little annoyances mount up and cause general anger. 2. a need or desire for a spiritual journey or "pilgrimage." 3. goals are achieved, dreams realized.

resuscitate 1. new beginnings in the offing, new friendships. 2. after hard work and perseverance, miracles can happen. 3. reverse: feelings of loss, grief and mourning.

retarded 1. self-esteem and confidence. 2. feelings of being socially "slow," somewhat alienated.

reunion 1. a need to revisit, better understand past events, possibly relationships. 2. to reacquaint oneself with various aspects of personality. 3. goals will be realized with a little outside help.

revelation 1. a very healthy, positive outlook on a seemingly difficult situation. 2. passion and excitement should be controlled.

revenge 1. previously unknown jealousies, bitterness or hurt feelings need to be addressed (to take revenge on someone). 2. use caution with the feelings of others, reassess behavior toward others (to have revenge taken on the dreamer).

reverse 1. a need or desire to gain a distance, a different perspective on a situation or problem. 2. reverse: gains are in the offing. 3. sadness, loss.

revival 1. domestic disturbances, quarrels. 2. a rekindling of feelings, the appearance of emotions after a period of distance or dormancy. 3. an urge for spiritual contact.

revolution 1. extreme changes in the offing, often regarding situations or circumstances. 2. a need or desire for fundamental changes. 3. nonconformity, going against society.

revolver 1. an ending to a phase of life or relationship, sometimes abrupt. 2. injustice, anger; use caution to limit outbursts of temper. 3. an emotionally charged, possibly dangerous situation.

revolving 1. a lack of forward movement, achievement. 2. cycle of life.

rheumatism 1. a good omen. 2. good physical health. 3. delay of activities, disappointment. 4. punishment.

rhinestones 1. social fun and excitement, "regal" entertainment. 2. fleeting pleasures.

rhinoceros 1. business matters and activities. 2. an aggressive personality, highly focused, straightforward and seemingly impenetrable. 3. sexual energy, prowess, usually male.

rhyme 1. a happy sense that love, including friendships, is in the offing. 2. reverse: concerns, worries about almost anything.

rhythm 1. social conformity or comfort levels. 2. a need or desire to get life in order. 3. possible concerns regarding the heart, possible health issue (as in "arrhythmia" or irregular heartbeat).

rib 1. suggests poverty and starvation, possibly spiritual (to see ribs). 2. reverse: unexpected pleasures, happiness (to break a rib or ribs). 3. a feeling that someone is being deceptive (to have hurt or broken ribs).

ribbon 1. social life and frequent love affairs, usually a good omen. 2. use caution regarding serious matters; they may be neglected. 3. femininity. 4. achievement (as in "blue ribbon").

rice 1. good omen regarding health, happiness, relationships and wealth. 2. basic nutrition, sustenance—likely emotional or spiritual—or a possible dietary need. 3. providing the basics of life (note the quantity).

rich 1. desire for wealth and security. 2. seeking an abundance of pleasure, usually emotional. 3. highly successful affairs, usually business.

rickety 1. feelings of instability, potential collapse. 2. a feeling of danger, likely regarding situations or circumstances.

riddle 1. feelings of inadequacy in facing problems, dealing with life. 2. a project will require more careful analysis than originally thought. 3. more obstacles than originally imagined.

ride, riding 1. sexual intercourse. 2. feelings of control—often in life, frequently in relationships. 3. the means or route to success in business, wealth. 3. social mobility (to ride a horse).

riding school 1. social mobility, usually upward. 2. more "life lessons" are needed, loss of direction. 3. a friend may not be what he/she appears.

right 1. analytical, logical and rational thinking. 2. correct action (as in "do the right thing"). 3. justice served, goodness.

ring 1. relationship commitment is in the offing. 2. wealth and security (a diamond ring). 3. to keep one's word or promise. 4. harmony, balance; completion (circular shape). 5. joyous announcement is to come (as in "ring a bell").

ring finger 1. union, marriage or commitment. 2. sexual availability. 3. success in usually social affairs and activities.

ringworm 1. possible health or hygiene issues. 2. an annoyance has turned into a profound irritation or "gotten under the skin," possibly from a friend with hostility.

riot 1. to take part in group destructive behavior. 2. loss of individuality, free-thinking. 3. financial disaster.

rising 1. upward movement, usually regarding wealth and business affairs. 2. overcoming obstacles. 3. new and happy beginnings (as in "rising sun"). 4. a new sense of social standing, perhaps superiority.

rival 1. competition, victory or defeat, pride or shame. 2. to lose social prominence. 3. obstacles, delays to success—usually in business, often in love affairs.

river 1. life's journey. 2. obstacles, turbulence in need of crossing.

roaches 1. feelings of anger, hostility, usually directed at self. 2. often feelings regarding sexual advances. 3. extreme adaptability, flexibility under adverse circumstances.

road 1. destiny. 2. immediate destiny in pursuit of goals. 3. good health.

roast 1. a usually good omen for wealth and happiness (except for vegetarians if it is roasted meat). 2. domestic difficulties in the offing. 3. feelings of worry, sadness, possibly loss, grief.

robbery 1. reverse: financial gains in the offing. 2. a sense of emotional loss in the offing. 3. feelings of a loss of self, being drained, possibly of identity.

robin 1. feelings of great joy, vitality. 2. great fortune. 3. domestic bliss (a nest of robins).

robot 1. feelings of emotional detachment, distance. 2. without a "soul," going through the motions.

rock 1. strength, fidelity and stability, often a relationship. 2. mother. 3. hard work ahead. 4. lasting forever, especially relationships (to sit on top of rocks).

rocket 1. a phallic symbol. 2. success is fleeting—usually business, often relationships. 3. rapid success, usually business.

rocking chair 1. wealth. 2. a warm, happy environment. 3. a short sadness, then contentment (to see an empty chair).

rocking horse 1. innocent, delightful pleasure is in the offing. 2. an inability to take life seriously or own up to responsibilities. 3. a strong need or desire for comfort, tender care, feelings of extreme fragility.

rocks 1. feelings of hardship, great difficulties will be overcome. 2. close friendship, trust and solidity. 3. wordplay on "between a rock and a hard place."

rod 1. a phallic symbol. 2. determination and will. 3. to draw attention to (as in "lightning rod"). 4. happiness, usually in relationships (note the material from which the rod is made).

rodent 1. close to the ground, extremely intuitive and sensitive. 2. feelings of poverty and displeasure at current circumstances. 3. a lack of cleanliness.

Rollerblades 1. fast forward motion, sometimes regarding relationships. 2. the ability to handle difficult emotional situations (note the level of expertise on the Rollerblades).

roller coaster 1. turbulent situation is becoming drawn out, absurd. 2. life's journey seems out of control. 3. modes of behavior are growing erratic.

roman candle 1. a sexual symbol. 2. use caution in affairs of life; they need to be taken seriously. 3. pleasure is in the offing (note the colors).

roof 1. intellect (with attic). 2. separation between the conscious and unconscious mind. 3. limitless success; ideas (on top of roof). 4. the thoughts and opinions of others are having a profound influence (leaking roof).

room 1. part of the subconscious, parts of self. 2. discovery of family secrets. 3. woman.

rooster 1. a particularly good omen, especially in regards to affairs of the heart. 2. "cockiness," superiority and arrogance. 3. severe arguments in the offing, often domestic (to see a "cockfight"). 4. dominance.

roots 1. origins, foundation of personality—sometimes hereditary or leading back to the parents. 2. deeply embedded situation or problem, not easily overcome (deeply planted roots).

rope 1. social "ties." 2. approaching difficulties regarding business affairs.

rosary 1. need or desire for meditation and spiritual contemplation.

2. seeking spiritual solutions to troubles. 3. to come full circle, start at the beginning.

rose 1. great fortune in affairs of the heart, joy and pleasure. 2. good news is coming (to smell a rose). 3. grace and purity (white rose). 4. infidelity (yellow). 5. pregnancy (to pick buds). 6. separation (fading roses).

rosebush 1. wealth (note the health and condition of the bush). 2. an improving situation or circumstance. 3. feeling threatened (to hide behind a rosebush).

rosemary 1. a good omen regarding domestic affairs. 2. reverse: an underlying sadness at home where things seem fine. 3. memory and nostalgia.

rose quartz 1. love and forgiveness, especially of self. 2. a need or desire for healing, openness and kindness. 3. a need for physical healing, possible health issues.

rouge 1. a sense that things are not what they appear—likely individuals and their intent, possibly situations. 2. possible health issues, possibly blood related. 3. a good omen, often regarding identity, especially for women.

roulette 1. arguments in the offing—possibly with friends, likely domestic. 2. use caution in risky emotional matters, usually in intimate relationships.

row 1. a good omen representing forward movement, sometimes change, usually in life. 2. goals and ambitions are far less difficult than they appear. 3. a need or desire for a spiritual "voyage" or journey.

rowboat 1. feelings of pleasure in social settings with friends. 2. business and opportunities for wealth (note condition of water and the boat).

royal 1. contentment, happiness and security. 2. feelings of superiority. 3. a need for discretion.

rubber 1. a feeling that concerns and difficulties are on the wane (as in to "bounce back"). 2. slang for condom, protection against the unseen. 3. financial security and possibly travel.

4. uncertainty or indecision, errors in judgment (to see an eraser).

rubber band 1. a negative omen for relationships, friendships, flexibility, helpfulness. 2. feelings about life, responsibilities and obligations (as in to be "overstretched" or on the brink of "snapping").

rubbish 1. a negative omen regarding business affairs. 2. a period of emotional turmoil or physical illness has gone (to throw rubbish away). 3. good times and success are in the offing. 4. harsh judgments and negative opinions.

ruby 1. a good omen for intimate relationships and professional matters. 2. desire, intense emotions, passion, perhaps obsession (note how deep the color is). 3. precision, almost surgical accuracy in emotional affairs or possibly actual surgery.

rudder 1. direction in life, sense of control over destiny. 2. travel, possible journeys, likely emotional (note condition of the ship or boat and the clarity of water). 3. fear of travel.

ruins 1. view of the past. 2. former way of thinking. 3. former relationships. 4. unexpected fortune.

ruler 1. feelings of inadequacy, not belonging. 2. a mystery reveals itself, news is in the offing. 3. attention to details, careful planning and precise consideration can achieve important goals. 4. ability to use good judgment.

rum 1. intellectual or moral flexibility. 2. possible addiction or illness. 3. a lack of refinement, being in a bad place, low period of time.

rumbling 1. news coming from a distance. 2. unquiet rest, uneasiness. 3. recovery, usually from illness.

runaway 1. feelings of social inadequacy, not belonging. 2. a fear of dealing with challenges—usually in life, frequently in relationships. 3. actions or activities are an immature diversion, an escape. 4. feelings that life or situations are extremely out of control (as in "runaway" vehicle, train or most modes of transportation).

running 1. difficulty defining goals, exerting energy without apparent benefit (to run either to or from something). 2. avoidance of conflict or confrontations; fears and anger (to run from something). 3. enthusiasm toward goals (to run toward something). 4. good luck and happiness.

rupture 1. a feeling that responsibilities, stress loads, are about to "burst." 2. possible illness. 3. domestic disagreements. 4. emotional strain. 5. reverse: very good omen for sense of fortune and financial rewards.

rural 1. rusticity, simplicity, not cosmopolitan, usually an aspect of life or environment. 2. a need or desire to simplify life.

rush 1. caution against avoidable accidents. 2. impatience creates difficulties. 3. seeking thrills, adventure (slang). 4. desire, need to reduce stress.

rust 1. inactivity leads to breakdown, deterioration—possibly physical, maybe spiritual. 2. neglect allows business to suffer. 3. inevitable loss, persistent feelings of doom.

rye 1. prosperity and future prospects, usually a very good omen. 2. individual character with elements of refinement, a steady, cheerful temperament and good judgment regarding business matters.

rye bread 1. happy domestic life and prosperity. 2. good taste and refinement.

S

sabotage 1. fear of being waylaid by someone one is dealing with. 2. realization that one's approach to life doesn't work.

sack someone is about to be terminated.

sacrifice 1. if victim of a human sacrifice, one is feeling guilty about something. 2. heroic action.

sad some aspect of one's life is not working out.

saddle 1. sitting on a saddle indicates that one is in command of a situation. 2. empty saddle points to opportunity.

sadism one has extreme hostility toward someone.

sadness probably reflected from waking life.

safari return to the primitive, not governed by rules.

safe 1. questions one has about how safe one feels. 2. if putting possession in safe, indicates that this is the way one is treating one's life. 3. if locked up, the dreamer may feel trapped. 4. one has achieved a goal by hard work and/or daring. 5. a place where one hides secrets.

safety pin something in one's life needs to be held together.

saffron 1. sacred knowledge. 2. something is being predicted.

sage 1. purity. 2. clarity. 3. truth.

Sagittarius people under this zodiac sign are usually intellectual, enthusiastic, energetic, visionary, and love sports.

sailboat desire to get away from it all.

sailing 1. feeling free and easy. 2. on the way to achieving whatever one wants to.

sailor 1. a long trip is imminent. 2. females dreaming of sailors indicate dissatisfaction with their current romantic relationship.

saint 1. acceptance of a spiritual side to life. 2. one feels that a spiritual message is going to be presented.

Saint-John's-wort peace and tranquility.

salad 1. desire for a healthier lifestyle. 2. looking for more variety in one's life.

salary 1. potential in life. 2. if spending, how one is developing one's abilities. 3. how one can improve abilities.

salesperson don't trust the person one is now dealing with on a business matter.

salmon 1. wisdom, insights. 2. determination.

salt 1. one's life needs spice added to it. 2. if tasting salt, one is bitter over something. 3. if salt is being poured into an open wound, one is experiencing some type of agonizing situation in waking life.

saltpeter one feels very guilty over the inability to perform sexually.

salute someone has been very helpful.

salve 1. applying salve to someone indicates that one is helping the person in some way. 2. applying salve to oneself is also an act of healing.

samples 1. one is facing a decision. 2. one will have more choices in some area of his/her life.

sand 1. cleanliness, sterility. 2. desolation. 3. something coarse or abrasive.

sand dunes 1. fortunes may shift. 2. peace and harmony are in one's life. 3. protection from something.

sap 1. semen. 2. energy.

Saturn 1. individualistic (from those who buy Saturn brand cars). 2. mood of dark disapproval.

sauce one should add something to one's life to spice it up.

sausage phallic symbol.

scab someone has been hurt by someone.

scaffold support is needed to complete a job.

scales 1. need to take a "balanced" view of something. 2. one is expecting or needing to make a decision. 3. one is being measured, evaluated for something.

scandal one is afraid that some aspect of life he/she wants to keep private is going to become public.

scar(s) 1. memories of a painful past. 2. physiological difficulties which are preventing progress and success.

scarecrow 1. one is being warned away from something. 2. a barrier to achievement or happiness. 3. depression. 4. fear.

scared (being) 1. hidden anger at someone or something. 2. fear of numerous problems or persons in real life.

scarf 1. one controls feelings too rigidly. 2. need for protection or isolation from oncoming problems.

scenery 1. memories of past. 2. detachment from reality.

school 1. learning experience. 2. childhood memories. 3. performance anxiety.

school bus journey that will result in personal growth and/or knowledge.

scientist 1. realization that one's personality is more scientistlike than not. 2. eccentricity. 3. willingness to experiment with someone. 4. need to have aspects of one's life validated, i.e., proven with absolute certainty.

Scientology desire to find some radical religion to help solve one's problems.

scissors 1. if used to cut something, indicates decisiveness in one's life. 2. desire to find a way to resolve an issue.

scooter 1. need to be evasive. 2. get away (scoot) from a situation.

Scorpio 1. jealousy, hate, vindictiveness. 2. great energy and drive.

scorpions 1. "stinging" or retaliation. 2. biblical icon.

scratch(ing) 1. a minor annoyance or irritation. 2. a need to start a project, goal or relationship over again, i.e., "from scratch."

scream(ing) 1. fear and/or anger. 2. inability to scream in the face of threatening situation indicates a suppression of thought or emotion.

screw 1. sexual symbol. 2. feeling that one is being taken advantage of by others. 3. something in one's life needs to be assembled, i.e., "screwed together."

screwdriver 1. need to assemble something firmly (see "screw"). 2. need to assist someone in solving their problems, i.e., help someone who is "screwed up."

sculptor 1. desire to be creative. 2. need to reshape certain aspects of one's personality.

sculpture 1. a measure of one's self against an often unreasonably high standard.

sea 1. mother. 2. if drowning in sea, being overwhelmed. 3. emotionally insecure, particularly with one's mother. 4. if calmly swimming, riding or paddling along, good relationship with mother or maternal figure. 5. if fighting successfully against the tide, making progress in difficult relationship. 6. unconscious mind. 7. play on words which indicates one should "see" something.

seafood 1. desire to be healthy. 2. message that one should "see food" and change diet as needed.

seagulls 1. desire for freedom and flight. 2. feeling that one will survive difficult and trying situations.

sea horse 1. hope that something magical and miraculous will come into one's life to solve a major crisis. 2. new approach to life. 3. something playful, whimsical and strange. 4. grace.

seal (legal papers) something adhering or final in one's business dealings and relationships.

seal 1. desire to be a tough soldier. 2. something in one's life must be hidden from view. 3. playful. 4. need or desire to be playful or friendly.

séance 1. desire to communicate with deceased persons. 2. need to understand situations more clearly.

search 1. something missing in one's life. 2. seeking a solution to problems. 3. need for new knowledge or relationships.

seashells 1. desire for health and prosperity. 2. symbol of security and protection. 3. need for immediate change in direction or approach at solving problems.

seasick 1. hidden desire to avoid a trip or project that one is contemplating. 2. repressed emotional stress and conflict.

seasoning one's life needs a little perking up.

seat belt 1. need for security. 2. need for restraint in one's actions and emotions. 3. desire or inclination to take unnecessary risks (not using).

seaweed 1. mystery or problem in one's life that resists solution. 2. desire or need to relax.

secret 1. recognition of untapped power and ability that is being kept from others. 2. be careful; someone is being deceptive.

secretary need for organization and discipline in one's life.

security (sense of) possible lack of confidence and well-being in one's life.

sedation 1. need to avoid upcoming problems or projects. 2. trying to avoid making a decision. 3. escape from reality.

seduction 1. sexual desire, either as a seducer or as the person desired. 2. feeling lured into a situation that may not be good or honorable.

seed(s) 1. there is an idea that one should pay careful attention to. 2. spreading or planting ideas. 3. human sperm or egg.

seesaw 1. one is involved in an up-and-down affair that is going nowhere. 2. one is indecisive about something.

seizures 1. one is gripped by forces one cannot control or understand. 2. fiscal hardship and stress.

selling ridding one's self of something of value, but not really needed.

semen sexual desire or prowess.

semigloss on a current question one is taking a middle-of-the-road position.

seminar 1. seeking to increase one's knowledge. 2. seeking to increase one's intelligence.

semiprecious stone not totally satisfied with one's efforts.

senility one feels abilities and intellect diminishing, despite not being old.

sentinel 1. be on one's guard; danger approaches. 2. help needed.

separation 1. feeling that relationships are coming apart. 2. one feels he/she is about to leave or be discharged from a job.

sequel something previously experienced in one's life is about to play out again.

sermon someone is trying to give one advice, which should be listened to.

serpentine one has a long way to go before reaching one's emotional destination.

settle 1. feeling one has given up something of value in order to "settle" a dispute. 2. desire to bring problems to a closure and move on.

seven, number luck is on the way (lucky 7).

sewer 1. symbolic of negative thoughts or relationships. 2. to achieve goal one must "crawl through a sewer."

sewing 1. mending a relationship. 2. if making clothing, one is trying to create a new image. 3. achievement of skill and maturity.

sex indicates questioning about one's own sexual persona.

shack 1. symbolic of one's life. 2. hint that suggests that one should embark on a romantic relationship with someone.

shackled beware, or one might do time on a "chain gang."

shadow 1. someone may be following one. 2. commitment of relationship one is reluctant to make. 3. rejection of one or more aspects of one's personality. 4. one's real self is being hidden or repressed.

shaking 1. discarding old ways of acting. 2. one is "shaking things up." 3. one is afraid of someone.

shaman 1. someone is trying to send a spiritual message. 2. hint to seek out someone to talk to for help.

shampoo 1. one needs to "wash" someone or something out of his/her life. 2. getting cleaned up to present a new image to someone.

Shane need for heroic father figure, boyhood hero.

shark 1. signifies one is dealing with someone who has the characteristics of the shark. 2. projected self which is now feeling like a shark.

sharpen 1. sharpening an object may be an attempt to enhance one's abilities, intelligence, etc. 2. someone sharpening a knife is someone getting ready to defend oneself.

shave (face) 1. need to change. 2. need to present a better image to the world. 3. someone shaving the dreamer means that one is willing to trust others.

sheep 1. feeling that one is unable to function well on one's own. 2. goes along with the crowd. 3. defenseless in the face of adversity. 4. useful to others.

sheet music the need for harmony in one's life.

shell 1. one wants to hide away. 2. one wants someone to protect him/her.

shelter 1. one needs shelter from some sort of emotional storm. 2. one seeks shelter from some sort of threat.

shepherd 1. one wants to be "shepherded," protected by someone. 2. someone is leading the dreamer in a good direction.

shield 1. one needs help against some sort of threat. 2. one sees oneself as protecting others against a threat.

ship 1. desire to go on a trip, get away from it all. 2. sinking ship suggests that part of one's life is out of control. 3. ship in rough seas means the dreamer is also in rough seas.

shipwreck emotional turmoil, view of one's life.

shire 1. mother. 2. the unconscious or unknown. 3. sadness or depression. 4. reaching the "bottom" of existence.

shirt 1. how it looks is reflective of one's inner persona. 2. if one gives a shirt to someone it may represent a large gift ("the shirt off one's back").

shock 1. some surprise, good or bad, has come into one's life. 2. a fresh awareness.

shoelace 1. essential part of some shoes. 2. loose shoelaces—deep desire not to be able to go somewhere (shoes not available).

shoes 1. changing shoes means a new approach to life. 2. if shoes are worn out, one has tried very hard to succeed. 3. wearing baby shoes signifies that one's approach to life is innocent and pure. 4. to be shining shoes signifies hope for the future. 5. if one can't find shoes, it means that the dreamer is sabotaging his/her own success.

shoofly one senses one is being followed.

shooting 1. shooting a person indicates deep hostility toward the person. 2. one is shooting for a particular goal in one's life. 3. if the dreamer is being shot at, then he/she feels like a victim in waking life.

shooting star 1. one's dream of better times can come true. 2. changes will be occurring in one's life.

shop place where one is seeking out certain emotional "products" that will help complete one.

shoplifting 1. feeling guilt over some kind of petty crime one committed. 2. expressing anger toward someone by taking something from him/her.

shopping cart 1. if one is pushing a filled shopping cart it is tangible evidence of success. 2. if shopping cart is empty, this symbolizes lack of success.

shore 1. if approaching a shore, one has almost reached a destination that has been striven for. 2. one needs to "shore up" some area of one's life.

shorts 1. one is comfortable with showing more of one's feelings and thoughts to others. 2. one may be selling oneself "short." 3. longing to return to childhood.

shot 1. if wound is self-inflicted, one is punishing oneself for some action one feels guilty about. 2. if someone else is shot, that person is being punished for some shameful action.

shoulders 1. to see one's shoulders symbolizes strength. 2. the ability to support others.

shovel 1. ready to find out (dig for) answers to long-standing questions. 2. trying to understand oneself better. 3. change of life is suggested as indicated by the presence of shovels.

shower 1. the need to cleanse oneself of bad experiences. 2. forgiveness.

shrew one feels very oppressed in one's romantic relationship.

shrimp 1. one feels small, insignificant. 2. one should eat healthier.

shrine 1. too much energy is being placed on one element of one's life. 2. something or someone one admires greatly and aspires to emulate.

shrinking (sense of) 1. sexual exhilaration or climax. 2. lack of confidence. 3. need to escape situation or realities.

sibling 1. when a brother or sister shows up, it indicates unresolved conflicts with the person. 2. reflection of a good quality or qualities that one should incorporate in oneself.

sick address certain mental concerns which are incapacitating.

sickening one's image of oneself is false.

sickle 1. hard work. 2. fear that one might be sick ("sickle-cell anemia").

sidewalk 1. if sidewalk is cracked or otherwise damaged, making walking difficult, life is perceived to be difficult. 2. if sidewalk is in good condition, one's life path is perceived as easy.

sideways 1. one is heading in the wrong direction in life. 2. one is trying to avoid a confrontation.

sign 1. one needs assistance, as reflected in what the sign says. 2. one needs to sign some important document.

signature 1. one is admitting responsibility for something. 2. one approves of something. 3. one is not afraid to reveal everything about oneself.

silhouette(s) obscuring the total reality or thought.

silk 1. feeling silk means someone is longing for luxury. 2. if wearing silk, one is vaunting one's importance, but it is at heart false.

silo 1. phallic symbol. 2. indication that one should save for a rainy day.

silver 1. the female aspect of oneself. 2. how the moon, in particular, figures in romantic events.

singing 1. happy, optimistic. 2. able to express oneself fully, to sing one's song.

sinking 1. one's career, life, etc., is heading in the wrong direction. 2. someone is pulling one down. 3. something important in one's life is ending.

sirens 1. being drawn, as in Greek mythology, to situations that can hurt one badly. 2. a problem that is leading to a lot of stress in life. 3. warning.

sister 1. ally. 2. someone to call on for special help.

sitting 1. unwillingness to get up and take a chance on something. 2. indecision.

six, number 1. disguised reference to "sex." 2. be reasonable.

size 1. to dream about whether something or someone is small or large may relate to penis size. 2. the power one has or others have over one. 3. the relative importance of things or events.

skateboard 1. one needs to be daring. 2. ability to perform with style and grace in difficult situations.

skating 1. indicates an ability to keep one's life balanced. 2. if skating on thin ice, one is getting into a hazardous waking situation that could mean disaster.

skeleton 1. something or someone is not fully developed. 2. if one attaches a person's name to the skeleton, it suggests that the relationship with the person is dead. 3. one needed to get to see all of a problem.

sketch 1. if one sketches oneself, it relates to self-examination and evaluation 2. trying to view a problem from a different perspective.

skiing 1. taking a risk. 2. unafraid to act as an individual.

skin 1. short for "skin deep"—one is shallow or in relationships that are shallow. 2. one does not feel very protected.

skinless 1. one's sense that he/she has no protection against the psychological onslaughts of others. 2. yet to develop, young.

skipping 1. stop wallowing in the minutiae of a project and move more quickly. 2. one has left something out in a project.

skirt 1. one is skirting an issue. 2. desire to wear a skirt, be sexually provocative.

skull 1. great danger. 2. one should work harder in developing one's mind. 3. in seeking a solution to a problem, seek the help of others.

skunk 1. one may be repelling others. 2. one does not like something about a particular situation.

sky 1. sense of freedom. 2. if the sky is blue, one is filled with hope. 3. if the sky is gray, the future looks grim.

skydiving 1. willing to take a risk. 2. high ideals.

skyscraper 1. high ideals. 2. one "thinks big"; the "sky's the limit."

skywriting 1. willing to take a risk to have this occur. 2. other meanings, depending on what is written.

slap 1. something one fears getting for an indiscretion of some sort. 2. if slapped, one feels disrespected. 3. if the dreamer slaps someone, it indicates a disrespect toward that person or his/her ideas.

slaughterhouse 1. a place where someone "can't win." 2. if one continues on one's present course, one will be "slaughtered."

slave 1. one is being led by others, and to no gain. 2. one is filled with anger toward a superior. 3. one is not taking charge of one's own life.

sled 1. desire to return to childhood. 2. ready to take a chance. 3. confidence in one's ability to navigate life.

sledgehammer 1. ready to break down or break up obstacles one faces. 2. a powerful weapon at one's command.

sleeping 1. peace of mind. 2. not fully aware of something. 3. the awareness of trying to find the answer to something by dreaming.

sleeping bag 1. one is protected. 2. the desire to go back to the womb.

slide 1. out of control; one has lost one's grip. 2. one should be able to accomplish a task easily.

slime 1. if one feels it is on him/her, guilt about something. 2. if slime is on someone else, the dreamer feels he/she is not able to trust that person.

slip 1. one is doing things one really doesn't want to do. 2. one has not yet decided what one's full identity is.

slippers 1. if wearing, one has a relaxed persona. 2. symbolic of tranquility in a situation. 3. a suggestion from one's unconscious to relax. 4. a suggestion that one is being lazy.

slope 1. problem one is determined to solve. 2. a problem in one's life that one is trying to surmount.

slot machine 1. willingness to take a chance on something or someone. 2. engaging in potentially self-destructive behavior.

slow motion one does not like whatever one is engaged in.

slugs 1. one is making very slow progress through life. 2. certain aspects of one's life are loathsome.

slums if living in the slums, one is not happy with one's achievements.

small 1. one's sense of self-esteem is low. 2. if one perceives someone else as small, that person is not regarded highly.

smile 1. if one is smiling warmly, he/she is satisfied with achievements. 2. if someone is smiling warmly at the dreamer, that person is satisfied with the dreamer's achievements. 3. if someone is smiling sarcastically, then the feeling is critical.

smog in a moral fog created by oneself.

smokestacks 1. phallic symbols. 2. if stacks are smoking, a situation must be dealt with ("where there's smoke, there's fire"). 3. hard work is being conducted. 4. thoughts from the unconscious.

smoking 1. playing a role, putting up a "smoke screen" to keep others away. 2. if smoking a cigarette, one may want to give the habit up. 3. if smoking is enjoyable, one is trying to escape cares, pressures. 4. phallic symbol.

smuggling 1. one is running a risk in waking life. 2. taking forcefully what one feels is rightfully his/hers.

snail 1. one is traveling slowly but surely. 2. individualistic, not concerned with impressing others.

snake 1. penis. 2. deviousness, either by the dreamer or by someone who will behave this way toward him/her. 3. period of growth (shedding skin). 4. gossip, spreading "venom." 5. if subject to constriction by snake, feeling emotionally strangled. 6. being sabotaged. 7. killing a snake indicates the ability to handle a fearful problem. 8. feeling vulnerable, not knowing what to do. 9. fear. 10. temptation. 11. willingness to change course or thinking.

sneakers 1. a hint to engage in exercise. 2. one leads an active life. 3. one way to engage in theft and be prepared to flee the scene.

sniper one senses that he/she has a secret enemy who may be suspected but not known.

snorkeling taking a chance and exploring one's emotional life, perhaps in psychotherapy.

snow 1. if snow is falling, it reflects an inner emotional life of tranquility. 2. playing in the snow suggests one is happy with oneself. 3. shoveling snow suggests one is clearing away emotional blockages. 4. desire to cover up problems, however temporary the cover-up may be. 5. desire to return to childhood.

snowboarding 1. overcoming fear of something. 2. using one's potential.

snowdrop 1. consolation. 2. hope.

snowflake 1. perfection. 2. an ideal to be reached.

snowman 1. if the snowman looks "mean," it reflects one's inner fears. 2. if jolly-looking, it reflects one's inner joy.

soap 1. one needs to clean oneself of certain habits and fantasies. 2. need to purge guilt or shame. 3. one needs to confess something.

soaring freedom.

soccer 1. from a Freudian perspective, sports serves as an arena for acting out sexual drives. 2. a projection of how one plays the game of life. 3. encourage abuse (sounds like "sock her").

sock punch.

softball sexual game one plays (i.e., bat is a phallic symbol, the ball a symbol of the female).

soil 1. potential for growth. 2. a solid foundation for living is present.

soldier 1. if one identifies with the soldier, it may reflect one readying oneself for battle. 2. one feels guilty about aiding someone.

son 1. oneself disguised as one's own son. 2. desire to have a son. 3. desire to see a little "sun" in one's life.

soot 1. if soiled by it, one feels guilty of having done something wrong. 2. there has been a fiery confrontation, and all that remains of the conflict is soot.

sorcerer determination to achieve one's goals by any means possible.

sore one is angry or irritated at someone for treating him/her a certain way.

sores 1. sores on one's body indicate suppression of negative emotions. 2. still smarting, as it were, over former relationship, as expressed by the sores.

soul 1. someone is spiritually lost. 2. one is looking for one's soul.

soup 1. spiritually hungry. 2. someone needs healing.

south 1. desire to go to a place where one is safe and warm. 2. love and passion. 3. someone's plan to do something has gone wrong ("gone south").

South America desire for a change of life of some sort, but something that is not too far away from what one is doing now.

sow 1. someone with piglike habits. 2. one is planting the seeds of one's future.

spa 1. need to go to a place where one can be refreshed re life. 2. need to cleanse oneself of hidden feelings.

space 1. need to be free. 2. need to not feel so crowded by a situation.

spaceship one is traveling with others to a place where freedom can be achieved.

spades evil is unseen but present in cards, particularly if one is the ace of spades.

spaghetti 1. one is involved in something very complex. 2. one is not sure of what one is feeling. 3. something Italian may be involved in a situation.

spanking if one is being spanked, he/she is getting or deserves punishment for doing something wrong that is childish.

speech 1. if giving a speech, one is expressing long-repressed feelings for all the world to hear. 2. if listening to a speech, one is hearing feelings from another person previously rejected. 3. if making a speech at a conference and one is booed off the stage (or from whatever forum one is speaking from), one feels his/her ideas are not being accepted. 4. if one is speaking and is accepted, one is respected for one's ideas.

speeding 1. compelled to finish something quickly. 2. feeling a threat. 3. moving too fast in a situation or relationship.

sperm 1. desire to have a baby. 2. sense of one's virility. 3. one has the capacity to grow.

sphinx 1. fear of some threat, but an unknown one. 2. intrigued with a foreign culture.

spice 1. one needs, as the saying goes, "variety in one's life." 2. to better deal with a situation, one needs to look at it from a different point of view.

spider 1. danger. 2. dangerous enemy. 3. dangerous to oneself. 4. fear of being rendered helpless.

spill 1. carelessness when it comes to the feelings of others. 2. if one spills a drink, it may be a message to cut down on that drink or cut it out entirely. 3. to spill food may be a message to cut back on eating.

spine 1. one knows he/she is going to have to be courageous in the near future. 2. one knows someone else is going to have to be courageous in the near future.

spiral 1. out of control. 2. taking a new, albeit risky, direction.

spire 1. pride. 2. striving for something.

spirits 1. hoping for a religious solution to one's problems. 2. belief in spirit equals belief in an afterlife. 3. someone is not who he/she seems to be. 4. drinking too much.

spit 1. if spitting, one is disgusted with something. 2. if spitting, one is trying to purge oneself of something. 3. if spitting on someone, expression of contempt.

splash 1. if being splashed with water, one needs to "wake up." 2. if splashing another, the person needs to be awakened to certain realities.

splinter if one has a splinter he/she is allowing petty things to get the better of him/her.

sponge 1. one should be ready to absorb new knowledge or experiences. 2. one is leeching off someone else.

spoon 1. need for something, perhaps emotional nourishment. 2. someone needs to be "spoon-fed," taught something gradually.

sports 1. if one gets a general sense that what unfolds in the dream represents sports, then it is a message to abide by all the rules and regulations of sports, as well as to be a team player. 2. people one knows are very fair about something.

sports car 1. if driving, one is immature. 2. trying to be "cool."

spring 1. a new season, new hope. 2. if a water spring, one should draw on inner resources to help deal with a current crisis.

sprinkler 1. one is nurturing something. 2. one is celebrating something.

spy 1. one doesn't trust others. 2. one is meddling in other people's business without their approval or knowledge.

square 1. feeling like a "nerd," in the slangy, critical sense of the term "square." 2. feeling boxed in.

squeeze 1. one is "putting the squeeze" on someone. 2. one feels squeezed by something or someone, such as finances. 3. short for "main squeeze."

squid 1. fear of becoming entangled in something. 2. one is not seeing something clearly (ink from the squid).

squirrel 1. industrious and efficient. 2. good planning. 3. at risk for serious disease.

stab 1. if stabbing someone, an expression of hostility. 2. encouragement to "take a stab at something." 3. one feels that one is being "stabbed in the back by someone."

stadium 1. the desire to be something big on a big stage. 2. one needs to work hard to achieve one's goals.

stag 1. one wants to be on one's own, romantically speaking. 2. one wants to get married.

stage 1. one does not feel connected with one's true self. 2. someone is being deceptive. 3. in a sense, life is more performance than substance. 4. one needs to be the center of attention. 5. everyone else is playing a role too ("all the world's a stage").

stained 1. one is seeking spiritual guidance. 2. the predominant colors in stained glass may have meanings.

staircase 1. if the staircase is leading up and one climbs it, there is an opportunity for change. 2. if one is coming down a staircase, one feels unsuccessful. 3. sexual activity (up or down), usually for men. 4. ambition.

stairs 1. climbing up stairs is an indication that all is going well in one's life. 2. climbing down stairs may indicate that one has failed at a particular thing. 3. climbing down stairs may indicate that one is giving the reins of one's job or other endeavor to someone else.

stalk 1. problems one is not confronting. 2. bad habits one can't break. 3. nameless fears.

stallion 1. powerful sexuality. 2. if riding a stallion, one feels imbued with its attributes of strength, courage and sexual power.

stammering hesitant about going forward on something.

stamps 1. one needs to communicate with someone. 2. if a roll or book of stamps, many people need to be contacted about something.

standing 1. one is assertive. 2. one is proud of oneself.

staples 1. more organization needed in one's life. 2. the basics that one needs to succeed. 3. the store, which contains everything one needs to achieve business success.

staring 1. challenging someone one is angry at. 2. feeling that someone is observing one too closely. 3. someone who is staring is attracted to the person being stared at. 4. someone is angry at the dreamer.

Star of David 1. an ideal to be reached. 2. a renewed sense of spirituality. 3. respect and regard for the Jewish faith.

starry sky 1. reaching as high as one can for something in life, particularly if the urge to reach the stars is present. 2. one bright star in sky: if goal is to reach or possess it, could be an inner desire to possess someone.

stars 1. aspirations. 2. need for fame and fortune. 3. anything is possible.

starvation 1. one is missing some emotional component or attitude. 2. if on a diet, one fears that he/she is not eating enough.

station wagon 1. if one owns a station wagon, it symbolizes the family, and what is going on inside the station wagon is going on inside the family. 2. if one rolls up the windows, it indicates concerns about one's family.

statue 1. unable to communicate with others (like a statue). 2. someone one idolizes.

Statue of Liberty 1. one is independent, able to function on one's own. 2. one is personally or culturally free.

stealing 1. if the dreamer is stealing, it indicates he/she does not feel adequate to succeed without using unfair methods. 2. anger at someone one is stealing from.

steam 1. one is very angry, ready to blow off steam. 2. headstrong.

steep to achieve what one wants will not be easy.

steering one is in control of one's life.

stew one's life is a lot of mixed things, but collectively good.

stillbirth an idea whose time has not come.

stingray danger ahead.

stitching one needs to strengthen one's support system.

stock taking one evaluates one's life.

stomach 1. something is difficult to take. 2. something is easy to take.

store 1. looking for what one needs. 2. if a new store with unusual items, one is dissatisfied with what one already has, including people.

stork 1. one wants to have a baby. 2. one is having a baby.

storm 1. represents emotional difficulty. 2. one is unsure if he/she can make it through something. 3. if lightning flashes, one may have an insight.

strawberry 1. lucky. 2. love.

street a path one must travel, good or bad depending on how it looks.

streetcar 1. taking a trip, but unable to deviate in it because the car runs on tracks. 2. desire (from the play *A Streetcar Named Desire*).

stroke 1. area of one's life where one is unable to take action. 2. former skill now unavailable to one.

strongbox 1. someone is hiding something. 2. someone is trying to deceive one.

stud 1. lover. 2. important building component.

sucking 1. one feels safe (breast-feed). 2. sexual urge.

suffocated 1. unable to reach one's intellectual goals. 2. unable to satisfy psychological needs. 3. being suppressed by someone with more power.

sundial 1. unrealistic activities. 2. old-fashioned.

sunflower 1. courage. 2. energy. 3. sunny.

sunrise 1. one is feeling positive, hopeful about the future. 2. one is at the end of a long ordeal.

sunset 1. sadness over something ending. 2. one is happy that an ordeal is ending.

suntan one is concerned with one's image.

Superman need for help from someone who is very powerful.

supplements 1. considering or taking a large number of vitamin pills reflects concern about the state of one's health. 2. if in a vitamin shop, considering various vitamins, one may be considering various actions that will energize one's life.

surf a place where one's daring will be required.

swan 1. beauty. 2. though one may be at a disadvantage now, things can change dramatically for the better.

swimming 1. if swimming where people one is attracted to are also swimming, it indicates sexual attraction. 2. if swimming in the ocean, it indicates one is very independent. 3. if swimming in a pool, one is less daring than an ocean swimmer. 4. if swimming anywhere one senses danger, such as from a shark, there is concern about where one is working.

T

table 1. personal relationships, society and community (note condition of table). 2. hard work followed by prosperity, especially a kitchen table. 3. domestic pleasure, joy.

tablecloth 1. a good omen for prosperity and social activities. 2. domestic disharmony, unhappiness, especially if the cloth is dirty. 3. family secrets or denials.

tacks 1. use caution; sharp words can hurt individuals, possibly damage relationships or reputations. 2. multiple irritations mount up and cause conflict, often in a relationship. 3. difficult times will soon come to an end.

tadpole 1. use caution with risky business affairs. 2. the beginning of great success, metamorphosis. 3. a good relationship has grown like magic.

tail 1. a good omen for most things. 2. something great is in the offing. 3. slang for sex. 4. wordplay for "story," possibly an excuse.

tailor 1. traveling, often business related. 2. a positive work environment. 3. feelings that a relationship may need "mending" or attention.

talisman 1. a good omen regarding social relationships. 2. judgment is sound and careful, usually concerning marriage.

talk 1. two-way communication, expression—often between two people, often between levels of consciousness. 2. family arguments (loud talking). 3. fear of not being heard or listened to (loud talking).

tallow 1. a negative omen regarding financial matters. 2. use caution to avoid careless words or deeds in intimate relationships. 3. situation or project is more difficult than originally thought.

talons 1. something long searched for is about to be reached, often in business affairs. 2. a feeling someone has bad intentions—often in business matters, sometimes in social activities.

tambourine 1. a good time is in the offing. 2. neglecting serious matters can cause problems down the road. 3. surprises are in the air.

tank 1. wealth and prosperity (an aquarium or fish tank). 2. use caution in expressing feelings; thoughtless words can be destructive (a tanker or army tank). 3. an overwhelming feeling of isolation and punishment (as in "to be thrown in the tank" or solitary confinement). 4. wordplay on drunkenness.

tannery 1. dissatisfaction in professional life. 2. good social skills. 3. possible contagious illness.

tape 1. a feeling of dissatisfaction regarding projects and endeavors. 2. joining two elements—usually social, sometimes in business affairs. 3. feelings of importance regarding domestic matters (videotape). 4. keeping a record, likely in legal matters.

tapestry 1. high living, wealth. 2. happiness is in the offing. 3. a feeling that happiness and prosperity are not deserved.

tapeworm 1. disagreeable feelings, lack of satisfaction, misery. 2. an emotional drain, likely from an individual. 3. possible illness, perhaps emotional.

tar 1. a negative omen regarding friendships, possible overly dependent person. 2. approaching obstacles, difficulty in forward movement. 3. use caution against gossip, possible injury to personal credibility.

tarantula 1. happiness. 2. repressed side of nature, usually angry or dark.

target 1. goals and ambitions. 2. a feeling of being a "target" or the object of gossip and unfriendly attention. 3. aspect of life is being neglected.

tarot cards 1. understanding the relationship between the past and the present (study the tarot and its message for clues to the many symbols). 2. a need or desire for a broad approach to an issue that requires healing (especially if individual tarot symbols are not noted by the dreamer).

tassels 1. happy news regarding friends or career. 2. hopes and plans will be fruitful. 3. negative news regarding business is in the offing.

tattoo 1. initiation, rite of passage. 2. important business needs attention. 3. bonding, friendship. 4. possibly repressed jealousy (tattoo seen on others).

tax 1. emotional drain—usually a situation, often a relationship. 2. success in money matters, affluence. 3. overcoming problems, obstacles to success. 4. sacrifice, hard work ahead (inability to pay).

tea 1. social status with ritual, dignity and style. 2. contentment.

teacher 1. a need or desire to control passion. 2. lessons need to be learned.

teacups 1. social pleasures and delightful companionship. 2. strong feelings of anticipation regarding the future, likely romance. 3. a negative omen (broken teacup).

teal 1. trust, loyalty and safety. 2. healing, faith.

teapot 1. feelings of dread. 2. a feeling that fate is already decided; upcoming events cannot be changed. 3. happy surprises in the offing.

tear gas 1. self-expression, likely a protest, is met with hostility. 2. feeling unable to "breathe," suffocated and in need of some personal space, likely in a relationship.

tears 1. a need or desire for emotional healing, cleansing. 2. reverse: great joy is in the offing. 3. possible illness, depression. 4. things learned through experience.

tease 1. innermost fantasies will come true and be satisfied, usually sensual. 2. social acceptability and regard, a general sense of being well-liked.

teddy bear 1. protection and trust, loyalty (to receive one from a partner). 2. immaturity, childishness, often in relationships. 3. sense of security, reassurance.

teeth 1. attack and defense. 2. stage of life or development (as in "milk teeth" or "cutting" teeth). 3. ability to communicate. 4. possible health problems.

telegram 1. fear of bad news. 2. an urgent message is trying to get through—usually from a friend, often from one level of consciousness to another.

telekinesis 1. emotional burden; emotions take on a life of their own, to the point of moving objects. 2. mental energy needs to be put to better use. 3. possible latent talents need to be explored.

telephone 1. a message is coming through from one level to the next, possibly the unconscious to the conscious or the heart to the mind. 2. telepathic communication. 3. difficulty in trying to communicate (to make a call). 4. someone relaying an important message, guidance (to receive a call). 5. delays, postponement.

telescope 1. a far-reaching view, exciting and vaulted ambitions, likely regarding aspects of life. 2. difficulties may not be as big or bad as they "appear." 3. a need or desire to expand, "lengthen" one's goals and ambitions. 4. an inability to "see" things in the immediate environment; overlook or neglect the obvious.

television 1. a distinct view of reality, not necessarily real or accurate. 2. intellectual movement; thoughts and concepts.

tempest a difficulty taken seriously out of proportion (as in "tempest in a teacup").

temple 1. inner state, especially spiritual. 2. a need for discretion; avoid gossip.

temptation 1. difficulties and obstacles, often tests of character. 2. good fortune in business (to be tempted to cheat on a spouse). 3. a feeling that someone has bad intentions.

ten 1. wholeness and the divine order. 2. having completed a phase of life or cycle.

tenant 1. loss, anger, usually in business. 2. future plans will be successful (to take money from a tenant).

tendon 1. disagreements, arguments. 2. a fatal flaw, a crucial vulnerability (as in "Achilles tendon" or "Achilles' heel").

tent 1. insecurity. 2. mobility and flexibility. 3. a phallic symbol (pole).

terrace 1. good health, society and prosperity. 2. a high, vaulted social position. 3. embarrassment.

terror 1. complete breakdown of trust. 2. a feeling that another harbors resentment, anger.

terrorism 1. lack of control, powerlessness through fear, intimidation. 2. violence with no apparent justification or gain. 3. pleasure at violence.

test 1. secrets will be revealed or mysteries solved (to have medical tests). 2. possible health issue (to have medical tests). 3. extreme difficulties, obstacles (an achievement test). 4. testing limitations and boundaries. 5. anxiety regarding tests and examinations.

testament 1. a message or document of grave importance (as in "last will and testament"). 2. changes in the offing. 3. suggestive of themes in either the Old Testament or the New Testament (make note of any other symbols for possibly related stories).

testicles 1. difficulties will soon be overcome (to have injured testicles). 2. social popularity. 3. a measure of competency, abilities.

testimony 1. social standing, achievement. 2. truthfulness, veracity (as in "to swear under oath").

text 1. a message being sent from one level of consciousness to the next. 2. a message is coming from a distance. 3. arguments are in the offing, especially involving close relationships.

thatch 1. depression and physical discomfort (to have a thatched roof). 2. rural charm, rustic tastes. 3. hair, especially in the pubic region.

thaw 1. a negative omen, trouble, perhaps even danger in the offing. 2. something once thought unchangeable can now change— likely a situation, often a relationship. 3. a change in character or personality, likely regarding attitude.

theater 1. a need or desire for emotional catharsis, cleansing. 2. a sense of the "dramatic"; overblown situation or event. 3. feelings of success in personal affairs and friendships.

theft 1. financial loss, loss of prestige in the offing. 2. fears of loss, usually of material things, money. 3. a feeling of time wasted (stolen).

thermometer 1. change, possibly in business or social standing. 2. possible illness. 3. an increase in emotional intensity, often regarding situations.

thief 1. financial security, gains. 2. love relationships, possible dubious candidate for intimate affairs (as in "stole my heart"). 3. feelings of self-doubt, unworthiness in regards to personal gains and successes.

thigh 1. strength and the ability to make the long haul. 2. pleasure and excitement. 3. use caution in affairs; behavior, judgment may be a little off right now.

thimble 1. industry, employment. 2. a happy domestic life. 3. happiness that comes from seeing to the needs of others.

thirteen 1. bad luck. 2. ability to see the future. 3. change and renewal. 4. maturity, coming of age.

thorn 1. hindered progress. 2. sin, guilt. 3. contentment to come.

thread 1. unity, continuity. 2. difficult journey to success. 3. commitments need strengthening. 4. connection between parent and child.

three 1. a symbol for the magical or divine (as in the "Trinity"). 2. signifies vital energy, power—often creative and intellectual, sometimes regarding growth. 3. a fascination with religion. 4. important messages or mysteries.

threshing 1. business and security. 2. community relationships and prosperity.

throat 1. communication and expression. 2. the ability to accept given situations. 3. point of extreme vulnerability.

throne 1. authority. 2. relationship with the divine. 3. fear of a loss of friends.

thumb 1. dexterity, ability to "handle" things. 2. success (large thumb). 3. dependence on others for mobility (as in "hitching a ride"). 4. direction in life.

thunder 1. inner rage. 2. loss and disappointment. 3. external forces, perhaps aggressive, calling for attention. 4. oversexed.

tick 1. difficulties in relationships. 2. a feeling that someone or some certain situation is draining, "parasitic." 3. possible health issues, possibly heart related. 4. anger (as in "ticked off").

ticket 1. new beginning. 2. admission to pleasurable activities. 3. journeys to come shortly (train or plane tickets).

tickle 1. a communication obstacle is likely to be overcome shortly. 2. reverse: unexpressed concerns regarding health or circumstances in life. 3. release of emotions in a physical way. 4. possible indiscreet or "delicate" situations in the offing (as in "ticklish situations").

tidal wave 1. turmoil in waking life. 2. being overwhelmed with emotions. 3. feelings of being overwhelmed in a relationship.

tide 1. good things are in the offing, good fortune (as in the "tide is turning"). 2. inevitable, natural change is about to occur. 3. a period of misunderstanding, unpleasantness, "misrule" or bad leadership is about to be overcome.

tiger 1. strength and readiness, possibly to strike. 2. an individual with bad intent, hostility, meaning harm. 3. a spirit guide, often representing feminine energy, physical prowess. 4. feelings of being overwhelmed—often by anger, likely by passion.

tiger's-eye 1. adaptability to change. 2. to feel a need for vigilance, to be "on guard." 3. a need or desire for confidence, to be free of anxieties.

tiles 1. business and financial matters. 2. use caution against recklessness or careless behavior (to see broken tiles).

till 1. success and financial gains. 2. a good omen for love relationships. 3. feelings of missing out, not belonging (to have a "short till").

timber 1. happiness, prosperity and financial security. 2. good relationships. 3. difficult times are in the offing (to see rotten or warped timber).

time 1. fear and anxiety over pressures of daily life. 2. "timely" activities and obligations are neglected. 3. feelings that "time is short."

time travel 1. a message from one level of consciousness to another concerning present circumstances or situations (note symbolism of time period represented). 2. an effort to avoid present difficulties or circumstances.

tin 1. intellect and the pursuit of knowledge. 2. adversity, often in business. 3. use caution bringing social relationships into personal or business financial matters.

tipsy 1. social pleasure, delight in company and a cheery temperament. 2. neglect or carelessness regarding important affairs or relationships. 3. a feeling that someone is a bad influence on the psyche.

tiptoe 1. a need or desire to avoid confrontation. 2. satisfaction and happiness with relationships. 3. a focus on details.

tire (car) 1. emotional well-being. 2. hard work is just ahead.

tire (fatigue) 1. depletion, drain—usually emotional, sometimes physical. 2. arguments ahead (others being tired).

toad 1. concealed nature or character. 2. transformation, magic (tadpole to maturity).

tobacco 1. professional and financial matters, often a good omen. 2. warm feelings regarding friendship. 3. an event or agreement of great importance.

tocsin 1. messages or warnings from the subconscious to the conscious mind. 2. reverse: the ability to cope well with difficult situations or events. 3. difficulties will soon be overcome.

toddy 1. important change is in the offing, often regarding life circumstances. 2. an important idea or concept is "fermenting" or ripening.

tofu 1. nutrition that may run contrary to popular tastes, likely in regards to character and intellect. 2. happiness, likely in marriage. 3. a good omen for energy, vitality and overall health.

toilet 1. emotional release, expression (note whether or not the toilet is clogged or flushes smoothly). 2. a secure, happy future. 3. sexual desire toward an individual.

tomatoes 1. a good domestic life. 2. good health and well-being. 3. strong feelings of embarrassment (as in "red as a tomato"). 4. feelings of intense sexuality, excitement.

tomb 1. forgotten or concealed aspects of self. 2. repressed or trapped spirit or "soul."

tombstone 1. aspect of self set aside, repressed until now. 2. a message from the subconscious, usually about direction in life (inscription). 3. long life ahead.

tongue 1. phallus. 2. language and communication. 3. indiscreet gossip, chatter. 4. manipulative, malignant character ("devil-tongued," "serpent's tongue" or "forked tongue").

tools 1. industry, productivity and skill. 2. phallic symbols. 3. prosperity and security.

toothache 1. good tidings, old friends are coming from a distance. 2. a need to express painful, repressed emotions or memories.

toothbrush 1. defensiveness and arrogant attitudes. 2. possible dental health or hygiene issue. 3. a concern with appearance.

toothless 1. difficulty in expressing oneself. 2. feelings of vulnerability, defenselessness. 3. possible health problems. 4. obstacles in the offing.

toothpaste 1. a coating or defense against bad thoughts and bad intentions, often regarding the intellect. 2. cleansing—likely of thoughts, possibly from the harsh words of others. 3. a possible dental health or hygiene issue.

toothpicks 1. a negative omen; use caution to avoid careless actions. 2. a need or desire to look at the larger picture. 3. small anxieties and annoyances are mounting up.

top 1. a need or desire to take life a little more seriously. 2. too much free time. 3. possible health problem (if feelings of dizziness accompany the top). 4. feeling emotionally overwhelmed.

topaz 1. balance, contentment and harmony. 2. feelings of insecurity, lack of safety, a need for protection. 3. a need or desire for restraint and control, often sexual.

topless 1. sense of vulnerability, exploitation regarding love, affection. 2. good sense of self-worth (high comfort level). 3. poor self-esteem (low comfort level).

torch 1. a good omen for the intellect and ideas (as in "illumination"). 2. a positive omen for business and professional matters. 3. lingering feelings of attraction, infatuation (as in "to carry a torch"). 4. deeply repressed anger, possibly over sexual tension (to "torch" or set something on fire).

tornado 1. feelings of potential disaster. 2. tantrums and emotional explosions in waking life. 3. overwhelming, likely destructive relationship.

torrent 1. feelings of unease, fear and dread. 2. being overwhelmed—usually by emotions, often sorrow or grief. 3. difficulties or problems in the offing.

torture 1. feelings of powerlessness and persecution—usually from a situation, often a relationship. 2. difficulties in home life, unhappiness. 3. attempt to eliminate feelings of love (to torture oneself).

touch 1. a desire for communication or physical, nonverbal expression. 2. feeling disconnected, "out of touch." 3. lunacy or craziness (as in "touched in the head").

tourist 1. difficulties in the acceptance of others, distance and anxiety with people. 2. travel and adventures in the offing. 3. a strong sense of unfinished business.

tourniquet 1. a need or desire to stop a loss of energy, vitality; a dangerous physical and/or emotional drain. 2. feelings of repression, "cut off" from the flow of emotions or ideas regarding a situation or important circumstance.

tower 1. a phallic symbol. 2. strength, protection and isolation. 3. lofty hopes, goals or ambitions. 4. a long period of happiness.

toy chest 1. childhood issues, often repressed. 2. rejecting immature behavior. 3. secure, happy family life.

toys 1. happy and safe domestic life. 2. appreciation for amusement, free-time activities and the healthful benefits of childlike behavior. 3. longing for more carefree behavior.

track 1. a need or desire for a search for self, identity. 2. obsession, enmity—sometimes over a situation, sometimes over an individual. 3. forward movement (as in "leaving tracks"). 4. feelings of alienation, not belonging, being out of step (as in following railroad tracks).

trade 1. feelings of loss, being cheated and depressed (as in an "unfair trade"). 2. success in business. 3. the ability to support oneself, self-sufficiency.

traffic 1. the flow of life, ambitions and goals (note the flow of traffic). 2. family difficulties, arguments. 3. difficulties can be overcome by asking for help.

train 1. social conformity. 2. progress of the dreamer's life. 3. progress of business deals.

traitor 1. feelings of betrayal regarding aspects of self, self-undermining, self-defeating. 2. a feeling someone has bad intentions, is being false or deceptive.

tramp 1. drifting, without responsibilities and obligations. 2. carefree times to come.

trampoline 1. the ability to cope in the face of change and adversity (as in "bounce back"). 2. a feeling of a lack of forward movement, exerting energy without seeming to get anywhere.

trance 1. a need or desire for introspection, time alone to think. 2. something or someone has a virtually hypnotic hold on the dreamer. 3. an effort to avoid obligations or responsibilities.

transfiguration 1. an extreme concern or obsession with outward appearances. 2. a need or desire for a new identity, a fresh start. 3. renewal of the soul or outlook on life, a spiritual awakening.

transformation 1. changing situations or circumstances, possibly beyond expectations. 2. difficulties over self-esteem issues, self-contempt. 3. a strong fear or unhappiness over a loss of control over a situation.

transfusion 1. the ability to share one's energy or emotional resources with others. 2. a good omen for business and financial matters. 3. possible health issues.

transmission 1. the ability to adapt to society or life's demands (vehicle transmission; note the condition of transmission and ability to "shift gears"). 2. the ability to communicate in general terms, broadcast self-image and intent. 3. a message is attempting to pass from one level of consciousness to the next.

transplant 1. a sense of fatigue, feeling drained (note the organ used in transplant). 2. a need to heal an emotional injury, likely from a relationship. 3. possible health issues. 4. feelings of not belonging, newness to a place and people or set of circumstances.

transportation 1. movement, mobility. 2. a measure of control (depending on who is driving or steering).

transsexual 1. feelings of confusion regarding the gender roles of the inner self, discomfort with one aspect or another. 2. issues concerning one's sexual identity. 3. a message from one level of consciousness to the next regarding the handling of a situation or relationship; may suggest the need to alter one's views or behavior.

trap 1. feelings of having been tricked or outmaneuvered. 2. deception is afoot. 3. unpleasant surprises or bad news is in the offing.

trapdoor 1. an unpleasant yet astounding surprise. 2. use caution to avoid snap decisions in sudden, difficult circumstances. 3. an urge or desire to avoid or escape certain conflicts or encounters, often wisely.

trapeze 1. a need or desire to take life a little less seriously. 2. use caution not to avoid responsibilities and obligations. 3. sexual adventure.

travel 1. change in business or affairs. 2. enlightenment brings new ways of thinking, usually spiritual. 3. disagreements.

tray 1. a measure of success and good fortune (note what and how much is on the tray). 2. use caution against wasting valuable resources.

treasure 1. use intuition, gut feelings; good sign of favorable success (finding treasure). 2. bad fortune in business, unsettled affairs. 3. hidden abilities revealed.

trees 1. relationships, friends, lovers and family. 2. self (note type of tree). 3. wealth and prosperity. 4. a measure of hopes and dreams (note condition of tree).

trenches 1. conflict, arguments and struggle. 2. a sense that someone harbors hostility. 3. use caution to be reserved with strangers or new situations.

trial 1. judgment, prosecution. 2. an experiment in behavior. 3. seeing an injustice. 4. very emotional period in life or situation.

triangle 1. energy, power. 2. a good omen for personal circumstance, general good luck. 3. direction, pointing the way, usually spiritual. 4. symbolic of genitalia, male or female.

tripe 1. a strong feeling that something is not as important or helpful as some believe it to be. 2. health and security. 3. possible illness. 4. approaching sadness and disappointment.

triplets 1. great joy, a surprise is in the offing after a great period of suffering. 2. a feeling that obstacles can be overcome, usually in business affairs. 3. destiny or divine intervention is at hand.

trophy 1. a feeling that rewards are unjustified. 2. feelings of insecurity, self-doubt regarding relationships; attraction may seem superficial (as in "trophy wife"). 3. a measure of feelings of pleasure.

trousers 1. use caution in business activities with friends (to see dirty trousers). 2. words without the meaning or deed to back them up are worthless and possibly hurtful. 3. financial gain is in the offing (to lose or not have trousers). 4. intimate relations may be out of control (if the trousers are on backward or not fastened properly).

trout 1. a good omen for personal finance matters and a change for the better. 2. a positive, cheerful attitude in life. 3. approaching success, pleasure in social affairs.

trowel 1. difficult times are about to be overcome and financial security is in the offing. 2. bad luck. 3. the ability to share a good attitude and feelings of goodwill.

truck 1. carrying a heavy load, burdens and responsibilities. 2. pregnancy is in the offing.

trumpet 1. exciting, surprise announcements are on the way. 2. achievement; dreams and desires are about to be fulfilled. 3. a feeling that someone would like to get better acquainted.

trunk 1. travel is in the offing (especially if the trunk is empty). 2. a need or desire to address feelings or memories long neglected. 3. a negative omen concerning relationships and finances (if trunk is lost, overstuffed or damaged).

truss 1. a need or desire for support, help in difficult, overwhelming times, often regarding business affairs. 2. possible sickness or injury.

trust 1. self-trust, ability to accept oneself. 2. issues of trust with loved ones are coming to the surface.

trusts 1. a stagnant career and/or urge to look for new ways of supporting self. 2. luck in speculative business concerns.

tsunami 1. turmoil in waking life. 2. feelings of being overwhelmed with emotions. 3. feelings of being overwhelmed in a relationship.

tub 1. a happy and secure home life (note how full the tub is). 2. difficulties in personal relationships (to see a broken or rusty tub).

tumble 1. great effort for little reward, often in relationships. 2. feelings of escapism and avoidance of responsibilities. 3. use caution against carelessness and neglect (to accidentally tumble). 4. good luck (to see someone else tumble).

tumor 1. repressed emotions emerging. 2. once small annoyances are becoming an issue. 3. possible illness. 4. forgotten event or wound needs to be addressed.

tunnel 1. vagina, birth. 2. insecurity (dark and feeling anxious). 3. secrets revealed. 4. limited perspective.

turf 1. something or someone new and exciting is in the offing. 2. being overwhelmed, in over one's head. 3. possessiveness, territorialism.

turkey 1. abundance is in the offing, often in terms of family life. 2. taking things seriously (as in "talking turkey"). 3. not taking things seriously, playing the fool.

Turkish bath 1. feelings of being overwhelmed or frustrated with health issues. 2. a good omen for social affairs. 3. a need or desire to be more open-minded, likely regarding health and sense of well-being.

turnips 1. prosperity and good fortune are in the offing, especially in financial matters. 2. little annoyances mount up and cause anger. 3. possible health issues.

turpentine 1. a good omen regarding intellect and thought processes. 2. a sense of upcoming disappointments, sadness. 3. current difficulties need careful research (to use turpentine to dress a wound).

turquoise 1. a sense or belief that hopes and dreams are attainable. 2. protection and safety, being "blessed." 3. purity, virtue and innocence.

turtle 1. obstacles will be overcome but it will take time. 2. slow but steady advancement. 3. protection, the ability to retreat or find shelter from situations.

tuxedo 1. a positive omen for upcoming social affairs. 2. a level of culture and sophistication. 3. a desire for social advancement, a greater sense of self-importance.

tweezers 1. extreme discomfort, intrusion—possibly in relationships, likely in situations. 2. a good omen for new relationships.

3. too much attention is taken with details, possibly neglecting the larger picture.

twelve 1. holiness, perfection, a high point. 2. good government and leadership. 3. cycles of time, life and relationships. 4. judgment (as in a jury).

twin 1. other self, identity symbol (in a non-twin dreamer). 2. doppelganger, mirror image, representing conflict, opposing values. 3. pregnancy with twins. 4. domestic joy.

twine 1. a negative omen regarding business. 2. fun and flirtation; use caution not to neglect serious matters or stable relationships. 3. a relationship or situation needs to be released or "cut loose" (to cut twine).

two 1. partnership, unity and interdependence. 2. diversity, duality, sometimes opposite individuals standing together. 3. balance and symmetry.

type 1. communication and ability to express feelings. 2. a message from one level of consciousness to another. 3. a feeling that a matter is of great importance (to note a typeface). 4. wordplay denoting a tendency to categorize or "stereotype," usually individuals.

typewriter 1. a need or desire to communicate or improve communications within specific relationships (note who is typing and to whom it is addressed). 2. forward movement in business.

typhoid 1. a feeling of being overwhelmed—usually by fatigue, often with social situations. 2. a sense of someone with repressed hostility, bad intentions. 3. possible health issues.

U

udder 1. nurturing desired. 2. sexuality.

UFO 1. spotting a UFO can mean that one is about to be helped in an unanticipated way. 2. spotting a UFO may mean that one is facing danger. 3. indication that the dreamer is a little "spaced out" in some way.

ugly 1. if an ugly face, someone is hostile toward the dreamer. 2. if home or property is ugly, prospects for the future seem dim.

ulcer one is deeply concerned about something.

Ulysses one's journey is going to be difficult.

umber makes something darker.

umbilical cord 1. the emotional bond between parent and child. 2. if cutting the cord, one is attempting to be free.

umbrella (open) 1. protection from emotional onslaught. 2. higher aspirations.

umpire 1. a strong authority figure who will guide, even command, one to take the right path. 2. someone who is able to keep one healthy and well. 3. uncomfortable feeling that every action one takes is being judged.

unassuming one desires something but doesn't "announce" it.

unavailable someone one needs for emotional help is not there.

unblemished someone is very honest.

unbuttoning trying to loosen up, have a more open relationship with someone.

uncircumcised sexually rambunctious.

uncivilized emotionally, someone is not worthy.

uncle 1. willingness to "give up" in a certain situation. 2. one seeks the counsel of someone wise.

Uncle Tom's Cabin concern over civil rights issue.

undertaker 1. authority figure who "undertakes" something the dreamer can't. 2. taking on too much responsibility. 3. leading a funeral procession.

under the weather beware of drinking excessively.

underwater 1. overcome by life, unable to fight back. 2. one needs to learn how to navigate one's life better. 3. in "over one's head." 4. if breathing underwater, one has returned—temporarily and emotionally—to the womb.

underwear 1. if in underwear and people are observing, one feels unworthy of respect, ashamed. 2. boldly, angrily displaying oneself. 3. one is suffering embarrassment over some situation. 4. if someone else is in underwear, the dreamer is embarrassed for him/her.

undress 1. if one is undressing in front of others inappropriately, the act expresses anger, defiance. 2. sexual yearning. 3. desire to be free of someone or a certain situation. 4. desire to shock someone. 5. if one is undressing someone, he/she is romantically drawn to that person.

undulate desire for sexual contact (the motion of intercourse).

unearth if one digs hard enough, one will find what one is looking for.

unemployed 1. lack of self-worth. 2. unemployed and longing for a job.

unfaithful indicates that whoever may be cheating in a relationship feels guilty about it.

unfortunate 1. feeling worthless. 2. if one feels someone else is unfortunate, that person is perceived as worthless.

unicorn 1. phallic symbol. 2. gentle approach to seduction of a female.

unicycle 1. one wants to "go it alone," in romantic, business or other relationships. 2. one has the confidence to run one's life alone.

unilateral one can make one's own decisions.

union united with others in a common cause.

unit 1. type of person. 2. treat things in a careful way.

Unitarian desire to be religious but without strict rules.

United Arab Emirates 1. fear of terrorists. 2. different worlds.

United States 1. freedom. 2. protection. 3. an ideal to be achieved in one's own life.

university desire to return to school to educate oneself.

unknown 1. if an unknown person appears in one's dream, that person represents a part of oneself that is not known to the dreamer. 2. one is wondering where to seek help and advice to solve a problem.

unsteady 1. one has a drinking problem. 2. one is not sure of one's opinion.

unvarnished one needs finishing.

unzipping 1. need to develop a more relaxed relationship with someone. 2. need to relax.

up 1. if one dreams of moving up, it signifies one is emerging—or wants to emerge—from a situation that is depressing and enervating. 2. one is ready to take on a difficult project.

uproot 1. one feels disconnected from others. 2. broken family ties. 3. lost job or other disruption.

upside down one is wrong about something, particularly in making assumptions.

Uranus 1. desire to travel far away. 2. disguised way to curse someone. 3. unusual in the way one thinks.

urination 1. clearing oneself of a problem. 2. not in control of one's life. 3. one feels exposed, spied on by others.

urn 1. worry that one might die soon. 2. longing for a more noble ending. 3. one is feeling exhausted, "dead tired."

usher 1. authority figure who is reminding one of obligations. 2. one should sort out certain things.

utensils one will take a practical approach to a matter.

utopia one has problems and would like to escape to utopia.

U-turn 1. changing the direction of one's life. 2. seeing a NO U sign indicates that one should continue on the same course. 3. a marker for a serious change in one's life.

V

vacation 1. a desire or need for rest. 2. to remove oneself from a bad situation or emotional state. 3. good fortune and happy times. 4. time to take life more seriously.

vaccination 1. to provide protection, immunity—usually emotional. 2. to inoculate against unforeseen assaults, usually from especially manipulative individuals.

vacuum 1. lack of fulfillment, emptiness. 2. feelings of loss, isolation. 3. to clean up—usually emotionally, sometimes in waking life.

vagina 1. femininity and female power. 2. possible feelings of guilt or shame (to dream something is wrong with a vagina). 3. feelings of a need to be more discreet, less exposed (to dream one's vagina is exposed).

vagrant 1. bad company, a leech. 2. end of prosperity. 3. escapist, free spirit; without obligations and responsibilities.

valentine 1. excitement, joy in relationships. 2. a need or desire to "rekindle" a relationship with self, work on issues of self-esteem. 3. too much focus on relationships causes neglect of other important matters.

valley 1. fertility. 2. low point in energy, vitality; often health related. 3. period of peace and contentment 4. good times, better prospects ahead (lush, green valley). 5. female sexuality. 6. possible illness.

vampire 1. seduction, sensual pleasures. 2. drain of vitality, life force; often in a relationship. 3. bad bargain has been made (as in "bargain with the devil").

van 1. employment, team efforts. 2. a measure of burdens and obligations (note how loaded the van is). 3. good news is in the offing.

vanilla 1. a pleasant seduction, delightful allure, often involving potential relationships. 2. a phallic symbol. 3. vagina. 4. the commonplace, boring.

varnishing 1. superficial or cosmetic enhancements will not fix deep structural problems, possibly in character. 2. feelings of having been deceived. 3. hard work and endurance bring rewards. 4. a bad omen regarding the truthfulness of matters and self-deception.

vase 1. feminine sexuality. 2. display, usually emotional. 3. extreme sorrow, loss (broken vase).

vasectomy 1. feelings of impotence, infertility, usually regarding creativity and the imagination. 2. a fear of not being able to fulfill obligations, responsibilities. 3. fear of impotence.

vat 1. a measure of financial security (note what the contents are and how full the vat is). 2. a bad omen regarding current emotional state. 3. sorrow and pain, usually regarding relationships.

Vatican 1. wealth and prosperity. 2. feelings of social inadequacy and inferiority. 3. some rules are unjust.

vault 1. obstacles are a little more difficult than originally thought. 2. a need to be cautious with valuables. 3. use caution regarding appearances of wealth; they can be misinterpreted.

vegetables 1. happy family life. 2. nourishment—usually physical, often spiritual. 3. modest financial rewards.

vehicles 1. personal mobility, often in life. 2. feelings of a loss of control over life (not driving, cannot drive or invisible driver). 3. stuck in old behaviors, mode of thinking (vehicle broken down, no gas, flat tires, etc.).

veil 1. hidden information, secrets. 2. lack of vanity, modesty. 3. concealed aspect of personality (woman wearing a veil). 4. mystery revealed (to remove).

vein 1. great sorrow. 2. use extreme caution in activities, a possible message to avoid careless injury (to be bleeding).

velvet 1. prosperous business ventures. 2. regal and wealthy, honors bestowed. 3. pleasurable sensations, softness, suppleness—usually emotional.

veneer 1. a strong sense or feeling of deception, that someone has been false. 2. a tremendous concern with appearances. 3. use caution with first impressions, they may be deceiving.

vengeance 1. guilt, usually for a misdeed or harsh words or actions toward an individual. 2. a need or desire to get even, usually from being made to feel ashamed or embarrassed.

venison 1. wild, unruly behavior. 2. a need to avoid harsh words or actions that may injure close friends.

venom 1. repressed rage, "poisonous" feelings. 2. difficulties with feelings about self, a lack of self-acceptance. 3. negative thinking can cause problems in the future.

vent 1. a need or desire to relieve anger or frustration. 2. feelings of being constricted, restrained.

ventilation 1. an inability to "breathe," thrive; feelings of repression. 2. a need or desire to reveal something, bring it into the open. 3. a need or desire for off-time, relaxation.

ventriloquist 1. use caution when speaking in front of strangers. 2. use caution against uttering possibly dishonest or deceiving words to intimate friends.

Venus 1. good beginnings to projects, explorations. 2. great success in romantic affairs. 3. feminine balance, harmony; love and compassion.

veranda 1. after some difficulties there will be success, usually regarding business. 2. happiness regarding intimate affairs (to be on the veranda with a lover).

vermin 1. delays and setbacks, usually regarding projects and activities. 2. a good omen regarding personal wealth and finances. 3. possible health or hygiene issues.

vertebrae 1. a need or desire for courage, the ability to stand up for oneself. 2. possible health issue—likely back related, possibly about to cause pain. 3. flexibility, ability to adapt to different situations.

vertigo 1. a negative omen regarding domestic affairs. 2. feelings of being overwhelmed—usually with activities, often with emotions. 3. possible health problem.

vessels 1. a general omen of work, security and prosperity (note size and condition of vessel and what and how much cargo is being carried). 2. news from afar.

vest 1. a negative omen regarding character and integrity. 2. empathy, caring for others.

veteran 1. wisdom through trial and experience. 2. quiet heroism, stoicism.

vexed 1. a large number of small annoyances that need to be addressed—usually anxieties, often over money, sometimes domestic affairs. 2. little quarrels will not soon be settled.

vicar 1. a need or desire to regard personal affairs more seriously. 2. petty arguments may be caused by jealousy. 3. a need for fatherly guidance. 4. a need to use caution against excessive behavior.

vice 1. a feeling that someone is being deceptive, perhaps cheating (to act out a vice). 2. a need to assess behavior regarding moral questions (to see others acting out a vice). 3. a need not to judge others for their behavior. 4. reverse: life progresses on a morally upright path.

victim 1. a sense of danger; issues of personal safety need to be addressed. 2. difficulty in accepting responsibility for actions. 3. to suffer from self-doubt, loathing. 4. feelings of being dominated by someone or something.

victory 1. a negative omen regarding sense of self, self-esteem. 2. dread or anxiety over the completion of a project or activity. 3. adversity can be overcome, success achieved.

video camera 1. expresses a need or desire to distance oneself from family or close friends. 2. current situations suffer from a bias, lack of objectivity. 3. a need or desire to be more focused on activities—likely regarding family, possibly where children are concerned.

videocassette recorder (VCR) 1. a past event, possibly traumatic, needs to be addressed. 2. a message from one level of consciousness to another regarding repetitive behaviors. 3. a need or desire for escapism.

video game 1. manipulation and emotional control. 2. an inability to accept responsibility, avoidance of obligations.

village 1. isolated or restrictive social circle, closed-minded. 2. rampant gossip. 3. a desire for a simple, traditional way of life. 4. effort needed in an approaching task.

vine 1. social or community relationships, possibly family. 2. a good omen of success, abundance and wealth. 3. possible health issue (note the condition of vine).

vinegar 1. hard work pays off but only after time. 2. a desire to seek out extreme pleasures of a sensual nature (to make vinaigrette). 3. use caution to act according to principles.

vineyard 1. an extremely good omen regarding sensual activities. 2. wealth and prosperity. 3. a good omen for judgment and risky affairs.

violated 1. feelings of being dominated, abused by another. 2. repressed memories of violation. 3. possible difficulties with self-esteem, self-doubt in need of attention.

violence 1. reverse: happiness, comfort and security. 2. a feeling that someone has bad, even harmful, intentions. 3. repressed hostility, rage. 4. use extreme caution in expressing emotions to others; avoid harsh words or arguments.

violet (color) 1. faith, gentleness, peace and serenity. 2. communication and happiness in intimate relationships.

violets 1. represent innocence, honesty and chastity. 2. happy events in the offing. 3. a good omen for intimate affairs.

violin 1. contentment, happiness, especially in domestic situation. 2. sadness. 3. sorrow will be comforted. 4. anger, arguments (broken violin strings).

viper 1. a bad omen representing an individual with bad intent (as in to "harbor a viper"). 2. a need or desire for serenity, peace and balance in life. 3. a fast-moving, relentless attitude and personal drive, a possible need to slow down (to dream of an automobile).

virgin 1. potential, purity. 2. innocence, emotional, intellectual or spiritual. 3. spiritual harmony (Virgin Mary). 4. great happiness (embracing a virgin).

visa 1. being allowed, permitted and free to take on an endeavor. 2. debt that needs to be addressed and possibly repaid.

vise 1. feelings of being forced, "squeezed" and dominated by another's personality. 2. to lose the ability to communicate effectively, often business related. 3. a feeling of having been manipulated into wrongdoing.

vision (a mystical vision) 1. extreme anxiety, fear—usually regarding individuals, especially if they appear in the vision. 2. success. 3. possible health issue.

vision (eyesight) 1. view of life and the world. 2. possible health issue. 3. a need to focus on current issues.

visit 1. pleasant events are in the offing. 2. obstacles, usually the questionable attitudes of others. 3. use caution against people with false intentions. 4. feelings of worry or concern over a loved one.

visitors 1. the care and concern of others, hospitality. 2. good news and positive changes in the offing. 3. use caution to reassess motives regarding others.

vitamins 1. a need or desire to strengthen and fortify oneself—often physically, sometimes emotionally. 2. possible vitamin deficiency.

vitriol 1. use extreme caution toward loved ones; reassess motives carefully. 2. a feeling that someone harbors resentment or hostility. 3. feelings that a harsh situation will benefit no one without careful consideration.

vodka 1. pleasant social activities. 2. confusion, usually regarding business affairs.

voice 1. difficulties in business (to hear a voice). 2. a good omen for relationships, reconciliation and forgiveness. 3. a need or desire to listen more carefully, focus more on the needs of others. 4. difficult times ahead (to hear voices arguing).

voiceless 1. an inability to communicate. 2. a need to find alternate means of communication, especially regarding intimate relationships. 3. feelings of loss and sorrow, usually regarding aspects of self.

volcano 1. repressed emotions: rage, passion. 2. violent disputes. 3. uncontrollable events in the offing (erupting).

volunteer 1. desire to help, lend assistance. 2. selflessly devote time or energy to a project or cause.

vomit 1. to disgorge or express repressed emotions. 2. a process of cleansing—usually emotions, often buried memories. 3. poor reputation. 4. false or self-serving behaviors in others is revealed (to see others vomiting).

voodoo 1. feelings of powerlessness, helplessness and a lack of control. 2. an urge toward earthly spirituality. 3. an attraction to a darker side of nature or self.

vote 1. a need or desire to assert oneself, to "be counted." 2. feelings of hopelessness, insignificance. 3. expresses a longing for peace, hopes for the future.

voucher 1. a feeling that someone is trying to cheat. 2. feelings of mistrust of friends or family members.

vow 1. a solution to problems, often domestic. 2. use caution in affairs to avoid carelessly breaking vows or promises. 3. reverse: unswerving integrity and fidelity (to break a vow).

voyage 1. news is in the offing. 2. a new phase of life is beginning. 3. an inheritance or legacy is in the offing.

voyeurism 1. disassociation from desire, affection—often emotional. 2. shyness, afraid of intimacy (to watch).

vulnerable 1. reverse: a sense of safety, security. 2. a feeling that someone is about to be hurtful or injurious, usually emotionally. 3. feelings of personal safety and security need to be addressed.

vulture 1. insight into difficulties. 2. irreconcilable differences, relationships. 3. purification, cleansing, end of difficulties.

W

wad 1. wise guy (chewing gum). 2. sexuality (porno).

wading a rebirth, baptism of sorts.

wager signifies good fortune coming one's way.

wages 1. if one is not satisfied with wages, one is likely not satisfied with oneself. 2. if wages are high, one is satisfied with oneself.

wagon 1. an empty—or full—wagon reflects one's life situation. 2. driving a wagon up a hill indicates a difficult situation is being contended with. 3. driving a wagon down a hill indicates a potentially hazardous situation. 4. driving a wagon which one is in control of downhill indicates one is in control of one's life.

waif 1. feeling alone. 2. if one dreams he/she adopts a waif, then someone close to him/her is in need of help.

wail 1. the dreamer who wails is afraid he/she may die. 2. if someone other than the dreamer wails, fear of death is also present.

wainscot concern with the condition of one's house.

waist 1. sex object. 2. if large, concern about one's health. 3. dietary concerns.

waiter 1. symbolic of the "good life." 2. if waiter is rude, he/she represents someone who is mistreating one in life.

waiting 1. if waiting for someone one is romantically or otherwise involved with, one feels subordinate. 2. if aware that someone is waiting for one, he/she feels dominant in a relationship. 3. one is waiting to take action.

wake 1. if at the wake of a friend, one fears for the future of the friend. 2. if the wake is for the dreamer, his/her fear is failure. 3. looking back on the past.

walking 1. one is able to control one's own life. 2. commentary on the pace that one is conducting one's life at; the faster one walks, the greater the pace and corresponding stress. 3. if competing against other walkers, one's position or standing in the race is revelatory, and if one keeps walking, then one's feeling is that the problems will be solved. 4. to walk at night says that a person is willing to take chances.

wallet 1. a fat wallet indicates one is well-off. 2. a lost or stolen wallet indicates that one fears someone might be trying to take advantage. 3. losing a wallet is fear of losing identity. 4. sense of being betrayed or violated.

walleye 1. determined (salmon upstream). 2. dead.

wallpaper 1. covering up something that one does not want others to see. 2. attempt to make one's life brighter, better. 3. stripping wallpaper means trying to change one's life.

walls 1. a barrier or barriers that someone has to get through. 2. if one is surrounded by walls, they may represent barriers that one has erected to keep others away emotionally. 3. breaking walls down is clearing access to oneself—or others.

wall-to-wall whatever the problem is, it is extensive.

walnut 1. something is being hidden inside the shell. 2. cracking a walnut means enabling others to see the secret inside. 3. Christmas.

walrus 1. dominance. 2. to see oneself as a walrus indicates one is willing to protect others.

waltz 1. admired by others. 2. a good relationship with someone.

wampum concern about money.

wand 1. phallic symbol. 2. magical. 3. in command. 4. the ability to change things with a single stroke. 5. good intentions.

wander looking for a direction in one's life.

want 1. to want something represents a desire perhaps more frivolous than needful. 2. one is in a state of misfortune.

war 1. chaos in one's personal life. 2. hostility toward someone or a group. 3. feeling that a problem can only be settled with violence.

wardrobe 1. condition of wardrobe reflects one's life situation. 2. longing for new wardrobe.

warehouse 1. if empty, loneliness. 2. if full, security.

warrant 1. to dream that a warrant is being served on one denotes that one will be involved with some important matters which will lead to uneasiness. 2. to dream that a warrant is served on someone else signifies misunderstandings and quarrels.

warrant, death 1. one has done something very wrong. 2. loved one has done something very wrong.

warrior to see or dream that one is a warrior represents life's challenges and one's ability to confront them.

warts minor imperfections in one's persona that are easily removed.

washboard old-fashioned approach to cleanse oneself is fine.

washbowl 1. to see a washbowl in a dream denotes that a new interest resulting in much joy and contentment will occupy one's time. 2. to see a broken washbowl signifies small pleasure for the dreamer while giving pain to others.

washerwoman to see a washerwoman in a dream signifies infidelity and/or a peculiar adventure.

washing 1. to dream that one is washing one's face and/or hands in a washbowl signifies that the dreamer will be consumed with passion for someone close to him/her. 2. to dream that one is washing one's feet signifies that the dreamer will change his/her line of work and undertake a more fruitful venture.

washing machine 1. one has the means to cleanse some part of one's life, such as guilt. 2. watching a washing machine in action means one's life is humdrum.

wasp 1. anger. 2. white Anglo-Saxon Protestant. 3. away from the nest. 4. if one kills a wasp, it indicates that one is not afraid of one's enemies.

waste take note of which part of one's behavior or life should be eliminated.

watch 1. if one sees a working watch, troubles will soon pass. 2. to see a broken watch indicates that one's problems may not go away so quickly.

watching 1. to dream that one is watching something represents one's lack of initiative to take any action; it may also symbolize neutrality in some situation. 2. one's neutrality in a quarrel.

watchtower religious fervor.

water 1. if clear and clean, indicates that problems can be solved. 2. if water is muddy the problems are more difficult to solve. 3. if dirty, then much difficulty lies ahead. 4. birth. 5. rescue. 6. the unconscious. 7. the womb. 8. sorrow. 9. emotions.

water carrier 1. signifies favorable prospects in love and business. 2. one will rise above his/her current position.

water bed 1. longing for sex. 2. need for relaxation. 3. womb simulation.

waterfall 1. deep sadness, tears. 2. releasing of blocked emotion. 3. if being pelted by waterfall, one's emotions are overwhelming.

water lily grief, sorrow, and bereavement.

watermelon 1. longing for leisure times, summer. 2. pregnancy. 3. sexuality.

water mill 1. hard work. 2. use whatever is available, however simple, to achieve one's goals.

water-skiing 1. one feels self-confident. 2. willing to take risks.

waterslide 1. willing to take a risk. 2. able to face the unknown.

waves 1. instability. 2. sense of being "swallowed" or engulfed.

waving 1. trying to draw someone into your life. 2. saying goodbye to someone who is out of one's life.

wax 1. candle with wax dripping may be a phallic symbol. 2. candle with wax dripping may also indicate the passage of time.

Wayne, John 1. heroic. 2. indomitable. 3. false self-image (as revealed in a biography about him).

weak 1. if the dreamer is physically weak, this could mean he/she harbors feelings of being inadequate. 2. it may also refer to time—a week. 3. physically weak.

wealth 1. if wealthy, one feels secure. 2. striving for wealth is symbolic of achieving one's goals.

wean desire to return to the womb.

weapons 1. if holding a weapon, one feels threatened emotionally or physically. 2. depending on the weapon, a phallic symbol.

weasel 1. an untrustworthy person. 2. the dreamer him/herself is deceitful.

weather 1. one's emotional state. 2. also a question: "whether." 3. predicting the weather means one has a good grasp on what the future holds.

weaving 1. putting something together in one's life. 2. one is an orderly person. 3. one is under great stress because one's life is bogged down. 4. plotting or planning to do something.

web 1. one is afraid that he/she may be getting into a situation where he/she will be trapped. 2. the dreamer's desire to protect him/herself, laying out a trap for others. 3. one feels trapped, unable to escape a situation, such as a bad job.

wedding 1. a new beginning. 2. fear of involvement, commitment to someone. 3. if remarrying the same spouse, it reaffirms one's happiness with that person. 4. dreaming about marrying anyone indicates the yearning for love.

wedding ring 1. a new beginning. 2. sign of commitment to someone. 3. if one sees a ring on someone else's finger, it may mean one wants to cheat.

wedge 1. the desire to separate from someone. 2. the fear that a loved one is separating from one. 3. the fear that someone is driving a wedge between one's love and oneself.

weeds 1. one's life is dotted with problems that need to be dealt with. 2. relationships that have gone bad.

weeping 1. bad news. 2. joy at something in one's life.

weight 1. if overweight, one's sense of self is negative. 2. if trim, one's concept of self is good. 3. burdens one carries. 4. if one feels lighter, then a "weight" may have been lifted off one's shoulders. 5. overweight may also mean that one is carrying too many responsibilities.

welcome 1. whatever one is doing is accepted. 2. if the dreamer welcomes someone, he/she accepts whatever the other person is doing.

weld makes something stronger than it was before in the place where it was broken.

welter many difficult issues to deal with.

werewolf 1. some part of the dreamer has extreme hostility buried within him/her. 2. one has hidden a strong sexual component.

west 1. the desire to succeed ("go west, young man") but it also applies to females. 2. the end of something.

wet 1. trying to cleanse oneself of painful emotions. 2. spiritually reaching.

wet nurse 1. one seeks to return to childhood. 2. if one imagines that one is a wet nurse, it may indicate that one feels she is in a relationship with someone who has a childish personality.

whale 1. one is concerned with overeating, weight. 2. something in one's life looms large, but not necessarily fearsome.

wheat 1. a field of wheat indicates that one's efforts are ready to be harvested or used. 2. one feels capable of supporting a large group of people.

wheel(s) 1. life, eternity. 2. the sun. 3. the divine.

wheelbarrow 1. to see or use a wheelbarrow in your dream represents hard work, labor, and difficulties. It also symbolizes your body and the way that you are moving about through life.

wheelchair 1. if in a wheelchair, one's life has been difficult to manage. 2. if one is pushing someone else in a wheelchair, that person is dependent on the dreamer.

whiff gave something one's best try and failed.

whip 1. one needs to have more control over one's life. 2. one needs to exercise better control over someone else's life.

whiplash certain actions have hidden payback.

whipped 1. punished. 2. make lighter.

whirlpool anxiety that one will be pulled into a situation and not survive.

whirlwind 1. beware of danger from seemingly nowhere. 2. one is very fast and efficient.

whiskers 1. maturity. 2. not caring.

whisky 1. need to deal with the anxiety in one's life. 2. observing a great number of bottles of whisky indicates a desire for a wilder life. 3. one would like to retreat from life's responsibilities.

whispering 1. one wants to know something but is afraid. 2. bad things are being said about the dreamer.

whistle 1. if whistling sound is heard, the listener is being alerted to something. 2. if dreamer is whistling, it reflects happiness. 3. warning. 4. romantically attracted to someone.

white (color) 1. purity. 2. truth. 3. cleansing. 4. religious experience or revelation.

White House, the 1. leadership, power. 2. concern over national issues or problems. 3. knowledge or wisdom.

whiten 1. try to clean up. 2. try to purify emotionally.

whitewash 1. covering up something. 2. cleaning up something.

white whale 1. significant adversary. 2. challenge.

wholesale 1. look for a bargain. 2. large amount of something.

whoopee cushion something is laughable.

whore 1. low regard for someone. 2. looking to identify someone ("who her?"). 3. someone interested only in money.

widget sometimes one has to be inventive to make something work.

widow(er) 1. lonely, isolated. 2. desire to end relationship with one's wife.

wife 1. reaffirmation of one's love. 2. indication that one's relationship is troublesome.

wig 1. if wearing, one feels that part of oneself is false. 2. feeling foolish about something. 3. longing to get work in some theatrical venue.

wilderness 1. if traveling through it, one feels he/she is able to handle anything that occurs. 2. if traveling through it, one may feel unable to cope with its dangers.

will 1. one is willing to share whatever. 2. problems can be solved if one is willing to go after them.

willow 1. emotional balance. 2. flexibility.

wilted 1. tired, wasted, unable to carry on. 2. feeling old. 3. feeling sexually inadequate.

Wimbledon 1. the best of the best. 2. competition. 3. grass.

win 1. one pictures oneself as a winner. 2. need a "win" in upcoming waking situation.

wind 1. a problem is uncontrollable, but walking on through the wind suggests that one has the ability to solve the problem. 2. fiercely blowing wind indicates the need for a change in one's life, either business or personal. 3. if wind is fiercely blowing into one, dreamer is facing adversity.

wind chimes 1. time passing. 2. longing for tranquility.

windmill 1. a sense of power. 2. longing to be old-fashioned. 3. one's state of mind.

windows 1. eyes. 2. if windows are blocked, it means that one is determined not to see a particular something. 3. opportunity. 4. observing situations or people from a distance.

windows (broken) 1. change or upheaval. 2. violence. 3. fear of self-destruction. 4. lost opportunities.

window washer 1. bravery. 2. desire to see things clearly. 3. one has the ability to clarify a situation and shed some perspective on an issue.

wine 1. blood. 2. recklessness. 3. intoxication. 4. temptation.

wine cellar 1. rich. 2. "cool."

wineglass 1. desire to be healthy. 2. desire to escape or numb oneself against some sort of pain.

wings 1. desire to be free of some situation. 2. reflection of one's angelic qualities, or those of someone else.

winter 1. one is going through or suspects he/she will be going through a bad time. 2. death. 3. old age. 4. the lost or forgotten.

wire 1. signal to contact someone. 2. police may be investigating one. 3. need to "wrap up" something.

wires 1. frustration or confusion. 2. need to "connect" or understand.

wise old man 1. God. 2. guardian or parent. 3. advice about the future or unknown.

wish something is missing in one's life.

witch 1. someone who is evil, heartless. 2. a person with seemingly magical powers.

wizard looking for a quick, easy solution.

wolf 1. someone beautiful but vicious. 2. the need for others, so one becomes part of a group. 3. hated by some. 4. someone who is devious. 5. someone who is romantically very active.

woman 1. love and nurturing. 2. may mean unknown desires are emerging. 3. feminine aspects of self. 4. fear of growing old. 5. if an old woman, laden with advice. 6. if a woman is pregnant, the dreamer looks on the pregnancy in a positive way, forecasting abundance.

woodpecker a role model, in terms of hard work, to be emulated.

woods 1. one's overall view of life: if the woods are healthy, the view is positive; if the woods are broken down, etc., then one's life view is not positive. 2. adventurous.

wool 1. the real thing. 2. seeking the best kind of protection.

work if one is at work, some sort of stressful situation has presented itself.

workman 1. some task needs to be completed. 2. one is getting an admonition ("work, man!") to work harder on something.

workshop 1. one's skills are being honed. 2. one admires what is good and basic in life.

world 1. if the world is going to end, this refers to one's own world. 2. a task seems much too great. 3. one thinks of oneself as minuscule.

worm 1. fear that someone will work his/her way into one's life. 2. one's image of oneself is very negative. 3. someone is perceived to be taking advantage of someone. 3. to view oneself as a worm is to think of oneself as a potential victim. 4. if the dreamer is baiting a hook, he/she is planning to trap someone else.

wound 1. a warning that what a person is doing may result in a disaster of some sort. 2. a physical wound may actually be a psychological wound.

wreath 1. fear that someone, perhaps oneself, will die. 2. happy thoughts, reminiscent of Christmas.

wreck 1. fear of the future, that one will end up a wreck. 2. obstacle in one's path.

wrestling 1. if wrestling with a member of the opposite sex, sexual activity. 2. one is grappling (wrestling) with problems that need to be brought under control.

wrinkles 1. awareness of time going by, one getting older. 2. what one has learned from experience.

writing if writing, an attempt is being made to communicate with someone.

Wyoming desire to move to a wilderness environment.

X

---

x 1. negative feelings or bad intentions toward an individual or oneself, hostility (to see an "x" near a name). 2. a sense of place and the present. 3. reward or financial gain in the offing (to see an "x" on a map).

xenophobia (fear of strangers or foreigners) 1. reverse: happiness, contentment. 2. feeling as if a friend has been lost. 3. domestic difficulties.

X-ray 1. a need to look under the surface of an affair—possibly business, sometimes in a relationship. 2. a repressed difficulty or anxiety trying to come to the surface. 3. possible health issue. 4. reverse: good health and well-being.

xylophone 1. a good omen regarding social circle and friends, sometimes business or personal achievement (note the kind and quality of the music). 2. good news is in the offing.

Y

---

y 1. a fork in the road. 2. a bird's foot.

yacht 1. the desire for a break from it all. 2. the desire to be wealthy. 3. the desire to be free of current problems, to take off. 4. longing for the good life. 5. one needs more time to oneself, on vacation.

yahoo 1. joy over something. 2. thinking about communicating with someone.

Yalta one is considering coming to terms with people who have common interests (meeting of Stalin, Roosevelt and Churchill at Yalta).

yam warm family get-together and celebrations.

Yankee 1. if one thinks of him/herself as a member of the baseball team, the dreamer has high regard for him/herself. 2. if Yankees baseball team visits one's city or town, the dreamer is optimistic about something. 3. set in one's ways. 4. a winner.

yap desire to make someone one knows and dislikes stop talking ("shut your yap").

yard 1. if well-kept, signifies the ability to maintain order in one's waking life. 2. if messy, signifies the inability to keep things orderly in one's life.

yard sale 1. trying to survive. 2. using everything one knows to succeed.

yardstick 1. ready to measure one's success in some area. 2. about to measure something to see if one has done it correctly. 3. fear of being "trimmed" (old-fashioned).

yarn 1. a propensity for telling stories that are not true. 2. one is conducting one's life in a numbingly repetitive fashion. 3. bring aspects of one's life together. 4. if there is a problem with the yarn, there is a problem with someone in life.

yarrow 1. clairvoyant. 2. divine.

yawning 1. boredom with life. 2. if another person is present in the dream, not feeling high regard for him/her. 3. if facing a potentially hazardous situation, one is unafraid.

yearning 1. if the dreamer is yearning for someone, it may be that simple. 2. if someone else is yearning for the dreamer, that also may reflect a life situation.

yelling repressed anger toward someone that should be expressed.

yellow 1. optimistic. 2. if dull and murky, may represent problems.

yellow bird 1. if the bird is deceased, the dreamer is worried—and warned (e.g., canary in mine that inhales gas). 2. a good omen, fiscally speaking. 3. not good, romantically speaking.

yesman 1. someone without character. 2. perhaps it describes oneself, and a desire to change.

yew 1. death. 2. rebirth. 3. immortality.

yield 1. willingness to yield one's ideas for the sake of peace. 2. curb one's erratic driving habits.

yodel 1. desire to visit a foreign country. 2. need something sweet.

yoga 1. one has achieved a large degree of calmness and control. 2. self-discipline.

yoke 1. desire to change to a simpler time in one's life (when oxen were used). 2. able to corral great power. 3. if wearing a yoke, one feels trapped, frustrated. 4. one feels enslaved, perhaps in a romantic relationship.

young 1. a desire to return to days of innocence and happiness. 2. hope. 3. a new outlook.

Yucatan 1. desire to learn about Mexican culture. 2. desire to go primitive.

yule log a yearning for happiness and contentment.

Yuma be expecting a showdown with someone (from the movie *3:10 to Yuma*).

Z

zebra 1. balance. 2. a feeling that current activities or projects are fleeting, a lot of work for little reward. 3. possible long-distance travel is in the offing, a dream journey.

zenith 1. success, achievement. 2. a feeling that an intimate partner might be "the one."

zephyr 1. a preference for romantic, poetic pleasures over all else. 2. too much focus on searching for love relationships, and low self-esteem.

zero 1. complete freedom. 2. circular motion, unproductive. 3. feelings of nonexistence, a void. 4. double cross (two zeros). 5. the beginning (as in a countdown or "zero hour"). 6. divinity.

zigzag 1. hesitancy, indecision and incertitude. 2. possible health issues, mental illness or addiction. 3. evasiveness, attempts at deception.

zinc 1. achievement—usually in business affairs, often personal goals. 2. energetic pursuits and activities, usually a good omen. 3. possible health issue, mineral deficiency.

zipper 1. invitation to lovemaking. 2. a need for discretion (to be caught with an open zipper). 3. wordplay on nothingness or "zip."

zodiac 1. conscious being, self (attributes of given sign). 2. very good luck, random (as in lottery win).

zombie 1. emotional detachment or stoicism, not necessarily negative (if not frightened). 2. a stage of inertia or immobilization, feeling a lack of control of fate.

zoo 1. confinement and exhibition. 2. controlled instincts. 3. feeling unnoticed, abilities underappreciated.

zoom 1. to focus on detail to the exclusion of all else (to zoom in). 2. to see a larger picture—usually of a situation, often an aspect of behavior. 3. versatility of views and opinions.

zucchini 1. a phallic symbol. 2. love and affection. 3. disappointments in the offing (bad or badly cooked zucchini).

Bibliography

Boa, Fraser. *The Way of the Dream*. Boston: Shambhala Publications, Inc., 1988.

Delaney, Gayle. *Living Your Dreams: The Classic Bestseller on Becoming Your Own Dream Expert*. New York: HarperCollins Publishers Inc., 1996.

Francis, Valerie. *Illustrated Guide to Dreams*. New York: Smithmark Publishing, Inc., 1995.

Freud, Sigmund. A. A. Brill (translator). *The Interpretation of Dreams*. New York: Modern Library, 1994.

Garfield, Patricia. *The Universal Dream Key: The Twelve Most Common Dream Themes Around the World*. New York: HarperCollins Publishers Inc., 2001.

Grant, Russell. *The Illustrated Dream Dictionary*. New York: Sterling Publishing Co., Inc., 1996.

Hearne, Keith and David T. Melbourne. *Understanding Dreams*. London: New Holland Publisher UK Ltd., 1999.

Hobson, J. Allan. *An Introduction to the Science of Sleep*. New York: Oxford University Press, 2002.

Innes, Brian. *The Book of Dreams: How to Interpret Your Dreams and Harness Their Power*. New York: Smithmark Publishing, 2000.

Jung, C. G. Gerhard Adler (editor); R. F. C. Hull (translator). *Dreams*. Princeton, NJ: Princeton University Press, 1974.

———. William McGuire (editor). *Dream Analysis: Notes of the Seminar Given in 1928–1930*. Princeton, NJ: Princeton University Press, 1984.

Koch-Sheras, Phyllis, and Amy Lemley. *The Dream Sourcebook: A Guide to the Theory and Interpretation of Dreams*. Los Angeles: Lowell House, 1995.

Miller, Gustavus Hindman. *10,000 Dreams and Their Traditional Meanings*. Cippenham, Berkshire: Foulsham, 1995.

Parker, Derek. *Parker's Complete Book of Dreams: The Definitive Guide to the Meaning of Dreams*. New York: Dorling Kindersley Publishing, Inc., 1995.

Richmond, Cynthia. *Power: How to Use Your Night Dreams to Change Your Life*. New York: Simon & Schuster, Inc., 2000.

Rock, Andrea. *The Mind at Night: The New Science of How and Why We Dream*. New York: Basic Books, 2004.

Zolar. *Zolar's Encyclopedia and Dictionary of Dreams*. New York: Fireside, 1992.

On the Internet

A Buddhist approach to dreams, Reverend Heng Sure, http://www.urbandharma.org/udharma7/dreams.html, 2004.

Dream Central's Dream Dictionary, http://www.sleeps.com/dictionary, 2004.

Dream Moods, http://www.dreammoods.com, 2004.

Dreaming at Swoon, http://www.swoon.com, 2004.

Gods, Heroes, and Myth: World Mythology, http://www.gods-heros-myth.com/namerican/asymbols.html, 2004.

A gynecology site, Nelson Soucasaux, http://www.nelsonginecologia.med.br/index.htm, 2004.

Hyper Dictionary, http://www.hyperdictionary.com/dream, 2004.

Symbolism: The Numbers, http://www.vic.australis.com.au/hazz/Numbers.html, 2004.

The University of Michigan, Online Dictionary of Symbolism, http://www.umich.edu/~umfandsf/symbolismproject/symbolism.html, 2004.

Working with Color in Dreams, Bob Hoss, http://www.dreamgate.com/dream/hoss/, 2004.

About the Authors

TOM PHILBIN has been a full-time freelance writer for thirty years. He is the author of *The Psychic in You: Understand and Harness Your Natural Psychic Power,* coauthored by psychic Jeffrey Wands, and over the years has published forty-five nonfiction and fiction books. He has written extensively for such publications as *Woman's Day*, *Parade* and *The Reader's Digest*. He is married, with three children and seven grandchildren.

JOAN SEAMAN studied Media Communications at Hunter College in New York City with an emphasis on symbols and their meanings; she has a passion for how they work on the human mind. Her passion extends to the dream world also through years of therapy, a never-ending quest for self-awareness. As a writer, Joan has worked on many projects for more than ten years under the thoughtful and skillful tutelage of Tom Philbin. Their most recent project was *The 100 Greatest Inventions of All Time*. She spends her time dreaming with the family she adores in Huntington, Long Island, just up the road from Tom and his family.